BARBARA BERG WRITES . . .

"During those years in which I yearned for and tried to have a child, I felt very much alone. But I know now that other women, even those who have had healthy, normal pregnancies, have shared bits and pieces of my experience and will identify with it. So while the story is my own, it is also every woman's who has wanted something desperately and finally succeeded in achieving it against overwhelming odds."

"This is *Our Bodies, Ourselves* writ large and personal. Women will love this book."

—*Library Journal*

NOTHING TO CRY ABOUT

Barbara Berg

BANTAM BOOKS
TORONTO · NEW YORK · LONDON · SYDNEY

This is a true story, but the names of many of
the people mentioned have been changed.

*This low-priced Bantam Book
has been completely reset in a type face
designed for easy reading, and was printed
from new plates. It contains the complete
text of the original hard-cover edition.*
NOT ONE WORD HAS BEEN OMITTED.

NOTHING TO CRY ABOUT

*A Bantam Book / published by arrangement with
Seaview Books*

PRINTING HISTORY
*Seaview edition published in 1981
The author and publisher gratefully acknowledge permission to reprint,
at the end of Chapter 6, lines from* My Rainbow Race *by Peter Seeger
Copyright © 1970, 1972 by Sanga Music Inc.
All rights reserved. Used by permission*

Bantam edition / August 1983

*Bantam Books are published by Bantam Books, Inc. Its trademark,
consisting of the words "Bantam Books" and the portrayal of a rooster,
is Registered in U.S. Patent and Trademark Office and in other
countries. Marca Registrada. Bantam Books, Inc., 666 Fifth Avenue,
New York, New York 10103.*

PRINTED IN THE UNITED STATES OF AMERICA

H   0 9 8 7 6 5 4 3 2 1

*To my mother and father for
showing me the joy of parenting*

For their ideas, comments, and time generously given at various stages of this book, I would like to thank Anne Borchardt, my agent; Sherry Huber, my editor; Nina Cobb, Rosalind Konigsberg, Marjorie Madigan, and Susan Maier, my friends. For their professional advice, I am grateful to Drs. Alfred J. Ainbinder, Doris Bernstein, Sheldon H. Cherry, Stephen K. Firestein, Herbert Jaffin, Alan Roland; and for their enthusiasm and love, Arnie, Laura, Alison, and Andrew.

NOTHING TO
CRY ABOUT

Chapter 1

One hand grasping the seat of the taxi, the other clutching at Arnie's shirt, I stifled a cry.

"Is it *very* bad?" Arnie asked, bringing his face close to mine.

I struggled to speak, my voice hoarse and whispery. "I think the contractions may be slowing down a little. Maybe they'll stop. No one in my family ever had a miscarriage. They run in families, don't they?" I asked pleadingly.

Arnie looked at me without speaking, his eyes dark and deep. He put his hand on my pulsating belly, trying to feel the baby kick beneath the taut skin.

I rested my head on his shoulder, breathing in deeply his faint scent of nicotime, sweat, and leather. Through my half-closed eyes, I could see New York stretch sluggishly. Someone's morning begins.

My morning had begun hours before, red and sticky and scared, with phone calls to an answering service, returned by a sleepy doctor.

"Bleeding? Some pain?"

"A lot of pain. Really, doctor, I'm in a *lot* of pain."

"Think we better have a look. Come right to the hospital. I'll meet you there."

The cab hit a pothole, sending us bouncing into the air.

"Are you all right?" Arnie asked.

1

I nodded.

"Jesus, I wish this guy knew how to drive. Hey, my wife is five months pregnant. Would you *please* try to be careful."

The driver continued chewing his gum loudly.

I tried to fix my gaze out the window. We were driving past the neighborhood where Arnie and I had lived when we were first married. The cleaner, the florist where he'd bought me a dozen roses after my oral exams, the coffee shop where we used to eat on our way downtown.

It wasn't so long ago: the two of us tall and flat-bellied, carrying our briefcases in our outside hands, our inside hands tucked around each other's hip, resting, teasing, grabbing. We were in love with our lives, the city, each other.

Things had been going well for us. Maybe too well. I should have known it wouldn't last. I'm not pessimistic. Not really. But sometimes I believe there are two drunken gods up there, looking to create trouble for those whose lives seem a bit too simple.

Now, our lives were never exactly simple, but those first years of our marriage were rich and full and good. It had been that way from the start. Both of us were fugitives from troubled marriages. Arnie's had been tempestuous; my own so boring that the only diversity had been the differing sports events on TV.

I'd met my first husband the start of my freshman year in college, and by that Thanksgiving had decided that I wanted to marry him. Tall, blond, and blue-eyed, he came closest to fulfilling my fantasies of a WASP husband without being one. He played varsity basketball, was president of his fraternity, and seemed the perfect all-around American boy.

Well, we were all into that in those days of crew-neck sweaters, knee socks, panty raids, and dorm parties. I was only sixteen, thrilled with being away from home, with my boy friend, my roommates, my classes.

It was the early Sixties, and we were the "Just Before Generation," just before chants like "Hell no, we won't go" replaced the college alma mater on campuses across the nation, just before the boycotts of Dow Chemical and grapes, and just before draft-card burning.

My politicization came later, with graduate school, our Student Strike Committee, the escalation of the bombing, napalm, Bob Dylan. It was a crazy, sad, exciting time when everything seemed possible except my marriage. It had gone flat almost immediately, my husband remaining the all-American boy he had started as. It wasn't his fault. He'd never promised to be more.

I stayed with him longer than I should have, willing myself to make it work, forcing myself to feel something more than friendship. Divorce? I mean, it *just didn't happen*. Not then. Not to a nice Jewish girl from Brooklyn. And of course everyone thought we always *looked* so happy together. Who could believe how miserable I was?

I think, though, there comes a time when the human spirit must break out and nourish itself or die. For me, there was no big production, no stage lights, no walking in on him with another woman. Instead, there was just a slow wearing away of the self, until I knew I had to act or it would be too late; I would become resigned to it, like the women I used to see in Flatbush, their skins slack and loose, pushing a baby carriage with one hand, holding a bag of groceries in the other, their eyes flat and dull. Resignation.

The divorce was wrenching. I had married Hank before I was twenty, going straight from the dorm to our studio apartment in Brooklyn. It had been like playing house: dinner at my mother's one Friday, his mother's the next. And we were always sent away with "care" packages—from *his* mother, that is, "to make sure our boy keeps up his strength, you know."

Hank was the only man I'd known, in the biblical sense and otherwise. When we were in college there was a dorm mother, a sweet-faced, gray-haired woman who let the boys come up to our rooms once a month—and then only if the door was open and *three* feet were on the

floor. Hardly adequate preparation for the singles' bar at
Maxwell's Plum!

Once, after my divorce, a friend of mine persuaded
me to go to Maxwell's with her, promising me that she
wouldn't leave me for a second. But when we got there a
tall Texan with cowboy boots and a fringed vest you-alled
his way between us, and for twenty minutes tried to you-
all me right up to his bedroom.

It wasn't my scene—and besides, I was too busy for
it. Between working to support myself, taking courses,
and looking for an apartment, I hardly had time to date.

A little bit of avoidance, perhaps? Probably a whole
lot of avoidance. Here I was, this presumably worldly,
sophisticated feminist, whose last crisis in dating was
whether I should let myself be kissed goodnight on the
first date. I was experiencing culture shock, plain and
simple.

My friends kept after me. "C'mon," Roz said. "You
can't hibernate. I'm giving a party. There'll be some nice
men there. One of them just got divorced."

Before I even saw him, I heard him. His voice rich
and deep like a warm blanket. Talking about—what?
Politics? The stock market? I strained to listen. His
daughter. *His daughter?* What kind of man comes to a
singles' party and talks about his daughter?

One that I wanted to meet. I turned toward him.
He was leaning against a wall, talking to a young blonde
woman in fishnet stockings and the shortest miniskirt
imaginable. I immediately regretted my subdued green
dress. I looked like a Girl Scout next to her.

He was wiry and dark with easy features and a
boyish grin. In one hand he held a beer glass; his fingers,
wrapped around it, were long and sensitive, I thought.

Feeling my gaze, he looked out over the head of his
companion. I smiled tentatively. He smiled broadly. And
that moment of our meeting established the pattern of
our lives together.

Arnie is exuberant, outgoing, and completely up
front. He loves people, has an abundance of restless
energy, and is a natural optimist who believes that

everything is possible. I'm quieter, more pensive, needy of hours of solitude, a little shyer and a lot more skeptical.

We are the right amount of different. Arnie's neatness for my—well—sloppiness. My punctuality for his constant lateness. My restraint for his spending. His confidence for my insecurities. And it works. Most of the time.

It almost didn't with my doctoral dissertation. I started writing it about two years after we were married. Arnie is a midtown lawyer who was happy to moonlight as my editor in chief. He'd rush home from work each day eager to subject my prose to the scrutiny of his legal training.

I was writing on the origins of American feminism and was deeply and passionately involved with the subject. I had discovered a whole history of women who cared about each other, who worked for each other's improvement, stretching back to the early 1800s. They even used the term "sisterhood." My involvement with my work was so complete that I didn't know where these women began and I ended.

So every time Arnie said "This doesn't make sense" or "This is an exaggeration," I took it as a personal affront. "For God's sake, don't be so sensitive," he would shout.

"You don't have to be such a perfectionist. This isn't a goddamn legal brief, you know," I would yell. Then I would storm into the bedroom and sulk, and he would stay in the living room and sulk, until one of us—usually me, because I hate to argue—would go to the other.

"This is silly."

"This is childish."

So we figured out a way. Arnie would make his comments in pencil in the margins instead of out loud to me. I would read them the next day, make the corrections I agreed with, and erase those I didn't. The dissertation became almost as compelling for Arnie as for me. It was our project. Our most important project. We discussed it constantly, over our breakfasts out, on the telephone during the day. "Arnie? Are you busy? Listen, I just had this thought. . . ." And, yes, we took it into bed with us.

Saturdays we would browse through antique-book shops and print shops, looking through crumbling papers for pictures, stories, clues to the minds, the imaginations, of women who lived a hundred and fifty years ago. I felt like a detective on a case. It was so absorbing, I couldn't imagine *anything* more satisfying.

I remember one Passover, my whole family was assembled for the seder, the table set with special dishes, a bowl of glistening hard-boiled eggs at one end, matzos at the other, the glasses full of sweet dark kosher wine, and my cousin, who instructed Lamaze classes, turned to me and said, "Isn't it time you did something creative?"

"You mean procreative?" I retorted, angry, insulted. What could be more creative than my work? As for a baby, I'd have one when I wanted—*if* I wanted.

It wasn't so much that I didn't want children ever, it was that I didn't want them *then*. I was only twenty-eight, Arnie thirty. We had time. But I couldn't imagine when the *right* time would be.

First of all, there was my work. If the Sixties were the era of letting it all hang out, the Seventies were the era of the "role conflict." A fancy term for something we all knew: No one can do everything.

Oh, yes, of course, there was the myth of the superwoman, that new partner at a Wall Street law firm, exemplary mother to her children, lover to her husband, who jogged three miles each morning, then went home to prepare eggs Benedict for her family before heading downtown.

But I didn't buy it. No matter how I looked at it, full-time work and full-time family amounted to fragmentation, not fulfillment. How many women—or men, for that matter—have been successful in all areas of their lives? If one thrived, the other usually withered. And I had no reason to believe it wouldn't happen to me.

I didn't need to read the studies of professional

women in which their children were termed "professional liabilities," or the books which told me that a "continuous work history is a prerequisite for good achievement." I saw it around me. I saw it in the tired, drained faces of those friends in graduate school who had young children. Carting them to the school day-care center, or running home from the library at two each day to relieve the baby-sitter, sometimes falling asleep in seminars, and handing in papers late because their children were sick.

How could you study with a baby screaming? How could you write with a toddler bursting into your room? How were they doing it? *Were* they doing it? Could I?

And even if I wanted to take the chance with my work, what would a child do to our way of life? To the freedom, the openness to new possibilities, opportunities? Arnie had just become the cochairman of the New York State Lawyers' Committee for McGovern. Although we had both worked in campaigns before, this one was special. Many old friends joined us, and new friendships formed fast if not deep. We felt involved and wonderfully hopeful.

Between our work and the campaign, Arnie and I were hardly ever home. We were spontaneous, ready to run down to headquarters, ready to go out for pizza, ready to jump into bed or out of it at any time. We were easy and breezy, with no ties except to each other. *And to Laura*.

The rabbi joined the three of us together in every way except in name. I was keeping Berg, Arnie and Laura were Schlanger. I wasn't just marrying a man, I was marrying his daughter also. She was almost four at our wedding, a special blend of child: vulnerable and wise. Standing next to us in her blue-and-white ruffled dress, her brown eyes like a fawn's, she proclaimed shortly after the ceremony, "People marry, have babies, and then get divorced." Litany of a twentieth-century child.

I knelt down and hugged her, feeling her soft curls against my cheek. "Daddy and I aren't going to get divorced. We're going to stay married forever," I whispered. Not knowing as I said this that she *wanted* us to get divorced, so that Arnie could remarry Charlotte, her mother.

I saw Laura as frightened and insecure, needing someone to turn to, to trust in. She was with us every weekend, and I embarked on being a mother to her then. Not a stepmother, another mother. And it was rough going at first.

Probably I overdid it. Tried too hard and too fast, and Laura rebelled.

"But, honey, you *have* to wear the new mittens I bought, your hands are like ice."

"I hate them. They're ugly. My mommy thinks so too."

Or, "C'mon, sweetie, get into your nightgown and I'll read you a story."

"I don't like that book, it's boring."

"Okay, then pick out one you like."

"I don't like any."

"But honey, we have a whole bookcase full of books for you. There must be *one* you like." Exasperation creeping into my voice.

"They're all dumb."

By this time we are both close to tears.

"Okay then, you'll have to go to sleep without a story."

"My mommy always reads to me. I wish I were home with my *real* mommy."

Now we are both in tears.

So she would retreat; and I, who should have known better, would retreat also. Until the next weekend, when I would try again.

I don't know why I kept trying. Maybe sheer stick-to-itiveness. Or my pledge to Arnie that I would, or my sense that Laura was starting to reach out to me, if only a trifle. But I stayed with it for a year, and gradually, finally, we became friends. Good friends. Playing together, bathing together, dressing together, shopping together. A real team.

And we had fun together. Certainly, *I* had fun, making hand puppets, playing with clay. I started planning for the next weekend as soon as this one was over. And I thought about her, even missed her, in between.

It was the Friday after Thanksgiving, our second Thanksgiving together, and I woke her up after Arnie had left for work. She threw her arms around me and said, "Just think, mommy, a whole day together by ourselves." And then for the first time I allowed myself to tell her what I already knew: that I loved her, not because she was Arnie's daughter and I was supposed to, but because I did. I really did.

So, of course, we *couldn't* have children of our own, not just as Laura was starting to feel she had a place with us. A baby would be terrible for her.

Anyway, how would we manage economically? During the early Seventies, studies estimated the cost of raising two children in a typical American family from birth through college at between $80,000 and $150,000—and that was before double-digit inflation. My earning ability was limited. If I did stay home with a baby, I'd have to rely on adjunct teaching jobs, which were as unprofitable as they were unpredictable. Arnie's income also was uncertain. Fully one-half his salary went to Charlotte for "family payments," as his separation agreement so delicately called them. I had my own words of description.

So during the first few years of our marriage, we justified our decision not to have children, in terms of role conflict, life-style, self-fulfillment, and other grafted words. Every so often, when we saw my parents after a lapse of time and they looked older and worn, or when a friend became pregnant and I watched her belly swell with life, a yearning rose up inside me for a child of my own. But on the whole, drifting into nonparenthood was comfortable and easy. I was mommy to Laura two days a week, a dedicated career woman the other five: a perfect balance. Then Charlotte remarried, Oxford University Press asked to see my dissertation when it was completed, Arnie and I took a trip to Norway, and the scales went haywire.

We began our vacation in Bergen, and our enchantment was immediate. We were captivated by the fishing boats, the outdoor markets, the freshly cut flowers, the old Hanseatic League warehouses surrounding the town with their wooden fronts of red, white, and pink and high gables. We felt as if we had stepped into a children's storybook.

A young American woman guided us through the old buildings, pointing out hidden doors for the women who visited the presumably celibate merchants. She had arrived three years ago as an undergraduate at Barnard and stayed on. "I couldn't go back. Norway had become—well, it just became a part of me," she told us after the tour.

"But your family, your friends . . ." I protested.

She shrugged her shoulders, bunching up her long hair as she did. "We all have to make choices, I guess."

Her words were prophetic.

We felt an unexpected sadness as we left Bergen for a three-day tour by bus and steamer through the fjords. Nature seemed sometimes gloomier here, painting the water a gunmetal gray, and sometimes resplendent, revealing glistening waterfalls and red-topped houses. Tore, our guide, told us of the magic of the mountains. We could almost feel the trolls watching us as we visited stave churches and small country inns. Everywhere we went, Grieg's haunting melodies filled our ears.

Our first night out we stayed at a lovely old hotel that smelled slightly of burning wood. The interior was ornate with old Norwegian carved rose designs, to insure indoor flowers during the harsh Nordic winters. After dinner we stood on our terrace looking at the slim Naerø Valley, surrounded by mountains of rugged grandeur.

We were an unlikely assortment of tourists. Most of the group were Scandinavian Americans visiting their heritage; then there were three victims of the same Nazi concentration camp reunited for the first time on this trip, a nurse from California, and a young couple from

New York. Yet by the time we reached Oslo, following a night of heavy snow in the mountain town of Tyin, we exchanged addresses, promised to keep in touch, and really hoped that we would.

It seemed strange to be alone again with nonstructured days. We lunched on reindeer meat, which tasted better before we knew what it was, and then we headed for a stroll in Frogner Park. As we approached, the air became sweet with freshly cut grass. Mothers and flaxen-haired children picnicked and sunbathed under the scrutiny of Gustaf Vigeland's awesome statues. Vigeland is Norway's most famous sculptor, his works dominating the seventy-five acre park. The statues, set in groups separated by streams and ponds, depict the passage from birth to death. In one cluster, a joyous mother holds her baby high above her. Next to her is an infant in a fit of temper. Nearby an adolescent girl, with hands cupping her young breasts, plunges into adulthood. In another group, some old men sit together, their faces reflecting wisdom, pain, fear.

For three afternoons we made pilgrimages to the statues, not quite grasping their meaning for us. On our last day there, a small boy climbed into the lap of one of the elderly figures. I stood transfixed. The vital young body against the still gray form it would become, that *I* would become. I felt our frail human mortality. The cycle of life.

I wanted to become part of it, *needed* to become part of it. To grasp the continuum. I wanted . . . I wanted . . .

"Arnie, I want to have a baby."

He took me in his arms and lifted me slightly off the ground. And the statues regarded us benignly as we kissed for a very long time.

But a whole year passed after Frogner Park, and I was still using my diaphragm. "I know how it'll be with you," joked a colleague. "You'll wait till after your dissertation is published, and then till after your first year of teaching, and then till after you get tenure."

That really scared me, but I knew he was right. I wanted to have a baby, thought that I did, *felt* that I did, but I was . . . I don't know. Afraid to take the step. I needed a sign, a push. And I got one, all right. But not one that I would have imagined.

It was, I'll never forget, a hot day late in August. I'd been writing all afternoon and now was feeling bored and restless. I pushed back my chair and put my feet up on the desk. It was Wednesday already. In only two more days Laura would be here. I walked into our bedroom and dialed her number.

I began with my usual perfunctory "Hi, Charlotte, how are you? Can I please speak to Laura?"

"No."

"What?"

"No. I don't want you calling the house anymore, and I've told her she can't call you. She can speak to her father at his office."

I felt the blood drain from my face. My hands became cold. I fumbled to put the receiver back on the phone, but it fell to the floor with a crashing noise.

I tried to get in touch with Arnie. He was on his way into a meeting, rushed and hassled. "Don't worry about it. Something must be bugging her. Laura will never put up with it."

That evening we decided that Arnie would go out to Long Island early on Friday and talk to Charlotte while Laura was out at a friend's house. With luck the entire thing would be resolved by the time he and Laura left for New York.

I waited impatiently for them to arrive. The doorbell rang at a quarter to seven, their usual time. I could hear them laughing all the way from the kitchen. So far so good. I threw open the door and drew Laura into my arms. She pulled back slightly. Or did I imagine it?

Laura went to put her things away, and I followed Arnie into our bedroom. "It's no use," he whispered. "Charlotte won't budge. We'll have to discuss it with Laura."

Our dinner-table conversation began with the usual

things: day-camp, friends, sleep-over dates. I found it tempting not to bring up the subject at all.

We were halfway through the meal when I drew in my breath and said, "Laura, you know your mom doesn't want me to call you anymore."

"I know," she said, not even looking up from her plate.

"I'm very upset, and I'm sure you must be also," I ventured.

"My mother said she had her reasons." End of the conversation. Eyes fixed solidly on mashed potatoes.

I was so unprepared for this that I didn't know how to respond. In the past, when *my* husband and *her* mother had had arguments, Laura and I had discussed them completely. She was logical, open, even ironic. It always amazed me how, at seven years old, she could be so objective, so in touch with her own feelings. But now a part of her was suddenly beyond my reach, and it frightened me.

I felt what I now recognize as a sense of loss. It gnawed away inside like an ulcer. For the rest of the meal we sat in prickly silence, Arnie interrupting it every so often with awkward little jokes that neither of us laughed at.

After Laura went to sleep, Arnie told me of his conversation with Charlotte. "Laura pulled one of her 'if only I lived in New York' routines, and Charlotte got pissed."

"Well, Laura probably *would* be much better off living here," I began.

"All children play off one parent against the other. Laura's probably angry at Charlotte for getting remarried, and is trying to get back at her. Kids do that all the time."

"But this is so unfair to Laura. I mean, our relationship, hers and mine, is so important to her."

"Yes, but now that Charlotte has a husband, *she'll* probably be around more for Laura."

So that's how it was. I'd just been filling in. Dispensable. Obsolete. I'm sorry, your time is up.

I felt betrayed. First by Laura, and now by Arnie. Who's family is this? Mine or theirs? Suddenly something I had always known was becoming known in a different way.

Arnie had a child and I *didn't*.

Chapter 2

97.3°, 97.2°, 97.2° . . . For fourteen days I had been taking my temperature with my new oval-index thermometer, and plotting the results on the nifty graph included with the kit. I was as casual as a child playing follow-the-dots. But now, on the crucial fifteenth day of my twenty-nine-day cycle, this had turned into serious business.

"How'd you do?" muttered Arnie, still in his 7:00 A.M. semicomatose state.

"This isn't a test," I snapped. But I was secretly happy at the reading: 97.5°—a sign that ovulation had occurred. Good to know that my estrogen, that old perpetrator of teen-age pimples, had finally gotten together with my progesterone to produce a classic temperature curve.

"So this is the right time, then?" Arnie stretched lazily and reached over toward me.

"The right time, but the wrong month." I slithered out of bed.

I had planned it all. I would finish my dissertation while pregnant, deliver over the summer, and maybe be able to do some part-time teaching that fall. So this was a dry run, really. Just to make sure everything was working as it should. I had no intention of taking my temperature while I was trying to conceive. I wasn't going to get into that game. Husbands postponing business trips, wives rushing home from the library: "I gotta go now, sorry. This is *the* night." No thank you.

We were going to be free and spontaneous and natural, and if it took a little longer, who cared? We did have a preference, however, for the sex of our baby. A *strong* preference. We both wanted a girl. I don't think either of us realy understood why.

I guess I wanted a companion, a full-time Laura, or maybe I saw a daughter as a chance to raise myself again. Besides, what did I know about boys? With their sweat socks and footballs and french fries? Arnie, I think, saw a girl as less competition, less threatening. His only experience was with fathering a daughter, and that had been *so* good that he wanted another.

Many of our friends had tried for one sex or the other and half of them swore that the method worked, the other half that it didn't. We bought the book anyway, with its appropriate pink-and-blue cover, and decided to follow its directions.

The next month we ceremoniously packed up my diaphragm in its blue plastic container and stashed it away in my underwear drawer. (I wasn't going to throw it out, just in case I changed my mind.) We didn't talk much about the possibility of a pregnancy or think about it much either. But when my period arrived a few days late that October, I felt surprisingly disappointed.

November, though, quickly consumed me. I had deadlines to meet on my thesis, Thanksgiving dinner to prepare, and Laura's costume party for eight neighborhood munchkins only two days later. Arnie was going as the Sesame Street lamppost. I, embarrassingly enough, still fit into my Brownie uniform. What joy to be five-foot-six in the fifth grade!

But Laura's outfit would take more doing. She was set on dressing up as a Raggedy Ann doll. The clothes were easy, but Raggedy's incomparable hairdo posed a problem. For weeks we were inundated with red crepe paper, yarn, streamers, and glitter pasted on oaktag, as Laura, determined to make the wig herself, tried to find her right medium. I was so busy painting floor mops red and curling scarlet pipe cleaners, Laura's newest schemes, that day thirty-four of my cycle passed before I realized I might be pregnant.

The thought was thrilling and strange and scary. At night I would dream of intruders. Breaking into an apartment. Not the apartment where Arnie and I lived, but my parents' apartment. The one I grew up in, with the high ceilings and many coats of paint.

What did they mean, these dreams? That I wasn't ready to be a mother? Or was I afraid of replacing my own mother? *Displacing* her? À la Oedipus. Was it a stranger inhabiting *my body* or *my life* that I feared?

At night I was filled with the idea of a pregnancy, but during the day it only came to me at times. The thought crept sweetly into my imagination while writing, while chatting with a friend, and it warmed me. For seven days the possibility floated in and out of my mind, but on the eighth, when Arnie dropped off my urine specimen at a lab near his office, it occupied everything.

We decided to call for the results together. Arnie raced uptown at lunch and we met at our favorite coffee shop near Hunter College. The pay phone was right outside on the corner.

I was too nervous to eat. "When did you say they would know?"

"Not before one."

"What time is it now?"

"Ten to."

For fifteen minutes more I picked at my tuna sandwich, then went outside and tried the number. It was busy, and five minutes later it was still busy. I could hardly stand still. My fingers were getting numb from the cold. I kept switching from foot to foot to stay warm. I didn't want to go inside and give up my hold on the phone. Arnie kept peering out the door. "Nothing yet." I waved him back inside.

I began to watch myself doing all this, observing a woman clinging to an icy telephone receiver. Was this Barbara, who liked to read and study history and had a cat named Oliver, and lived with her husband in an apartment that had one bedroom and one study, where Laura slept? So eager for disruption? I dialed again.

"It's positive," the nurse told me.

"Arnie! It's positive, I'm pregnant!" I yelled through the glass window.

"Congratulations!" shouted a passing student.

"Hope it's a boy!" called another.

Arnie rushed out so quickly, the waiter had to come after him with the check. He swept me up in his arms and whirled me around. I kissed his nose, his mouth, his eyes.

"Arnie-dwarmie. I'm pregnant. Can you believe it?"

Neither of us could. It was awesome. Magical. Mystical. That human life was so created. That a conception had occurred without knowledge, without sensation, almost without permission. But there it was. The test was positive. We felt no ambivalence. Only the sheer joy of existence—and maybe just a tiny bit of pride in our achievement.

At home that night we drank wine and leaned lazily against each other. "Are you going to use Bentley?"

"I guess so." I hadn't really thought about it. Robert Bentley, head of Ob/Gyn at Manhattan General, a well-known teaching hospital, had been my gynecologist for the past six years. I had gone to him shortly after my divorce because I was staining between periods. My old gynecologist had tried to convince me it was just nerves. "The only thing I'm nervous about is that I'm bleeding for three months straight," I told him, and decided it was time for a change.

Bentley had taken it seriously. He'd performed two D&Cs six months apart and a cervical biopsy, "just to make sure." I didn't understand the logic of it, but the treatment worked. The staining stopped and my periods returned to normal.

Bentley parted his hair in the middle, wore baggy pants, and chain-smoked. I didn't particularly like him. "So you won't marry him," my mother said. I didn't particularly dislike him either.

My sister, Lucy, who was then in her seventh

month, was Bentley's patient also. And so far she had no complaints. I think that was the thing that clinched it for me. That he was Lucy's doctor.

A funny thing happened to me on my way to my Ph. D.—I forgot about my sister. A little older than I and so much a look-alike that we could be clones, she somehow got lost in the shuffle of my colleagues and professors. She lived close to us, always wanted to *be* close to us. And now I had the chance. We could go to our appointments together, and then out to lunch. We'd be sharers of a special bond, getting to know, at last, the adults that two little girls had become.

Actually, Lucy was the first one we told. She had become our in-house expert on temperature charts. She advised us to wait a while before spreading the news, but we began immediately. My mother-in-law told me I'd never get my figure back. My sister-in-law told me that my baby would be a Leo, stubborn and difficult to raise. And my mother—well, she became my mother in boldface letters.

"Barbara, are you eating enough? Are you sleeping enough? Are you drinking enough milk?"

We could talk pregnancy for hours—maternity clothes, names for the baby, and all the other special language that my "condition" supplied. We were closer than ever. And some of the time it was fun. But when she conducted a veritable pogrom against dust in Lucy's apartment as her due date approached, I became nervous. Comradeship was one thing, but this was turning into a complete takeover. When the risk of coup d'état seemed greatest, I would lash out and assert my independence. And then immediately feel guilty for being different, or for wanting to be different.

And my mother? How did she respond? I guess the way any mother responds when her daughter's life seems to repudiate her own—by being hurt.

She was the only child of Russian immigrants, born on Second Avenue in Manhattan where the life of the Russian intelligentsia centered around the Cafe Royale. My grandfather worked in a factory as a pattern cutter.

His hands were large and rough. He had a round callus on the second joint of his right thumb from the heavy scissors. When I was a little girl I thought that all grandpas had such hands. He knew everything there was to know about American history, and could recite the batting averages of a decade of Brooklyn Dodgers. His most cherished memory was of once carrying Eugene V. Debs's suitcase.

My grandmother was small, with eyes the color of faded denim. She made the best chicken fricassee, and carrots so sweet we'd always ask, "How much sugar did you put in, grandma?" knowing the pride she took in not using any. Their samovar, which is now mine, still has charcoal in it, left over from the days when they would sit and distill life along with their tea.

The two consuming passions of the household were opera and politics, but money was scarce. My mother grew up wearing hand-me-downs and yellow rubber shoes that her aunt got from the social-work agency where she was a caseworker. Those shoes were the bane of my mother's existence. The soles made a dreadful squeaking noise, and her classmates jeered. They teased her and mimicked her mercilessly, but still voted her the girl most likely to succeed when she graduated from James Madison High.

And succeed she did in 1930s terms. After working in Macy's while putting herself through Barnard, she married my father, a gifted young college professor of clinical psychology, had two children, and stayed home for fifteen years. Then, because they needed the money, or because she was bored, she decided to go back to work. She had always wanted to get a doctorate in history and be a college professor, but instead took a job teaching high school. Still working full-time, she got a master's degree at Pratt Institute and became a school librarian at the precise moment the Sixties generation declared reading irrelevant.

Had I stopped to think about all this, I would have understood her eleventh-hour mommying, but I was too preoccupied.

Two weeks after I had broadcast my news up and down Third Avenue, I began to stain. It started late Sunday afternoon, just after we drove Laura home.

Immediately, there was the self-blame. I shouldn't have told everyone. I shouldn't have taken such a long car ride. One of my books suggested that women who do a lot of traveling have a higher incidence of miscarriage. I was reading up on my symptoms while waiting for Bentley to return my call.

I already knew that any bleeding during the first three months could be the start of a miscarriage, but I had no cramping or abdominal pain, and that was a good sign. My pregnancy paperbacks, which were now crowding my history books off the top of my desk, offered treatments ranging from bed rest to hormone therapy, but Bentley took a *que sera sera* attitude.

"You can continue with normal activities, except— uh—for intercourse. I'll check you next week and we'll see what happens."

"Do you think we can go out to dinner?" Arnie asked when I told him what Bentley had said.

"He sort of implied that we could, but I think we ought to skip it. I'm sorry," I said, turning toward him, "but we can whip up something here."

We usually stayed in with Laura on Saturday nights, so our Sunday dinners out were special. We started planning where we would eat as soon as we dropped her off, and sometimes hadn't decided by the time we were through the Midtown Tunnel. I can be satisfied with anything, but Arnie's palate is—well, somewhat eclectic. He can eat Peking duck along with a Sicilian pizza and finish it off with a chocolate mousse. It's enough to send Craig Claiborne to an early grave. And the maddening thing is that he never gets sick from it, or puts on any weight, while I can gain from just reading a cookbook. I knew I was taking my chances when I asked him to make dinner that night, but I wanted to get off my feet.

It could have been worse. We had a watercress-and-salami omelet, with pickles, of course.

I kept a pretty low profile for a couple of days, staying home, resting a lot. I had read that most micarriages are caused by the failure of the fetus to develop properly, and Bentley had told me the same thing. But I felt I had to do *my* part.

The stock of Charmin toilet paper must have risen five points that week. I went through cartons of it, I was checking so often. But after six days the staining stopped as suddenly as it began. I had passed the danger point.

I was just starting, though, what Dr. Alan F. Guttmacher, the Dr. Spock of unborn children, calls the "common complaints" of pregnancy. I was nauseated and chronically tired. I had back pains and leg cramps and a postnasal drip that awakened me each day at 5:00 A.M.

And the amazing thing was that Arnie matched my symptoms one for one. I'm not sure whether womb envy has enjoyed quite the publicity of penis envy, but Arnie sure had it. Like Zeus, who carried Dionysius sewed up in his thigh until ripe for birth, Arnie was experiencing gestation.

I don't know if he worried about stretch marks or varicose veins, but I certainly did. The supposed improvement in my complexion never happened. It didn't blossom, it blotched. A bad day at the typewriter threw me into a panic. A thoughtless comment from a friend put me in tears. Sometimes I wondered if it would all work out. Sometimes I wondered if I wanted it to. . . .

We had not told Laura yet. Her response to my sister's pregnancy and those of my friends had hardly been encouraging. Little speeches about how "daddy and you already have a child and don't need another," accompanied by all kinds of regression, baby talk, crawling around, wanting to be carried, the whole schtick! So we waited as long as possible, waited until I could barely zip up my jeans.

We told her over a lunch at Rumpelmayer's. *A spoonful of sugar helps the medicine go down*. We were prepared for her anger, her tears, her jealousy. We *weren't* prepared for her response.

"A brother or sister!" she exclaimed. "I can't wait!"

What a relief! What luck! It's too good to be true! And, of course, it was. We wanted so much for Laura to accept our new baby, to sanction it, that we forgot that children, like adults, usually don't say what they feel. I even overlooked the one clue she gave us: her concern about sharing her room.

I didn't realize, then, that sharing a room really meant sharing love. I thought a room meant a *room*. After all, didn't Freud once say, "Sometimes a dream about a cigar *really is* about a cigar"?

Anyway, it seemed like a reasonable concern. Arnie and I also were worried about lack of space. Our closets already looked like the inside of a fully loaded Santini Brothers moving van. We were having our yearly "Should we move to the suburbs?" conversation on a biweekly basis.

There are very few things that I am narrow-minded about. Life outside of New York City is one of them. The thought of a house and garden gives me the hives. I'd rather quest after the best in water-processed decaffeinated coffee than quest after the best in lawn furniture. Besides, I'm a terrible coward. I prefer steel-gated windows and Medeco locks to glass sliding doors and easy-access bay windows. And I had vivid confirmation of this when Arnie and I took a trip up to his ancestral seat—Gloversville, New York.

Now Gloversville is a nice place to visit, a *beautiful* place to visit. In summer it is serene and smells of honeysuckle. In winter it is harsh and breathtaking. The snow stays white for months, icicles hang from trees like lollipops, and the pond freezes over for skating. For a Brooklyn kid it is a Currier & Ives come to life.

Arnie and I went up in February. My thesis was at the typist's and his parents were at a relative's. We built snowmen, took pictures of me with my arms encircling a barely noticeable belly, and bundled up for long, peaceful walks.

We had returned from one of these outings when we noticed that the back door was slightly open. "We probably just didn't lock it," Arnie said. And we forgot about it, until later, when he went out to get the Sunday *Times* and I went upstairs to lie down for a while.

I was just starting to fall asleep when a banging noise startled me into full concentration. I strained to listen. From the basement. Someone was in the basement. Of course we hadn't forgotten to lock the door, we *never* would have done that. My flesh tingled along my arms. I crept downstairs and took a large knife from the kitchen drawer. The logic of this I can only attribute to fright-induced insanity.

I slowly opened the door to the basement, flipped on the light switch, and was just about to make my attack when the phone rang. It was my in-laws. I kept talking to them until Arnie returned.

Together we searched the house, but noticed nothing, except that it was getting cooler. "It's really cold out there," I said, putting on one of Arnie's sweaters and pulling the sleeves down over my hands.

"I don't know about out there," he said, "but it's freezing *in here*. I'm going to check the basement again."

He came back laughing. "I didn't *think* there was a light switch near the door. You turned off the burner by mistake—that was how you got rid of your banging burglar. All oil burners make noise. They're sold with a warranty against quiet."

This episode, known forever as our Gloversville story, convinced us to start cleaning out our closets, for our baby would be bred as well as born in New York City.

At first I wasn't sure I felt it, but ten minutes later it happened again. Softly. A flutter. Like an eyelash brushing against skin, the baby was moving inside me. I put my hand over the spot and felt a gentle swell in my stomach. I sat back and closed my eyes. I would call Arnie, but not yet. My baby, living and growing silently for twenty weeks, was making its presence known. It was a glorius moment.

Odd that I who cherished my privacy, who when alone would draw the blinds and let the telephone ring, so loved the idea of sharing my body with another life.

With quickening, I started to feel better. I had boundless energy, felt capable of anything, of everything. I started to enjoy the pregnancy, *love* the pregnancy. I loved to eat three good meals a day, loved to order milk at a restaurant, loved the floppy, cutesy maternity clothes, loved my body, loved Arnie, loved the world. I was crazy, mad, head over heels in love with being pregnant.

I was the first woman in the world ever to do this, to feel this. I exchanged smiles of recognition with other pregnant women, talked intimately of leukorrhea, lightening, Lamaze, La Leche. I was finding another sisterhood of sorts. Right there under our eyes. A sisterhood. *Of course!*

I was the earth mother, the good mother, everyone's mother. Hands on my belly, self-satisfied smile on my face. Oh, I was high.

And it fascinated me so, my changes, the baby's. When the fingernails appear, when the hair appears, when the arms bend at the elbows, when a fist can be formed. When Bentley's nurse first heard the heartbeat. That loud dull thumping. Earnest, steady. Two times to my one.

"Arnie, you *have* to hear it. It makes everything so real, so believable. There's a baby in there. A real live baby. God, it's exciting."

I knew Arnie would come with me the next month. He wanted to experience as much of it as possible. We were, I think, closer in those few months than at any time in our marriage. As though the question of having a baby had weighed more heavily than we realized. No more defensiveness, no more justifications, no more "Well, *I* would if you would," or "*I* would if we had a bigger apartment," or "*I* would if you weren't so involved in your work." No recriminations, no blame. Just the acceptance and responsibility of something it seemed we both wanted, *really* wanted. Surprising how much we wanted it after all, and how happy we both were.

I had just gotten off the telephone with Arnie and was on my way to start dinner when suddenly I felt a gush of wetness. My pants were getting soaked. I ran into the bathroom and stood over the toilet. It seemed like minutes before it stopped. What the *hell* was that? Pressure on the bladder causing uncontrollable urination? It happened, I knew. But this seemed so forceful, so much.

I rushed to my books. "The sac surrounding the fetus can tear, causing amniotic fluid to flow out."

Could my membranes have ruptured prematurely? I was only in my fifth month. I was trembling, really shivering with fear. I called Bentley's service. It was after office hours.

I hate to do this, call a doctor when he's off duty. "I'm sorry to disturb you . . ." I began. Bentley didn't say that I hadn't, but listened to my symptoms.

"What month are you in?" he asked. "Fifth? Must have lost control of your bladder."

"Really? But there was so much."

"Yep. Lost the whole thing."

"Could it—could it have been amniotic fluid?" I asked nervously.

"In your fifth month? Are you kidding?" These women with their silly, crazy notions. "No, it was the bladder, all right. Happens when the baby gets larger. When's your next appointment?"

"Tuesday."

"Okay. Come in then. I'll check you in the office."

"Tuesday? But today's only Thursday," Arnie protested when he got home. "Why is he waiting so long to examine you?"

"How do *I* know? I'm not a doctor. He must see this thing all the time. He almost laughed when I suggested amniotic fluid."

I had confidence in him. I mean, how could you *not* have confidence in your doctor? That's why you went to him, right? To interpret symptoms and signs. It was unsettling, frightening, to question his judgment.

There was some dripping. No more gushing, but—yes, a definite dripping. Probably urine, probably the increased discharge of pregnancy, or—or—

"You don't really think it could be amniotic fluid, do you?"

"I don't think so, but . . ."

"I'm sure it isn't either, but . . ."

"Your stomach feels the same, but . . ."

"The baby's moving, but . . ."

But. But. But . . .

Saturday I called Bentley's service again. He was away for the weekend. I got the doctor covering.

"Well, *I* don't know what's going on, but I think you ought to stay off your feet until Tuesday."

"You mean—you mean it *might* be amniotic fluid?" I said, immediately sitting down.

"It *might* be anything."

"Could you please check me now? I'll come down to your office, the hospital, anywhere." I was pleading.

"Well, um—well, um . . ." He seemed flustered at my request. "We don't want to do too much poking around in there. Dr. Bentley will examine you Tuesday."

So that was that. Definitive. Forceful. Final. I had to wait.

I didn't know why everyone thought it was so dangerous to give pregnant women internal exams. Even Bentley on Tuesday morning said, "I'll do this very fast."

I was so tense I felt like rigor mortis had set in from the waist down. But the test was simple and painless. He took a small piece of nitrazine paper and touched it to my cervix. It turns blue-green or deep blue when wet with amniotic fluid. Mine was yellow—negative.

"See? I told you," Bentley exclaimed triumphantly, waving the paper like a flag. "Dry as a bone."

I rushed out to tell Arnie. He was sitting amid all the pregnant women, grim-faced and tight. Seeing him so always moves me. It makes me want to protect him from every imaginable hurt.

He broke into a grin at my smile. I was okay. Bentley was positive. I could resume all my normal activities.

Never could the thought of peeing in my pants make me so happy.

We were extravagantly happy. Everything about the pregnancy seemed more wonderful, more splendid than ever before. We celebrated the whole week—until Friday.

That morning I was getting my hair cut and I felt the slightest twinge. It was more like pressure than pain. I ignored it. Probably just the position I was sitting in.

I met Arnie to shop for baby furniture. The twinge grew to a spasm. Still faint. Still unfamiliar. Nothing much, but I mentioned it.

"Let's call Bentley," Arnie said. "We're so close to the hospital. Maybe he'll check you."

"Oh, I don't know. . . . I hate to keep bothering him. I was just there four days ago." I was tired of the drama, the panic. We'd had it for a week already. That was enough. I wanted to shop and play among baby things, with my new haircut and blue denim jumper.

But by lunchtime, I was getting concerned. The spasms were becoming tighter, even a little painful. Reluctantly, I asked Arnie for change.

Bentley was too busy to talk. His secretary was screening calls. "Only patients in labor can be put through. Are you in labor?"

"No. At least I hope not," I said with a little laugh.

"Well, try in a little while."

I called again and then again, but he still wouldn't come to the phone.

"He could call you back later," the secretary suggested.

I decided to go home and wait to hear from him.

Each time I felt my stomach harden, I clasped my hands together so tightly my knuckles turned white. Without even being aware of it, I was breathing in short, shallow breaths. The pain was sharp, angry, aggressive. Then it retreated. Maybe it would stop.

I went to the toilet. Something red on the paper. A tiny dot. No, this is impossible. I felt paralyzed. I stared at it again, then rushed to the phone. I told Bentley's secretary it was an emergency.

Bentley didn't seem to think so. "A little bleeding? Just a broken vessel, probably of no consequence. Sounds like you're having a few contractions, that's all. I'll be away for the weekend, so ask to speak to Dr. Abrams if you have any questions."

I kept walking around the apartment, trying to outdistance the pain. I didn't call Arnie. Maybe I'd feel better by the time he got home. Maybe the bleeding would stop. Maybe it had already stopped. I checked. No, still a little. But wait. Something. Oh, God, something that looked like a telephone cord was hanging out.

The white tile floor rose up to meet me. I grabbed onto the towel rack for support. Waves of nausea swept over me. My forehead grew damp with sweat. Steady. Steady. Walk into the bedroom to the phone. That's it. One step, then another. See how easy it is.

My fingers were trembling so, I couldn't dial. I held one hand with the other and tried again. "There's a—a white piece of tissue, something—like a telephone cord protruding from my vagina," I told Bentley.

"That's your urethra that's prolapsed. That's why you're having difficulty controlling your bladder."

"But what should I do about it?" I was terrified, but I tried not to sound it.

"Stick it back in." He sounded irritated, rushed.

I had seen him this way when I was sitting in his office. How he looked when a patient was keeping him on the phone too long. Impatient. Scowling. Puffing on his cigarettes.

"I'm sorry to keep you. I know you're trying to get away for the weekend—"

"That's right," he snapped. "And I'm an hour late already."

"But I'm in terrible pain. Could something be wrong with the baby?"

"Sounds as though you're freaking out. Just relax and have a good weekend." He clicked off.

I stared at the dead receiver as though it were an alien object. What should I do? Bentley had been my doctor for years. Lucy's and my friend Roz's also. *They* trusted him. Shouldn't I?

And his explanation. It made sense. I guess. If the urethra did prolapse, it would affect bladder control. It *sounded* logical. Or did it? I really didn't know.

But Bentley must know. He wasn't exactly a kid. He'd been in practice for a long time, had a nice office, with all the obligatory certificates and memberships and positions. Should I call him back? No point in being a nuisance, like the boy who cried wolf. He'd have me pegged as a nervous Nellie, probably did already. And then what if there were a *real* emergency? . . . At least nothing was wrong with the baby. He was definite about that.

I didn't tell Arnie how bad the pain was. He was looking forward to trying a new restaurant with our friends Terry and Mark. It might be good for me to go. Bentley hadn't said anything about restricting my activities. Maybe I would forget about the contractions. But as we started walking there, a fist socked me in the stomach so hard I crumpled over. Passersby looked at me curiously. Arnie became alarmed. "Barb, let's go home. It's all right. C'mon, let me get you to bed."

"No, I just need to sit down. I'll be better when I sit down."

He supported me until we got to the restaurant. But inside, it was worse. The pain was ranting, screaming, wild. I was holding on to the tablecloth, to the arms of the chair to keep from crying out.

"Barb, *please*."

"Yes, go." Terry reached out and took my arm. "Please don't stay because of us. Go home. We'll call you later."

I couldn't make it the last three blocks. Arnie had to lift me in his arms and carry me to the apartment. What was happening to me? Nothing was *ever* like this. My body was off on some crazy trip of its own. It was being crushed to death.

"Am I dying?"

"Of course not. Of course you're not dying."

"Then what is it? What's going on?"

"I don't know . . . I don't know." Arnie sat next to the bed and put his face in his hands. "You have to call Bentley, or whoever the guy is who's covering for him."

Abrams had been told I might call. "Sounds like you have a spastic uterus."

"What's that?"

"You know, like a spastic colon. Your uterus is just being irritable. Have a few drinks. That'll calm things down."

Arnie poured me a Jack Daniels. I had one, then another. The contractions were slowing, subsiding. Terry and Mark called to see how I was feeling, we invited them over.

They joined us in another drink, then left. I felt a drowsy, warm gratitude. The pain was slight, sporadic. I got into bed and slept heavily.

My baby was sick. I was running through water to find help. Help. I had to get help. But the water was so high, catching me, pulling me into it. I gasped for breath. Arnie. Arnie, help me. "Arnie," I called. Where was Arnie? I was drugged, hazy from all the liquor. "Arnie? Arnie?" He came rushing in from the living room, still fully dressed. He had been sitting there so as not to disturb me. Keeping vigil, I suppose. One of us alert, on guard. He held me in his arms until I fell asleep again.

The pains were riveting, relentless, agonizing. The contractions had started again. It was only 5:00 A.M. Could we call Abrams so early? No, better wait an hour longer.

His voice was thick with sleep. "You'd better go right to the hospital. I'll meet you there. And—er, honey, better not eat or drink anything," he added as an afterthought.

Arnie helped me out of bed. The sheet was sticky and wet with blood. I shuddered and turned away. I tried to get dressed, but had to keep stopping to sit down. To breathe deliberately, ride with the pain. At last I was ready. Arnie brought my jacket in. "I'm going to call for a cab."

"Wait," I said, fumbling with my makeup kit, "I have to put lipstick on."

"What do you need lipstick for?"

"I don't know. I don't know." I started to weep.

Manhattan General was still hushed and dimly lit. We went up to the maternity floor where Lucy had delivered a baby girl a few months before.

I expected Abrams to be there already, or at least to have called ahead. But no one seemed to know what to do with us. A large blonde nurse, liberally sprayed with Jean Naté After Bath, suggested that we wait in the fathers' lounge. Her associate whispered something to her about my traumatizing the expectant fathers. They conferred briefly while I stood clinging to Arnie's arm.

"I don't care where you put her, but my wife has to lie down. She's in a lot of pain and has been up half the night." Arnie was using his lawyer's voice, and, as always, it got the desired response.

"Let's see if we can find a labor room for her," the fragrant one suggested.

The word "labor" sent a chill down my spine. I looked at Arnie with such terror that he pulled me close to him and stroked my head like a parent comforting a frightened child.

The room was just a cubicle filled with monitors, oxygen tanks, intravenous poles, scissors, syringes. There were rows of these cubicles, little boxes made of ticky-tacky, and they all looked just the same. No, not all the same. In some, women were deep in the grips of their labor, welcoming it, groaning with it, birthing with it. While I . . . what *was* I doing here? Among menacing, cold equipment, a Charles Addams fantasy of a bedroom. I should be home sleeping next to Arnie, listening to his heavy, even breathing, feeling the warmth of his body.

"Why don't you get some coffee or something, honey?" I asked after a while.

He shook his head. "I want to be here when Abrams comes."

"But that may be a while and you haven't eaten anything since lunch yesterday."

"I'm not hungry," he said flatly. "I think I'll walk over to the nurses' station. Maybe *they* know when he's coming. Will you be all right until I get back?"

I nodded. The contractions had diminished to slight, insignificant ripples. Maybe they were stopping. Maybe Abrams would just observe me for a few hours, then let me leave.

Arnie came back smelling of nicotine. "No sign of him yet."

So we waited. Hours passed. Finally, around eleven, a resident poked his head into the room. His hair was greasy and his rumpled tunic spotted and stained. "Let's check the heartbeat," he said, hooking me up to the large monitor in the corner of the room.

I smiled. At last Arnie would be able to hear it. It would save him an extra trip to Bentley's office.

The resident tried one spot, then another. Three, four different places.

It had to be there. Of course it would be there. I was hardly in pain. I crossed my fingers. Another spot, then another. I started making frantic bargains with God. Please let them find it. I won't work. I'll stay home full-time. I always planned to do that anyway. *Please, please* let them find it.

"Try up here," I pleaded, pointing to the place where Bentley's nurse had heard it last. But there was nothing. No thumping, no beating two times to my one. Only the hollow sound of the machine making its own noise.

Arnie held my hand. I couldn't bear to look up at

him, his face was so contorted in fear. "Don't worry," I said after the resident had left. "That guy's just learning, he looked half asleep. He probably doesn't even know how to use the machine."

Arnie looked at me sadly, then turned away. "If only Abrams would come . . ."

As if willed to appear, he came bursting into the room minutes later, wearing a camel turtleneck sweater and plaid slacks. On his way to the golf course? His hair was still wet from his morning shower.

"I heard they couldn't find the heartbeat. Let me see what's going on," he said, putting on a rubber glove and asking Arnie to leave.

He took a piece of nitrazine paper and gave the nurse a knowing look as he watched it turn blue. I felt removed, distant from what was happening. It didn't seem to register, *nothing* was registering. Not even when he examined my cervix and said, "I'm sorry, honey, you're going to abort."

"But the urethra," I heard myself saying. "What about the urethra?"

Abrams knit his brows. "Urethra? Where did you get the idea that it was your urethra? My dear, that was the umbilical cord that prolapsed. That's why there is no heartbeat."

That penetrated like an arrow. I gasped and made some indistinct, barely audible sound, covering my face with my hands. Abrams stood a few feet away from me, peeling off his bloodstained glove. "Look, it's really better this way. It would have been worse to send you home knowing there was no heartbeat, waiting for you to go into labor." He walked out of the room quietly and sent Arnie in.

I watched him enter, his face expectant, maybe even a little hopeful. Abrams hadn't told him. Why had he left it for me? Why couldn't he have slapped his arm around Arnie's shoulder, man-to-man, and said, "Sorry, but I've got some bad news," or, "You better sit down, I have to tell you something," or any other of the half-dozen little prepackaged messages doctors used for such occasions? Why did I have to be the one? I, who wanted to wrap my body around Arnie's like a blanket and keep him from all sadness.

But I didn't have to say it, he knew from my face. He rushed to me and took me in his arms. "It's all over," I sobbed. "I'm six centimeters dilated." I could feel Arnie's body shaking underneath his heavy woolen sweater.

"It'll be all right, honey. We'll go away, we'll get over this. I promise it'll be all right," he said.

How long did we have together? A few minutes? Not more than five. Then the door flew open and in marched the entourage—residents, interns, nurses, aides. My medical history, my allergies, my vital signs. My vital signs again. They discovered my heart murmur and were lining up to listen. Literally four of them wanted to hear it.

Arnie pleaded. "Can't you leave us alone for a while? Please, we need a little time."

"But this is how we learn," student number two said, putting his stethoscope to his ears.

The intern started my intravenous drip.

"What's in it?" I asked, looking up at the two bottles swaying above me.

"One's glucose and water, the other's Keflin."

"What's that?"

"An antibiotic—chemically related to penicillin."

"Penicillin? But I just told you. I'm allergic to penicillin. My whole family is. My mother almost died from it."

"There's only a ten-percent crossover."

"I don't care. Can't you give me something else?"

They gave me Abrams. He came into the room and stood over the bed, so close to me that I could smell the coffee he had just finished. "You have to take the Keflin to prevent infection. You've been walking around for *over a week* with ruptured membranes," he growled accusingly. My fault. Completely mine. Not Bentley's. No, never blame the colleague, always the patient.

I tried to keep my voice calm and even. It came out

a little shaky anyway. "I'd like another drug. One with no risk of reaction."

"Look," said Abrams with obvious anger, "I'm giving up my whole Saturday to be with you, and you're not even cooperating. We'll be standing right outside with Adrenalin in case you need it."

I looked at Arnie, but he averted his gaze. This was *my* decision. Just then my body began to convulse in a new contraction. I didn't care anymore about the drug, about anything except the pain. "All right, give it to me," I said wearily. I just wanted the whole hideous episode to be over.

For the next hour or so, Abrams kept returning to check the cervix. The rest of his staff wanted a crack at it also, but fortunately he was sufficiently worried about the risk of infection to keep them away.

I saw them start to assemble their instruments.

"Wait. Aren't you going to put me to sleep? I don't want to watch this."

"No. We need your help," Abrams answered.

Before I could say anything, two residents grabbed my shoulders and pulled me to a sitting position. Hands inside of me, ripping out part of my body. A terrible tearing pain making me scream out as I would never have allowed myself to do. I saw a blurry pink form, and it was over.

"It's a girl, and she's normal," called out Abrams excitedly, as though he were announcing a birth instead of a death. It was too much. I gave in to my tears.

Slowly they gathered up their things. I was lying down, but I could see them take the shiny little body and put it in a jar. They filed out. The last resident glanced back over his shoulder at me. I was weeping loudly, uncontrollably. "It's nothing to cry about," he said, and closed the door.

I tried putting my hands over my ears. The pillow over my head. Nothing could drown out the sound of babies. High-pitched cries, like a meow. I could hear them from my room, two doors from the newborn nursery, a relentless reminder of what I'd lost. I was surrounded by those who held new life in their arms, who exchanged "Who does she look like?" talk and recounted their deliveries in exuberant tones.

Around five o'clock that evening a photographer burst into my room. "I'll be taking pictures in the nursery tomorrow morning—"

"Please leave." Arnie was on his feet instantly, almost chasing him out of the room. My husband, who has such respect for life that even misguided spiders and bugs are set outside and freed, looked as though he would have gladly killed that poor baffled man.

It was intolerable. My mother went down to Admitting. She refused to take their "It's the only available room" for an answer, and insisted that they page Abrams. He was less than delighted to see her. He had assumed we were Bentley's headache now. "They always go to maternity after a 'miss,'" he informed her. "That way we can check them on our regular rounds." Another way of saying "We won't have to take the elevator to another floor."

But my mother, formidable at five-foot-three, stood firm. So they placed me on Y-7, away from the women talking about their episiotomies and the babies wrapped in receiving blankets. I stayed there for three days surrounded by my family and my anger.

How could Bentley not have known what was happening? How could he not have cared? Never before had I felt such rage, so strong, so corrosive. It threatened to crowd out every other human emotion.

Chapter 3

I had rehearsed it many times. What I would say to Bentley when he made his appearance that Monday. I had even written down the points I wanted to make. The whole scenario was ready, just waiting to be played.

But Bentley had a different script. He came abruptly into my room, puffing furiously on a cigarette. "Heard what happened from Abrams. Just a fluke. You'll be back here next year having a baby." Looking at his watch— "Oops, gotta run." Exit.

The whole thing happened so fast I didn't have time to say a thing. All my fury, my accusations, burned inside me.

"Let's sue that bastard," Arnie said. Everyone was telling us we should. I mean, all our friends and relatives. The staff, Abrams, the residents—well, of course, they were silent on the entire topic of diagnosis and cause. If either Arnie or I mentioned it, they clearned their throats, averted their eyes, adjusted their collars, and said nothing. The vow of silence.

I wished him grief, I wished him misery. But did I wish him sued? I didn't know. "What good will it do? I mean, it won't bring the baby back."

"No, but if the case gets some publicity, other women may be spared your experience."

I gave my tentative consent.

Arnie wasted no time in setting up a meeting with a

lawyer specializing in negligence and malpractice. I couldn't bear to go with him, but I wrote down the exact record of the events and conversations preceding the miscarriage for Arnie to take.

He came home despondent. The lawyer had been discouraging. We could only hope to be compensated for our out-of-pocket expenses: hospital, doctor's bills. And the sum was so small, no able practitioner would handle it on a contingent-fee basis.

"But what about the loss of the baby?" I asked in astonishment.

"The law recognizes no compensable damages in the death of an unborn child—mainly because there is no way to determine her earning potential."

"But that's outrageous." Oh, yes, of course, I remembered from my course in American Constitution history: A wife dies in an accident, and the husband receives payment, not for the loss of a loved one, or a companion, but for the loss of consortium—the loss of services. "I wonder if they would have been more sympathetic to the loss of a *male* baby."

Arnie shrugged. "Look, we can still pursue it, you know. You'd have to give depositions, appear at the trial, and we'd need an expert witness, probably your next obstetrician, to testify against Bentley."

I didn't know what to do. I wanted to become pregnant again as soon as possible, and I was worried about how emotional sessions before a jury might affect me. Anyway, I didn't think it was such a great idea to involve my next obstetrician in a malpractice case. Doctors, it seems, are universally allergic to lawyers, and I wanted mine to be more concerned about my pregnancy than about the fact that my husband was a member of the bar. The statute of limitations gave us two and a half years to make up our minds. We decided to take our time.

Besides, after talking to other women, I began to think that suing Bentley was irrelevant. What we needed was a class action on behalf of our sex against the whole medical profession.

While I was still in the hospital I started hearing about other women who'd had problem pregnancies or problem doctors. A whole network seemed to spring alive. I was becoming a magnet for pregnancy stories as gruesome as mine. I've known Marcie since college. We had become the kind of friends who see each other about once a year but talk as though only a week had passed. She had gone through hell to become pregnant. After stopping the birth control pill, she never resumed ovulation. When Clomid (clomiphene citrate), a commonly used drug, failed to help, her doctor experimented with Pergonal (human menopausal gonadotrophins). It had to be administered in daily injections.

"For months I was racing uptown to get my shots, getting weighed, giving urine specimens, having daily pelvic exams, all during a fifty-minute lunch break," she said. "The strain was almost unbearable."

Marcie finally did become pregnant, only to miscarry in the fourth month. Afterward, she told her doctor how miserable she felt. "Too bad you didn't want a baby this much five years ago," he said. "If you had never taken the pill, you could have had two children by now."

Although she's now the mother of an eighteen-month-old daughter, Marcie couldn't control her tears as she talked about the guilt his remark engendered. "Imagine," she said, "making *me* feel responsible. He was the one who prescribed the pills in the first place."

Unlike Marcie, my friend Judy became pregnant fairly quickly, but by her third month thought she might be carrying twins. There were sets in both families, and she seemed to be gaining weight too rapidly. Yet each time she discussed it with her doctor, he snickered. "No one ever admits to eating too much." But Judy was convinced. As her pregnancy progressed, she felt more and more uncomfortable.

"My ankles and feet were so swollen, I couldn't get my shoes on. I had to stop work. I felt so much kicking, I was sure there were four arms and legs."

Still, her doctor, affiliated with a large maternity center in Boston, ignored her symptoms and thoughts about twins. Although a pregnancy involving twins is on the average twenty-two days shorter than the calculated due date and is likely to have a more complicated delivery because of the prematurity and low birth weight of the babies, Judy's doctors didn't bother to examine her when she arrived at the hospital in the beginning of her eighth month complaining of lower back pains and leakage of fluid.

But they had to see her when she came back nine hours later with the head of *one* of her babies already crowning. There was no time for adequate preparation, no time for emergency procedures. The twins, born alive, died within one hour of each other that morning.

My aunt told me about her friend's daughter's miscarriage. She had been bleeding for weeks. Every time she called her obstetrician, he said that pregnant women sometimes bleed for no reason. But when large blood clots started to appear, she and her husband rushed to the hospital.

She miscarried, the senior resident told her, because of a large uterine fibroid. When she asked her doctor how he could have missed it, he assured her he had known about it for years. He just didn't want to worry her.

And Arnie heard the next one from a colleague living in Raleigh whose wife had recently had a stillborn baby. She didn't know whether or not to give the baby a funeral, but finally decided against it. Better to let the hospital dispose of the baby in what they called "a manner consistent with the common traditions of human dignity."

But when she went to her doctor for her six-week checkup, he told her nothing had yet been done about the baby. She had visions of it being used for experimentation, or for demonstration. She'd have to make burial arrangements herself.

She followed the nurse to the hospital lab in the adjoining wing, and waited, signing the appropriate forms, when suddenly a doctor came out, handed her a gallon glass jar, and walked away. Inside was her baby, shriveled and discolored, floating in formaldehyde.

It is Octave, in Jean Renoir's film *Rules of the Game*, who utters the famous line "Everyone has his reasons." And I suppose that my obstetrician and those of my friends had theirs also. But what were they? Why would an educated person, one who had selected the health-care profession, treat another human being so shabbily? With such disdain? I didn't understand it at all. But in another way, I understood it completely. *Too completely.*

All the things I'd studied, all my "book learnin'" in feminism, began to make a new kind of sense. Had I believed it when I read it? I wasn't sure. That the development of radical surgical procedures during the Victorian era, like clitoridectomy, oophorectomy, and hysterectomy, related to the unconscious wish to control women; that gynecologists living then thought all women hovered on the verge of hysteria, insanity, and crime, and that these natural instincts were heightened during pregnancy. Books and books were written about man's secret dread of woman, about woman as the temptress, about woman as the destroyer.

And what about my feminist colleagues? The talks we used to have, corroding our stomachs with countless cups of coffee. Didn't *they* believe that birth should remain the all-female event it had started as, the expectant woman surrounded by friends and relatives and generally a midwife, all of whom provided comfort? Didn't *they* see the development of modern obstetricians as the attempt by man to take birth away from woman and call it his own?

Did I believe it now? I still wasn't sure. But I had to understand what had happened between Bentley and me. Why he had acted as he did. Why I had responded as I did. I had to sort it out, get it straight, so I could let it rest.

"I'm going over to the medical bookstore," I told Arnie the Saturday after I got out of the hospital.

"C'mon, Barb, why do you want to do that? You'll probably read a lot of things that'll be upsetting."

And Arnie was right. It *was* upsetting.

"*You probably lost control of your bladder; it sometimes happens as the baby gets bigger.*" "The diagnosis of ruptured membranes is obvious if the membranes rupture with a gush. . . ." (*Danforth's Obstetrics/Gynecology*, p. 623).

"*But today's only Thursday. Why is he waiting until Tuesday to check you?*" "Where membranes have ruptured ascending infection is a constant threat. . . . [It is] a very important cause of maternal morbidity and even mortality." (*Danforth's Obstetrics/Gynecology*, p. 633. *Williams Obstetrics*, p. 793.)

"*I'm going to do this fast.*" (*No speculum used.*) "To diagnose rupture of membranes: Perform one sterile speculum examination. . . ." (*Williams Obstetrics*, p. 742.)

"*You can continue with regular activities.*" "If membranes rupture prematurely and the patient is . . . months from term . . . it is routine to place them at complete bed rest at home or in the hospital." (Guttmacher. *Pregnancy, Birth and Family Planning*, p. 195.)

"*Something white that looks like a telephone cord is protruding from my vagina.*" "Unless prompt delivery is accomplished, fetal death results from a prolapsed umbilical cord." (*Williams*, p. 793.)

"*That's your urethra that's prolapsed. Stick it back in.*" "Primary repair of injury to the urethra . . . should be carried out once a diagnosis . . . is made." (*Operative Obstetrics*, p. 53.)

"*Barbara, I think you're freaking out.*" "In terms of women, we really must teach [male doctors] respect." (Dr. Marsha Storch, Assistant Professor of Gynecology at the Columbia University School of Physicians and Surgeons.)

I scanned the indexes of the heavy medical textbooks for miscarriage: emotional adjustment after; understanding loss; patient response; need for reassurance. Nothing. No advice about this at all. But plenty of advice about other things. Oh, yes. There was that.

One textbook instructs gynecologists to counsel their patients that "the frequency of intercourse should depend primarily upon the male sex drive. . . . The female should be advised to allow her male partner's sex drive to set their pace and she should attempt to gear hers satisfactorily to his." In another, the doctor is admonished to ask his patient certain questions to enable him to *appraise her character*, to pay attention to how she responds, whether in a "feminine way or whether she is demanding, masculine, [and] aggressive . . . in her attitude."

One author refers to a miscarriage as a "spilling of the products of conception," and still another claims that women who are habitual miscarriers are of two personality types: "the basically immature woman and the independent, frustrated woman."

And we wonder why doctors aren't more compassionate?

But what about me? I was at fault also. Why had I allowed Bentley to dismiss me so callously? Why hadn't I insisted that he see me? Why had I believed him so unquestioningly? All my instincts had told me something was wrong. Why hadn't I trusted them? Was I too afraid of the truth? Or too afraid of Bentley, that symbol of male authority, to acknowledge them?

Why had I so readily acquiesced in the role of good girl? Was it because it was so familiar to me? Or because I nurtured the fantasy that if I were compliant and docile, I would be taken care of? Or was it because Bentley and Abrams had encouraged it? Calling me by my first name, calling me honey, sometimes fatherly, sometimes patronizing, but always superior.

Well, those days were over. I would never again allow myself to be so ignorant of my condition, never again allow a member of the medical profession to treat me so contemptuously. I was going to become an assertive, educated consumer of health care, spend hours in medical libraries if I had to, but it *would not happen again*.

But after all this outpouring of righteous indignation, I didn't know where to begin. With the facts. *Just the facts, ma'am*.

The autopsy confirmed Bentley's initial judgment: I had lost a perfectly normal thirteen-ounce baby girl. Nothing being wrong with the baby meant that something was wrong with me. I didn't have heart trouble, high blood pressure, diabetes, RH factor, or toxemia. I decided to find out the other possibilities.

Back to the bookstore. By now I didn't even feel awkward about being there. And no one seemed to mind my sitting and taking notes. I think the staff regarded me a bit curiously, though.

At first I found the reading tough. But I took a medical dictionary from a nearby shelf and kept it beside me as I went along. And in no time, things began to make sense.

A miscarriage in the second trimester, when I had mine, could be caused by a weakness in the neck of the womb (the cervix), by fibroid tumors in the uterus (so *that's* what a fibroid looks like), or by other congenital malformations of the uterus.

I had no idea whether any or all of these were my problem, but it seemed clear that I needed an obstetrician who was also a skilled surgeon, instead of one who was strong in endocrinological disorders.

I swore that I would never go to another male doctor, but as I started developing my list I realized that if I stuck to this decision I would end up delivering the baby myself. Not that there aren't women obstetricians. Of course there are. But none whose name I was given as a specialist in high-risk pregnancies.

How did I get my list of names? From my internist, from Ob/Gyn departments at neighboring hospitals, from other women.

I didn't particularly care which of the three or four nearby hospitals my doctor was affiliated with, but I did have a strong preference for a group practice. Many of my friends like seeing a single practitioner and the continuity it assures. But doctors are only human, as we are *so often* reminded. They take vacations, they play golf, they visit their children at camp. And at those times their offices are covered by . . . by whom? Someone who doesn't know you, is not familiar with your case, and will not take responsibility for your problems. I wanted my obstetrician to have associates with access to my records, who would be concerned about me as if I were their own patient, because in a sense I would be. And there was another reason also. I didn't want my baby delivered by a stranger.

Of all my sources, talking to other women was the best. They were the ones with firsthand experience. They were the ones who could tell me the important things. Was he thorough? How did he respond to your questions? How did he act in a crisis? Did he treat you with respect?

Two names kept appearing. And since our insurance company would pay, I decided to see them both. This was taking up lots of time, but I thought I should shop as carefully for a doctor as I would for a new winter coat.

I didn't tell either of the doctors I was merely surveying the scene. I probably should have, but I didn't want to break into this bold new me all at once. It's tough to undo a lifetime of socialization in three weeks. I thought I'd go one day at a time. So I let the first think I was his patient.

Venerable and portly, he called me Mrs. Berg. He answered all my questions and recommended the same tests outlined in my medical textbook, which I was using as the criterion of his thoroughness.

But something about his office disturbed me. At first I wasn't sure what. Then I realized—it was messy. Records were strewn about haphazardly and the examining room was like the Mr. Clean commercial, before.

Now, as Arnie will readily affirm, I am far from the world's neatest person. But I didn't want my doctor's office to look like it qualified for federal aid. On to number two.

Dr. Ronald Morgan's Fifth Avenue office, which he shared with two colleagues, was a study of neatness and efficiency. Even my mother would have had a hard time finding dust there.

Minutes after Arnie and I were shown into the consulting room, Dr. Morgan walked in. He was a large man with salt-and-pepper eyebrows, a well-traveled face, and an even tan that I suspected lasted the whole year. He greeted us cordially and began taking a history. And what a history! Hearing the nuances and subtleties in our answers. Picking up on things that we'd forgotten or wanted to forget. And he not only asked, but *listened*.

He listened to our story, our rage at Bentley, closing his eyes, shaking his head sympathetically. Stopping me every so often to clarify things, asking again about my D&Cs.

Then he gave us his opinion. "It's too soon to know for sure. Certain tests have to be performed after you have completed two menstrual cycles, but from your history, it sounds as though you have an incompetent cervix."

"A what?" I almost fell off my chair.

"Incompetent cervix," he repeated.

Terrific. After all the time and money I've spent learning to like my body, it's what I suspected all along. *It's substandard*.

"Don't be upset by the name," he chuckled. "It only means that your cervix is weak, either congenitally or from the surgical procedures you've had, to the point that it cannot sustain the weight of the growing fetus. What happens is that the cervix opens, the sac balloons out, the membranes rupture, and the cervix closes again. That's why by Tuesday there was no trace of amniotic fluid. That test should have been performed *immediately*"—he pounded his fist on the desk for emphasis. "Actually, with your history of D&Cs, you should have been checked internally every other week to make sure the cervix stayed closed."

"You mean all this could have been prevented?" Arnie interrupted, almost lurching out of his seat.

"Sure—we see it very often." Morgan seemed to relax again. "As soon as the cervix begins to open, we rush the patient to the hospital and perform a simple procedure that saves the pregnancy. But we're getting ahead of ourselves. Let's wait and see if that turns out to be your wife's problem. If it is, it's easily correctable."

We left the office feeling relieved. Arnie more so than I, taking my hand and swinging it back and forth, suggesting we buy ice cream cones. As though by finding a doctor we both liked, we could close the door on this whole hideous episode.

But for me, the real pain was just beginning. Until now, my anger had sustained me. There were so many people to tell, so many exclamations of horror at Bentley's behavior, that it had consumed my sorrow. And I had made sure I was busy. *Very busy.* Too busy to think about it. Hadn't I rushed right to the medical bookstore three days after I got out of the hospital? Denying my grief. Intellectualizing it. Making it into a research project. And insisting on taking my dissertation defense the following week, even though my adviser suggested I postpone it. Oh, no! I had to show that I was strong and in control, that women could separate their professional and personal lives.

So it had been business as usual, with Arnie, with Laura . . . now *that* was a mistake. I had been so convinced that Laura would be disappointed, devastated, in fact, that I wanted to soften it as much as possible. We'd decided that Arnie would tell her after he picked her up, on their way back into New York.

"Be careful what you say about it," I cautioned. "Don't mention anything about a dead baby, be as vague as possible." I remembered from Psych. 101 that children identify with that kind of death and find it threatening.

Friends had offered us three tickets for the *Mikado* that night. "Do you think we ought to take them?" Arnie asked. "Sure. It'll be fun for Laura." A celebration? Were we nuts? How could we have fallen so easily into the patterns parents create for children? Shield, protect, deny, even lie. Didn't we know the way to teach feelings was to show feelings!

So we said nothing about being sad, and neither did Laura. But as she left the theater humming "Three Little Maids from School," I was beginning to think that we had hurt her more than we had helped her.

Even my friends had taken their cue from my attitude, giving me a huge surprise party the night of my dissertation defense. Forty of the people I love best in the world crowded into my friend Susan's one-bedroom apartment, munching on chicken wings and acting as though nothing had happened.

But *something had happened*, something of major consequence, although no one, including me, could acknowledge it.

I had never thought about it before. How little attention we pay to the loss of an unborn child. Strange in our society, where the family is so glorified, where pictures of happy, dimpled babies are used to sell everything from Pampers to used cars, that an unfinished pregnancy is barely noticed. We don't even know whether it's a baby or merely a fetus, whether it's really life or just a potential life.

There is no ritual, no funeral, no recognized period of bereavement, no visits of condolence. Instead there is a papering-over with conventional wisdom.

"It's so common." "You'll be pregnant again before you know it."

I thought I was doing the right thing by putting on a happy face. But it didn't work. How could I ever have thought it would? I, who have so much trouble with separations—from people, from things, from memories—who can't bear to throw away ticket stubs or evocative slips of paper but leave them where I find them, in old handbags, in raincoat pockets, so that the whole memory remains complete, unsullied. How could I have thought I could separate from my baby so easily, she who was attached to me, part of me, depending on me. Didn't I know that the contracting uterus would feel like the baby kicking? That my breasts would still have milk? That my whole body would yearn to nurture?

Didn't I know the anguish of seeing my sister's baby? Of seeing any baby?

And Arnie, what could he know of it? His jeans still fit him. He had no endless bleeding, no constant reminder. And Laura, so obviously relieved that there would be no sibling. I loved them and needed them and resented them like crazy for believing me. For believing that I was okay and happy. For letting me go on with my charade, when what I really wanted was for someone to take me in their arms and tell me it was okay to cry my heart out, to cry and sob until the hurting stopped.

We had just gotten into bed and turned out the lights, our cigarette butts looking like fireflies on a summer night. This was a new habit of ours—actually a recently revived old habit. Smoking. We had given it up years before, but started again the night before the miscarriage. We hacked and coughed and told each other we had to stop, but kept puffing away. It was our bedtime activity. The only one we were indulging in. Of course it was too soon for lovemaking, but I was feeling so depressed that I even resisted cuddling.

Arnie reached over to touch my arm. "What's wrong, Barb? You're so distant."

I didn't answer.

"Do you think it would help if we got away? We've been talking about going to the West Coast for years. We could do the whole thing—San Francisco, Yosemite, Los Angeles. Dr. Morgan said we could travel. What do you think?"

Even in the dark I could see his face become animated, alive with the thought of planning a vacation. Arnie loves adventures, excitement. Soon he'd be jumping out of bed to get a map. We sure as hell needed a vacation, and I couldn't feel worse than I felt being at home.

"Okay, let's go."

"Terrific!" He pattered out of bed. I didn't even have to ask. In a minute he was back with the atlas.

* * *

Our western trip got off to a bad start and never recovered. The cold I had been harboring worsened, and by the time we reached Los Angeles I had 102°. I urged Arnie to go off on his own, but he didn't want to leave me, so the two of us stayed in the room and sulked.

When I finally was well, we did the conventional things. Universal Studios, Disneyland. Now that was an experience I should have done without. It's everything you'd imagine it to be—apple pie and mom and your basic nuclear family complete with pigtails, freckles, and braces. I found it devastating.

"I know what we'll do," Arnie suggested brightly. "Let's go to Giorgio's. We'll buy you the presents my parents wanted to get you for passing your dissertation defense. And even if you don't find anything you like, the store's a real experience."

If chicken soup doesn't work, take her shopping.

Giorgio's is pure Hollywood, with its pool table and ferns and mirrored Art Deco bar. The saleswoman hovered over me attentively. "This is just darling, it's *you*," she gushed.

I tried on eight, maybe ten outfits, but nothing was right.

"I liked that blue one, and the plaid was nice." Arnie was trying to be helpful.

I shook my head. "No, they're awful, absolutely awful."

The saleswoman looked perplexed. "But these are some of our most popular numbers."

They weren't awful at all, of course. In fact, a few of the things were really beautiful. But I didn't want to be trim and slim, trying on elegant little dresses, I wanted to be loose and big and oozy.

"Well, maybe this one will please madame," she said, holding up a yellow-and-black suit. I glanced at it, then noticed the blonde who had just walked in with fringed leather boots and an aqua knit dress clinging to her seventh-month belly. No frilly pastel Little Bo Peep maternity outfits for her. This was California, and *she looked terrific*.

I took one look at her and burst into tears. "I just lost a baby," I cried, and rushed into the dressing room.

As the trip progressed, I started worrying a lot. All the walking was making the postdelivery bleeding heavier. I remembered Morgan's caution that there was still a slight risk of hemorrhaging. Was the flow increasing? I kept checking my Maxipads: the Rorschach test of my tension level.

By the time we reached Yosemite National Park, I was in a state of high anxiety. It was April. The medical infirmary wouldn't be fully staffed for another month. "In case of emergency there's a copter to take you to a hospital in Mariposa," the receptionist at the Ahwanee Lodge said reassuringly. She didn't know to whom she was talking: Isadora Wing incarnate. I'd rather bleed to death than fly in anything smaller than a 747.

"Stop it already," said Arnie irritably. "You're just building this whole thing up in your mind. You're not going to hemorrhage."

"Like I didn't have a miscarriage," I retorted.

I think that sooner or later it happens to all of us— when a parent dies, when we face serious adversity or illness; we lose that protective shell, that sense of immunity. For me it was the miscarriage: the blow to my ego, the betrayal by my body, the indifference of fate, and it diminished me.

But Arnie felt none of that. He thrilled at the surroundings. His exuberance, so wonderful at other times, was grating.

"Look at that! It's incredible!" he gasped.

"You must have said 'incredible' twenty times," I snapped.

"Jesus, Barbara, you're impossible. You're picking on everything. You don't want to take pictures, you don't want to hike in the woods. What do you want to do?"

"To have a baby."

"You'll have a baby," Arnie said. "I promise."

"But I feel so unhappy," I cried.

And that's how it went. All through Santa Barbara,

Carmel, San Francisco. We'd quarrel, then talk. But finally came close to understanding the two levels of my pain. Arnie could and *did* feel the sadness, the disruption, the disappointment, the need to make new plans. But the other part, the intensely personal part—that it happened in my body, like an amputation—this could be described, but not really shared. So we reached an uneasy truce. We realized that we had lost something very important—but most of it was mine to endure.

It never fails that the phone rings as soon as you walk in from vacation. I usually don't answer it, but this time I did.

"May I please speak to Barbara Berg," a male voice asked.

I was getting ready to hang up. Since I'm listed in the phone book, I get bimonthly calls from the telephone-titillation crew. But this didn't sound like the local breather.

"Speaking," I replied.

"I'm calling for Dean Wagner Roberts at Sarah Lawrence College. We'd like you to meet with the ad hoc Appointments Committee on May fifteenth."

"Sure!" I burst out. "I mean—er—let me check my calendar," I said, knowing of course it was blank. "Yes, that will be fine. Thank you for calling," I said, and I hung up.

The week before we went to California, a friend had called my attention to an ad in the *EIB* (*Employment Information Bulletin*, published by the American Historical Society and used by unemployed historians to convince themselves they should have gone to law school). Sarah Lawrence needed someone to teach women's and American history. I sent in my résumé and hadn't given it another thought.

The idea of the interview made me pretty nervous. I spent the next two weeks busily compiling reading lists and course outlines. I felt it would be a good experience for me to go through the process, although I didn't think

I had a chance for the job. And my meeting with the committee certainly confirmed that impression.

Halfway through the interview, Ada Webber, the prominent women's historian, turned to me and said, "I thought you were in twentieth-century history." (How she could have thought that is still a mystery to me, since everything in my résumé except my date of birth ended at 1865.) "We don't need another nineteenth-century historian here."

Well, so much for that, I thought as I waited for the train in Bronxville. They hadn't even offered to reimburse me the $5.80 for my transportation. At least I had met a few celebrities.

But a week later they called again. This time they wanted me to meet with the dean and the president. "And, oh, yes, it's part of the Sarah Lawrence practice for the students to interview you also. One of them will be calling to arrange it."

She did call. Three would meet me on campus, the other two in front of Butler Library at Columbia University. "We'll see you then, Barbara," she said. Barbara? What happened to the days when college teachers were called doctor or professor? Seven years spent on a Ph.D. so a freshman could call me Barbara?

As the interviews approached, I concentrated on the essentials: how to get from Bronxville to upper Broadway in twenty minutes, and what I should wear. My *Dress for Success* book advised low heels and a suit in subdued colors. That sounded fine for the first part, but what about the students? How about jeans, a peasant top, and a shell necklace? I couldn't quite see myself changing in the ladies' room, however, so I decided on a compromise. Studious, but not stodgy. I wore a plain blue knit dress. But it was all wrong anyway. The deans wore T-shirts and the students wore Gucci.

The meetings went well. But by the time I got the letter three weeks later, I had thoroughly convinced myself that it would be impossible for me to revise my dissertation for publication by deadline time *and* prepare two new courses.

As I reached into the mailbox, I remembered what we used to say about college admissions. A thin letter meant a rejection. This one was thick. There were forms in it. I ripped it open in the elevator. "We are pleased to inform you . . ."

I rushed in and called Arnie. "They're offering me the job. They want me. How could they do this to me? What am I going to do now?"

Chapter 4

My work hastened the summer months. Early in July I had made a vigorous schedule splitting my time between revising the thesis for publication and preparing for my seminars at Sarah Lawrence. It felt good to be immersed in the past again. The new history, arising from the demands of the Sixties generation, no longer just a study of leaders, policy makers, elites, but of the people, the neglected, the ignored. A history from the bottom up, some called it: of blacks, immigrants, women; a record of everyday events, everyday lives.

It was compelling, this new material, touching me as history never had before. Oh, I had read of thousands dying of yellow fever, thousands living in tenements, thousands sold at auction. But you can't suffer for thousands. Yet one young woman's account of her life as a slave invaded my dreams for nights.

Reading the diaries, narratives, notebooks of these ordinary people, reliving the sweat and sinew of their lives, helped erase the lines which called grief mine. Slowly the pain of the miscarriage lessened. Now whole days passed when I didn't think of it at all. But at other times it was back. Real, vivid, gouging. Diminished by nothing.

It was like that the morning of the hysterogram, a procedure Dr. Morgan had ordered. Because of its diagnostic value, it's one of the most common tests used in fertility studies. With the help of radio-opaque dye injected into the uterus, an X-ray is taken of the whole reproductive system, enabling doctors to find any abnormalities of the womb, tubes, and cervix.

One of my friends had this test done when she was having difficulty conceiving. Her doctor had told her it wouldn't hurt, so when she started having severe cramps, she became worried that something was wrong and asked about it. He was irritated, acted as though she were complaining about nothing, and continued without explanation, leaving her tense, embarrassed, and angry.

I'm not sure why doctors become so euphemistic when they talk about pain. "Mild discomfort," "slight distress." They could be talking about the weather instead of an operation. Is it that the idea of inflicting pain is too difficult to acknowledge? Or are illness and anguish threatening to their sense of omnipotence?

I thought about all this as I walked to the radiologist's office—how Bentley had acted, how I had acquiesced in his treatment, how most patients are totally accepting of their doctors, and how I had vowed not to let myself be so victimized again.

But when the nurse ushered me into a room with strange and heavy equipment, my resolve crumbled. I sat on the table, clothed only in a blue paper gown, feeling cold and clammy. I had nothing to read, nothing for distraction, and trying to figure out what all the instruments were for was hardly comforting.

Flashbacks to pictures of seventeenth-century obstetrical tools—crotchets, grippers, dilators—each so jealously guarded by the surgeon who designed and fabricated it that when Peter Chamberlain invented the forceps, it was kept a family secret for more than a century. *Men compete, women suffer.*

After what seemed a long time, Dr. Newman walked in and extended his hand in greeting. "I want to know everything you're doing, step by step," I said in a small voice, struggling to sound forceful.

"Oh, I always tell my patients what I'm doing as I go along," he said pleasantly.

He told me to lie back and pulled the X-ray machine close to my body. I got sweaty and tense.

"You'll feel a little pinch now," he advised. "There may be a feeling of pressure. Do you feel some cramps?"

For fifteen minutes he kept up the symphony of symptoms as he busied himself taking X-rays. "Only about five, maybe ten minutes to go," he sang.

This wasn't so bad. Painful? Yes. Unbearable? Not at all.

"Gotta leave for a minute," he called as he sashayed out of the room.

Immediately my body grew tight, crampy. So that was Newman's technique—parceling out the pain in small pieces so I could deal with it.

He came back again soon with good news. "Wanted to read those pictures as soon as possible. I don't see anything much to worry about. You look fine. Cervical incompetence maybe, but that's all. Lie on your stomach, you'll feel better."

And he sat down and talked to me, *actually talked to me,* about history, teaching, Sarah Lawrence. This couldn't be real! That dye must have contained some dream potion. But, no. I was wide awake. He was truly concerned about me and my pain. *Bravo!*

I felt so relieved after getting Dr. Newman's report that I concentrated on my teaching for the rest of the summer. I had to be on campus right after Labor Day because faculty presence was required for student registration. At Sarah Lawrence, students select their seminars after meeting and questioning the professors. All day for three days the interviews continued: Close Encounters of the Fourth Kind. "How will you teach the course?" "What books will you use?" "Is this your first job?" (Clearly, I was exuding confidence.) "Where do you live?" (West Side was in, East Side suspect.)

My office was poorly lit, poorly ventilated, and so small I practically had to move my desk in order to open the door. But Laura and Arnie were excited about decorating it. During my first class, which for some forgotten reason met on a Saturday, they rushed out and bought pictures, curtains, and plants. I frankly thought dollhouse furniture would have been more appropriate, but I didn't want to spoil their fun. When we were finished, I proudly hung up my poster, purchased for $5.95 at Womanbooks on Amsterdam and Ninety-second. In bold black letters on a gold-and-burgundy background: "Women's History Is a World Worth Fighting For."

I practically did have to fight to teach that, or anything else, the first few weeks of school.

"I hated that book you assigned." "The period was in the wrong place on the reading list." My morning litany, compliments of Joan Simons, graduate student par excellence and royal pain in the neck. After a while I began to wonder if she was a "plant" provided by my competitors for the job.

And it wasn't only Joan. Since seminars at Sarah Lawrence are not separated by level, the range of student background and knowledge is enormous. If I talked about women during the antebellum period, half the class didn't know when that was. If I stopped to explain, the other half yawned audibly. One student had spent the summer working in the Gay Task Force of NOW, another student had never heard of NOW.

The Sarah Lawrence system, though, is designed to cope with these disparities. Faculty must meet with each member of their seminars for forty-five minutes every other week. That's the time set aside for special assignments, tutoring, help with contracts, and general talk.

The stream of students in and out of my office was steady and seemingly endless. The office was always either too cold or too warm. I constantly yearned for coffee. Finally I decided to bring in an electric pot and make my own. I bought a mug for myself and paper cups for the students. They began to relax and so did I. We talked about their backgrounds, about history, what it meant to them, what it meant to me. They were open, honest, grasping in a way that only the young are. Some who never talked in class started to. Joan finally stopped. The conference system was working.

One morning, Miriam was telling me about a problem she had. She sat on the tiny stool, her long skirt and shawl floating to the floor like waves at a beach, her innocent face strained in seriousness. "So I really didn't know what to do," she was saying. "I mean, it was *that* difficult. Then I finally asked myself: What would Barbara do?"

I was so stunned I spilled my coffee across my desk. She saw me as a role model. Someone to be looked up to, emulated. I remembered that one sociologist I had read explained that students often became too dependent on women teachers. She had called it "academic momism."

My students clearly wanted mommying, but I had tried to keep some distance, tried to be sympathetic and interested but not nurturing. Gentleness, self-sacrifice, nourishment, all those domestic qualities for which we are so prized, are not exactly the attributes associated with a successful career. But what a Catch-22! When women display competence, independence, and leadership at their jobs, they are not admired by the majority of men or *women*.

A few years before, when I was working with an affirmative-action program, I had done a presentation at a large corporation, asking ten cigar-smoking, flannel-suited executives to name the qualities they looked for when interviewing. Ambition, assertiveness, and initiative headed the list. We read short descriptions of several female applicants. Every woman whose résumé indicated that she was either ambitious, assertive, or enterprising was turned down. Oh, I was eloquent that afternoon about the insidiousness of role stereotypes!

What a joke to think that I, too, was bound by them. I guess I was more than a little concerned because I knew how much I still wanted to have a baby. It might have worked the other way! Once I was teaching, involved with history, and my students, I might have found that enough.

But strangely, being at Sarah Lawrence made me crave a child even more. I was so happy and alive at work that I wanted to express it in every way possible. And the conference system, bringing me close to the daughters of so many other mothers, made me yearn for one of my own. Once in a seminar I called one of my students "honey." I don't think anyone noticed, but I did.

I didn't want to mother my students, and I didn't want to sublimate my wish for a child in my work. I hoped I'd become pregnant again soon.

It didn't happen the first month, but we were pretty sure I would conceive quickly. So when I didn't get my period in October, we assumed that I was pregnant. I couldn't wait to get positive confirmation. When I was ten days late, I rushed to Morgan's office, urine specimen in hand for the test. It was negative. "Try again next week," instructed the nurse, "and make an appointment, he'll probably want to examine you."

But the following Friday, the test was negative, and Morgan could find no trace of a pregnancy. "You'll probably get your period in a few days," he said knowingly.

"But I've never skipped a month," I protested.

"It sometimes happens even to women who are usually regular," he assured me.

There seemed to be nothing more to discuss, so I got up and left. But I felt let down and confused. Why would I suddenly start missing periods when I never had before? Were they going to become irregular, making conception more difficult? Or were they going to stop completely as one of my friends' had? The thought made me anxious.

A colleague at Sarah Lawrence had just told me of a poll she had taken in her psychology class: "Assuming your reproductive capacity was unharmed, would you choose never to get your period?" Every student but one voted against menstruation. I was surprised, but I shouldn't have been. Why should women want to get their periods when so many of their earliest associations with it are negative? "The curse." "Unwell." Boxes of sanitary napkins wrapped in plain brown paper. Something terrible, something unhealthy, something hidden.

Maybe it's a bit of perversity, but I actually *liked* getting my period. I counted on its regularity. The rhythm of my being. So when the weekend passed with no period, I felt distanced from the cycle of my body and depressed about its implications. But I was starting to feel pregnant, and I knew that the urine test, which checks for the placental hormone, is only about 95 percent accurate. I clung to a smidgen of hope.

That Wednesday, the day before Thanksgiving, Sarah Lawrence had no classes. I decided to have another pregnancy test. This time I went to a women's health center near our apartment. The tests were free and I liked the anonymity.

I walked into the reception area where a tired-looking young woman with wire-rimmed glasses asked me to fill out some forms. The adjoining room was sparsely furnished with a few shabby chairs sitting awkwardly on a rubbed-out linoleum floor. What a contrast to Morgan's office, with its rich, nubby fabrics and antique coatrack. But for women's centers it's a whole other story. Working on scanty budgets, dependent upon donations and grants, sometimes embroiled in disputes with the medical community. We really haven't come a long way at all. Elizabeth Blackwell established the first medical infirmary for women a hundred and fifty years ago, and we are still fighting the same battles.

I handed the receptionist my specimen and took a seat in the barren waiting room. Two women were already there, both with suitcases. (The center also does low-cost abortions.) I smiled at them. One looked away, the other smiled back shyly.

What must they be feeling? Fear, guilt, relief, maybe a mixture of all three? In college one of the girls on my floor became pregnant and had to leave school to try to get an abortion. Of course we knew nothing about that at the time. *Those things* weren't talked about. It wasn't until later that her roommate finally confided in us about the furtive visits to local doctors, the frantic calls to Planned Parenthood.

I hadn't known her well, and at seventeen still

regarded my virginity as my most precious possession, but her story threatened all of us, the way an under-forty cancer story does now. I hadn't thought about her in years, but today she came back to me, with her sandy hair, and freckles spilled across her nose, and I wondered how she had resolved it, and whether it ever really was resolved.

The receptionist motioned to me to follow her. "It's positive," she whispered apologetically, thinking I was a candidate for her services.

"That's wonderful!" I almost shouted. "I had two negative tests and my doctor said I'd get my period."

She wrinkled her face in disdain. "That's doctors for you. They think they know everything!"

That Friday Arnie and I were sitting in Morgan's waiting room. Holding hands, giggling, whispering, self-satisfied. Morgan was visibly pleased, and if he was surprised, it was deeply concealed. Had I expected some admission of error? A "Looks like you were right after all"? Maybe, but it never happens that way.

Anyway, none of that was really important, except, perhaps, to my ego. We had serious things to talk about. How we were going to manage this pregnancy.

"When you are about twelve, maybe thirteen weeks pregnant—" he began.

"No, not thirteen weeks," I interrupted. "I'm superstitious. Not always," I hastened to add. "Just about pregnancy. It has something to do with magical thinking."

Morgan knit his splendid eyebrows quizzically.

"You know, having control. If I don't eat such and such, things will be okay."

He stared blankly.

Well, of course he was skeptical, *he* had never been pregnant. What did he know about all the little rituals women invent for themselves to insure a healthy pregnancy? One friend didn't wear anything black for nine months. Another collected Kennedy half-dollars, although why she thought anything connected with that family would bring luck, I'll never know.

"Okay, then at twelve or fourteen weeks," he continued, "we'll put in the suture."

As he talked about the Shirodkar procedure—a purse-string stitch designed to reinforce a weakened cervix—his voice became alive with excitement. Saving babies was clearly his thing. "It's done under general anesthesia, and if all goes well, you can leave the hospital the next day and resume normal activities in a week, except"—he averted his eyes slightly—"except for intercourse."

What? In all my investigation, no one had mentioned this *tiny* restriction. I glanced casually over at Arnie; he shifted uncomfortably in his seat.

"You mean for the *entire* pregnancy?" I asked.

"Uh-huh. It can lead to infection for Shirodkar patients, and we're finding out it might for others as well. But think of it this way: We're not putting the suture in until around fourteen weeks, and we generally advise against intercourse from the thirty-sixth week on, so it's only a question of twenty-two weeks," he said brightly.

Even with this new math, I didn't feel too cheery. I wondered what else about this procedure I didn't know.

"What about the effects of anesthesia on the baby?" I asked.

"Nothing to worry about. The only real risks are possible rupture of the membranes or premature labor, while the suture is being put in or shortly after. But we just got the latest figure back and eighty percent of Shirodkar patients carry to term."

For the next few weeks we thought little about the pregnancy. Arnie's father was having surgery at a hospital nearby and our apartment became a hotel for his family, all of whom live out of town. When they had finally gone, Arnie and I rejoiced not only at his father's regained health but also at our regained apartment.

"C'mon," said Arnie, the Tuesday evening they left. "Let's do some Christmas shopping and celebrate."

There's something about the holiday season that always pulls me to it. I sat in the cab with my nose literally pressed to the glass as we rode down Fifth Avenue. First stop Saks's maternity department, where we looked through the racks together, selecting things to try on. With our arms full, we went into one of the spacious dressing rooms and laughed as I tried on a pillow they provided to simulate a belly.

I was just taking a knit dress off the hanger when I felt a gushing sensation. I looked down. I was bleeding, not just a stain but a real flow.

"Oh, God, I'm having a miscarriage," I said. Dots of red were spilling onto the floor. Instinctively I tried to mop them with a tissue.

"Don't worry about the carpet, let's get home," Arnie said.

We made our apologies to the saleswoman and left hurriedly. Arnie ran out in the street ahead of me to get a cab. But with only four shopping days left until Christmas, we had to walk blocks before getting one. I was practically shaking from fright, sobbing the whole way home. As soon as we reached the apartment, I lay down on the bed and called Morgan's service.

Five minutes later the phone rang. It was Matthew Davis, one of his associates. "Are you in a lot of pain?" he asked.

"No, no pain at all."

"Well, that's good. You're eleven weeks pregnant? Might just be the placenta invading the uterus."

I had a mental picture of my placenta armed with bows and arrows.

"Come in tomorrow at ten. Don't eat or drink anything. And"—he paused—"if you pass the fetus during the night, bring it in."

His words were chilling. I'd heard of it happening. Women miscarrying in the street, in the bathroom. My whole body shuddered at the thought. I kept my hands protectively on my stomach and my legs tight together as if the sheer force of my wishing it could keep the pregnancy intact.

The night passed torturously. Each time I rolled or turned over, Arnie startled and asked, "What's wrong?" And each time I went to the bathroom I closed my eyes, afraid of what I'd see.

Finally, bits of light seeped around the edge of our shade. I got out of bed. Still a little bleeding, but nothing else. Arnie packed an overnight case. I was sure I was going straight to the hospital.

Dr. Davis arrived at the office after we did. He was wearing a ski parka and looked young enough to still be getting allergy shots. He examined me. "The pregnancy is still in the uterus, so we have a chance."

"How much of a chance?" Arnie wanted to know when we were all seated together in the office.

"Well, that depends on whether you're an optimist or a pessimist," Davis responded. "I know you've had a rough time," he continued, "but the hysterogram was good, and that's important. You'll have your progeny," he said, "but maybe not this time. Stay in bed for a while—no lovemaking either. We'll check you again next week."

The next few days were like the first night. Every time I stood up, I felt queasy. Would the bleeding become heavy again? Would there be tissue? The fetus? My body a bundle of fear, I lay on my bed reading, visiting with friends who came by.

The weather turned to winter. Delicate snow crystals touched the window and disappeared. I yearned to go out. For two days now the bleeding had been replaced by a brownish stain. I called Morgan's office. He was away for the next two weeks. The secretary put me through to Dr. Roth.

"Hi, Barbara, how's the bleeding?" he asked. I had never even met Dr. Roth, and I found it impressive that he was so familiar with my case. But he was not as impressed with my news.

"Brown staining means there's still bleeding. I wouldn't go out if I were you. Try to take it easy a little longer."

I was so disappointed. I loved the snow. It made me nostalgic for my childhood—sledding in Prospect Park, skating on the lake, then home to rich hot chocolate. Days when no one was afraid, days when my parents were young enough to build snowmen.

I resigned myself to staying in. Sarah Lawrence was on a combined Christmas/intersession vacation and I had student evaluations to do. The college requires faculty members to write, in two hundred fifty words or more, a comprehensive appraisal of each of their students. Grades are hardly ever seen, but the evaluation is mailed to the student, and the school places great importance on them—so much so that faculty checks are withheld until all the forms are submitted to the dean. Ada Webber had suggested that new professors Xerox copies of evaluations written over the past few years to use as guidelines for their own.

I sat down with my packet and began reading. "Toby has difficulty blending diverse pieces . . ." "Joellen possesses the ability for fine synthesis. . . ." Blending diverse pieces? Fine synthesis? Were they talking about students or a Cuisinart? I couldn't write like that even if I tried. It seemed to take forever to do just one.

I was still staining. If it stopped in the morning, it started again by noon. It was frustrating, this new obstinacy of my body. For three decades, my body and I had lived pretty much in harmony. Oh, I had never liked it much. How many women do? But it generally responded as I expected. When I ran, my legs carried me; when I exercised, I got stronger; when I dieted, I got thinner. Once I had really abused it by doing the usual student things—not eating properly, not sleeping enough—and I became seriously ill. Doctors always start listening carefully to my medical history when I mention my almost simultaneous bout with viral pneumonia and pyelonephritis.

But the point is, I had really brought that on myself. And even the miscarriage I had come to see as understandable, almost predictable because of the horribly inappropriate and inaccurate medical treatment I'd received.

Now, however, I was doing everything the doctors and all my reading told me I should be doing and still my body would have its own way. It was a sobering realization that I lived with uneasily in those weeks.

The doctors, though, remained encouraging. The uterus was growing. "Hang in there," they said. I could hang in there if the baby could, but my vacation was almost over. I didn't know what to do about the commute.

Both Davis and Roth were concerned about the stairs at Grand Central Station and the pressure of the trip. Arnie and I decided to get a car. In the past we had rented for special occasions, but now we could justify our need for it.

She was secondhand and two-tone brown. We called her Glencora, after Lady Glen of Trollope's Palliser family; Glennie for short. I used to think people who got attached to their cars were nuts, but I found myself in lively chatter with her every morning. What a relief to be able to drive up to Bronxville. And how much more of a relief that the staining stopped five days before I had to!

My next doctor's appointment was with Morgan. This would be the first time I'd seen him since his vacation. Now that the bleeding had stopped, I felt relaxed and confident. And he, deeply tanned, looked relaxed and confident, too. But as soon as he examined me, his mouth drew into a taut line and the eyebrows came together.

"Your uterus is a little too small for thirteen weeks," he said grimly.

"Oh, no." The words came out like a gasp. I struggled to remain composed. "Can you please talk to Arnie and me in the office?" I asked in a voice that was barely audible.

"I think it's an incomplete miscarriage," Morgan explained to us. "The fetus dies, but for some reason remains in the uterus. Do you still feel pregnant?"

"Yes."

"Well, that's good. Look, I don't know for certain. Davis and Roth thought the uterus was the right size, but I don't. The pelvic exam is subjective. That's why I want you to go to Hillcrest Hospital for a sonogram. I'll ask Caroline to arrange it for this afternoon."

But the sonogram schedule was filled for Friday. Monday at 9:30 was the earliest possible appointment. We took the number and said we'd keep trying from home in case they had a cancellation, but there was none.

The weekend was our foe. Unrelieved and uncertain. It was tempting to believe that everything would be all right. I did still feel pregnant and maybe looked it a trifle. Some people, friends of mine, would have waited until they knew for sure; but we assumed the worst. I think we had to, as a shield against being caught unawares like the last time, to prepare ourselves while we had time to talk about it calmly, alone, before it became a matter of hospitals and intravenous drips and bright lights and operating rooms.

But still there were those nagging thoughts that leaped unbidden to my mind. The anxieties, the fears of worthlessness, the insecurities. And also that most sacred feeling blessed in Jewish homes along with the challah: guilt; for not drinking four glasses of milk a day, for resenting having to go to the doctor every week, for trying to have everything, i.e., more than my mother had.

We took a taxi to Hillcrest, Arnie instructing the youthful driver to go slowly and avoid the bumps. As if you could do anything *but* drive slowly in Monday morning traffic.

When we got there, we went directly up to J-2, the labor-and-delivery floor. Through dimly lit halls, we followed the signs to the ultrasound room. Linen carts seemed to idle aimlessly in the corridor, trash cans overflowed. I hoped the medical staff was more efficient than the housekeeping.

The room we wanted was at the end of the hall and we only had a short wait before our turn. Karen Walters, the technician, greeted us warmly. She had a strong, confident handshake and wore her hair in what used to be called a chignon. She led us into a room with a table and a large screen that looked like it could have been for a television. "Have you ever seen this machine before?" she asked; and then, without waiting for a reply, she launched into her spiel.

"The sonogram uses sound waves to produce a black-and-white picture on this screen," she said, pointing. "To map out intra-abdominal objects, I simply slide this transducer over your stomach. Since the technique doesn't depend on the density of calcified bone mass, like an X-ray, but on the existence of any mass that reflects sound waves, I can detect a fetus as early as the eighth week and the fetal heartbeat as early as the tenth week. If you have a viable fetus, this test will show it."

I lay back on the table and pulled up my shirt to avoid getting it stained with the mineral oil that Karen was generously spreading over my stomach. She began moving the transducer, which looked like a telephone receiver, back and forth over my abdomen. I grabbed Arnie's hand and held my breath. This was all too familiar.

"There's the fetus," Karen called out excitedly. "It looks okay."

Arnie and I sighed loudly.

"And wait—shh—I hear the heart beating, too. The fetus is small. Could you have miscalculated your date of conception?"

"No, I don't think so. My periods are regular. Maybe I'm just having a small baby."

Karen pointed out the head and arms on the screen. I nodded, but I really wasn't sure what anything was. Anyway, I was too happy to care. We waited out in the corridor for Morgan to come.

"I'm sorry I worried you," he said apologetically. "But you *did* seem small. We'll try to do the suture in about three weeks, a little later than we planned, but we'll give the baby a chance to grow. I don't want you too active until then—no lifting or climbing, and limit your walking. Come in next week, I'll check you in the office. I'm sorry I scared you," he said again, and left, I think to do a delivery.

Arnie and I walked back down the dingy hall, nodded to the abandoned linen carts, and talked about what I should do. My office at Sarah Lawrence was two flights up; so was one of my classrooms. The campus was spread out, hilly, winding. It was a real climb just to get from my car to the rest of the school. We were in the midst of a fierce winter with record-breaking cold and constant heavy snowfalls.

"Look," said Arnie when we were finally inside the coffee shop where we were going to have breakfast, "you'll just have to tell them you're pregnant and that you're having trouble."

I speared some greasy-looking scrambled egg with my fork and remained quiet.

The phrase "having trouble" reverberated through my head. I hated to admit it. That women could manage both careers and children, I accepted as surely as I knew the sun rose in the east. And I believed that those of us who wanted to do both had a commitment to the women who came before us and those who would come after us to do it in the best possible way.

And now, what was *I* doing? Confirming the convictions of those of my less liberated colleagues that children really *did* interfere with a woman's work, that there really *was* no point in admitting them to medical school or sponsoring their dissertations, because look what happens when they decide to become pregnant. Oh, how that tore at me!

"I guess I'll have to call them today," I said, sipping the lukewarm coffee. "If nothing else, it should be interesting to see how the sisterhood responds to motherhood."

And what a response it was! They not only switched my office to a beautiful airy one near the parking lot, they changed my classroom, too. Their concern was moving.

"Take a full week off after you're sutured," advised Ada, making it sound like a command. "We'll take turns covering your classes."

"Maybe you shouldn't commute up here," suggested Dean Roberts. "Why don't you stay in the guesthouse for the next three weeks? After all, the driving has *got* to be putting pressure on you."

Living at Sarah Lawrence for three weeks was an interesting idea. I didn't mind driving in the snow, and Glennie had never let me down, but she was old and didn't have snow tires. Suppose she got stuck? Suppose she skidded? Arnie and I looked at the guesthouse. It would have been great, except that all the toilet facilities were upstairs. Morgan had been definite about no climbing.

"Why don't you stay at a hotel nearby?" one of my colleagues suggested. "Arnie could commute every day, and you could go home for the weekends."

I started making inquiries. The Holiday Inn seemed like our best bet, cheapest and closest to the campus.

I have to admit, it wasn't so bad being in the suburbs. It did, however, reinforce our feeling about commuting *into* Manhattan. Friends who had moved from the city, no matter in which direction, no matter how far, whether to Larchmont or Poughkeepsie, swore it took "only thirty-five minutes door-to-door." Arnie was never able to do it in less than an hour, sometimes more. One day there was a fire at Grand Central Station; another day the switches were frozen, or there was a power failure, or signal trouble. I was glad I wasn't cooking dinner for him.

The meals out were an extra dividend. Bronxville is not exactly a college town, but some of the pubs reflect the student population. Sitting in small, dark restaurants with the music blaring recalled graduate-school days during the height of student protests; the pulsating energy, the hopes, the convictions.

Sarah Lawrence had recently used the Sixties as a theme for a dance. Students had painted doves and "Out Now" signs and had worn "War Is Not Healthy" buttons.

Six years after Kent State, and the antiwar movement was already something quaint!

But I had changed, too. I remember picketing stores that sold grapes; and iceberg lettuce, that symbol of wretched oppression, had been banished from my home and lips for years. I had marched for civil rights, for peace, how many times to Washington? And been chased and tear-gassed. And now as I sat there, my unborn child a barely perceptible swell, I could not imagine a single cause worth bringing it harm.

How remarkable, this fierce protective love, this turning so totally inward. Would my baby always be so strong a ballast, or would this intense intimacy pass with the pregnancy? I thought about that during those happy, pensive, peaceful weeks in Bronxville, and wondered how much change a child would bring.

My surgery was scheduled for a Wednesday, and I entered Hillcrest the night before. I had taught Tuesday, getting home just in time to change, pack an overnight bag, and leave. Even as we were in the cab headed for the hospital, my mind was still engaged in the seminar I'd just left—the questions I had asked, the students' responses, where it had faltered, how it could be improved . . .

Then I saw my hospital room, and fear rose up inside me. Small, stark, grayish, it looked out on a construction site; the crane and dump truck, covered with dingy, clotted snow, looked like huge prehistoric beasts.

I put my suitcase down and said heavily, "I guess this is it."

"Pretty dismal," Arnie, usually so optimistic, agreed.

My parents brought in some food from a nearby delicatessen to brighten things up a bit, then wandered around the corridor, looking at the newborn nursery, while I tried to get the TV picture to stop rolling.

After they left, I walked around the halls and then back to my room to wait for the anesthesiologist. He came around nine, but he could just as well not have bothered. He spoke and understood very little English. I did manage, though, to figure out that he had ordered some pre-op medication for me to take that evening. Pre-op medication for a pregnant woman? Would it affect the fetus? Did he even know I was pregnant? I tried to tell him.

"Yes, I know, deliver baby," he said, trying to reassure me. "Take pill."

Now *that* really made me nervous. As soon as he left I called Morgan to ask him about it. He checked with the nurses' station and phoned back to say that the medication was a sleeping pill. I could take it if I felt I needed it.

Only later did I realize how outrageous it was to have an anesthesiologist, the most important person in the operating room, the one responsible for the patient's life, not able to speak English. I hadn't known then that experts place the mortality rate from general anesthesia at one out of every two hundred and sixty operations. I hadn't known then the scarcity of competent anesthesiologists in this country, or how important it was to discuss the *anesthesiologist* as well as the anesthesia with your doctor before entering the hospital. I hadn't known then to insist that the anesthesiologist be board-certified or at least a resident physician trained in anesthesia.

That night I was just relieved to have the question of the pre-op medication settled. At least I thought it was settled when I told the nurse that I didn't want it. But about a half-hour later the door to my room was flung open wide. No knock, no anything. In walked a weary resident. "I hear you don't want to take the sleeping pill."

I explained my reasons. He made a halfhearted attempt to argue, then left, shaking his head.

"Why should he care?" I later asked the nurse.

"Oh, but he does. He's been up two nights in a row. If you become anxious later on and need stronger medication, *he's* the one who's going to be called."

"You mean sleeping pills are prescribed for the

convenience of the house staff?" What was this? A rewrite of *Coma?*

"Partly," she whispered, "but don't tell anyone I told you."

I read until about midnight, then turned off the light. But I couldn't sleep. I tossed and turned. Wind howled through the empty construction site like a pack of wolves. Cold crept into the room. I pulled the thin blanket up around my neck and hunched my shoulders. I was freezing. I rang for the nurse, but she said there were no extra blankets. Finally, I got out of bed and put on my velour bathrobe and a pair of woolen knee socks I had worn under my jeans. But still, sleep was shy. Oh, well, it really didn't matter. It was more important that Morgan slept well than I.

He had, he assured me when he saw me the next morning. I was in on of the labor rooms waiting to be moved into the OR. The nurses checked the heartbeat and gave me some liquid Di-Gel to drink. I was so hungry that anything would have tasted good.

When I finally got into the operating room, the clock read 10:20. Two residents were scrubbing along with Morgan.

"You're going to do this yourself, aren't you?" I asked. I had heard too many horror stories of residents performing surgery. My cervix was in bad enough shape already without being used for practice.

"Absolutely," he answered, coming over to stand next to me. A small, dark nurse began to put my legs in the stirrups.

"Why don't you wait until she's asleep?" asked Morgan, the consummate gentleman. She gave him a put-upon look, then loosened my legs. Morgan introduced me to the new anesthesiologist. This one understood me perfectly. He asked again about my allergies and started the IV drip. The nurse held my hand. I could see Morgan and the residents put their masks over their faces, and then darkness engulfed me.

* * *

The clock said 10:55. I was in the recovery room.

"It went fine," said Arnie's voice drifting over my head. I opened my eyes and smiled at him. Ten minutes later Morgan came in. He had changed out of his OR greens and was is a suit. "Any cramps?" he asked.

"No, just hunger pains."

"Good, you can eat when you get back to your room. Don't get out of bed until tomorrow. You'll be getting morphine injections to prevent contractions. I'll try to stop by later."

As soon as I got back to my room, I had my first shot. It made me pleasantly drowsy and hazy. But about an hour later, after I had eaten lunch, I became nauseated. I called for the nurse, but she insisted that it was merely a reaction to the anesthesia. I was skeptical. I'd had general anesthesia before and had never become sick from it. Maybe it was the morphine. All afternoon I willed my stomach to stay calm, taking deep breaths and trying to relax. But after my second injection I felt my diaphragm and stomach press together violently, and I began to vomit.

As soon as I stopped for a minute I called Morgan. I was still retching uncontrollably. He sounded concerned. "It's the morphine, all right. Don't take any more. The vomiting could throw you into contractions. We want to keep the uterus as calm as possible."

By that night I felt better, but stayed in the hospital until Friday, just to make sure.

I was home a week, then back to Sarah Lawrence, where everything seemed to be happening at once. My graduate students were panicking that they'd never get their masters' essays done. My undergraduates were panicking about life in general. And my colleagues were panicking about the advance copy of Anne Roiphe's *New York Times Magazine* article, "The Trouble at Sarah Lawrence." Roiphe had concluded the place was teeming with lesbians.

Lesbians there were, but, as one of my students put it, "I've never seen homosexuality made so boring." The straights and gays lived pretty much in harmony. We did our thing, they did theirs. No group proselytized the other. Some lesbians were conspicuous, most were not. Lois, one of my favorites, said, "It's getting very hard to be different." "It's always been hard," I replied, and felt annoyed at Roiphe.

The debates on compus were rampant and sometimes rancorous. If we tried to get the article squelched, would it be inhibiting free speech? If it was printed, would it call for a rebuttal? Would that be admitting or giving dignity to the charges? If we ignored it, would prospective students and their parents ignore it, too? As the publication date approached, everyone's tension level seemed to rise, except mine.

I was then in my sixth month and my psyche was blissfully languorous. Just as my books on pregnancy predicted, as my growing belly occupied more of my body space, so, too, it occupied more of my mind. I was floating through life, peacefully in harmony with the baby.

Everything seemed to be coming together for us. Sarah Lawrence had rehired me for the fall, and had agreed to let me come back on a part-time basis, two days a week. The campus was looking lovely with tiny fragrant buds. I started holding my seminars outside, sitting on the green surrounded by earnest young faces. The perfect fantasy of college teaching.

At home, things were calm and content. Laura's reluctant acceptance of my pregnancy was slowly changing into excitement about her role as a big sister. And Arnie and I—well, we were silly and giddy and caring and loving, smiling conspiratorially, coming home with little gifts, for the new baby or for each other. Once it was a dressing gown Arnie surprised me with. A slinky, sexy affair straight out of some Harlow movie.

"To take with you to the hospital."

"It's beautiful, Arnie. But for the hospital . . . don't you think it's a bit—um—a bit décolleté?" Actually, I had serious doubts that I would fit into it *then*, forget about in four months.

He looked crestfallen. I hated to spoil his fun. "I

could wear it here, though," I said, trying to hold my breath as I pulled it over my belly. He brightened immediately.

So for weeks I padded around the apartment putting cream cheese on bagels, dusting the furniture, wearing my big furry bedroom slippers and an outrageously ornate creation that Laura said made me look like a chiffon balloon and made Arnie very happy.

I was seeing Morgan every other Friday so that the position of the suture could be checked. So far it was in place, but I always worried until the examination was over.

On this Friday we had just listened to the heartbeat, a good strong sound, and Morgan started to check the cervix. He seemed to be probing a little more deeply. A frown spread across his face.

"This may be a little uncomfortable," he said as he reached for a speculum and placed a stool at the end of the table. "I want to get a good look at what's happening."

My breathing was the only sound in the room for a few minutes.

"The suture is slipping," he said, turning off the lamp and pushing back the stool.

"What?" I asked, raising myself up on my elbows.

"Slipping—moving down the cervix. Why don't you get dressed? I'll talk to you in the office."

I slid off the table and over to where I had hung my clothes. I was so shaky I pulled one of the buttons off my shirt as I tried to fasten it.

Outside, Arnie was pacing. "What's wrong?" he asked as soon as he saw me. "It took so long."

"It's no good." I swallowed back the tears.

Morgan looked almost as grim as we did. The suture wasn't holding and my cervix was effacing—shortening in preparation for labor. It was already 50 percent effaced, and, with over three months to go, he was worried. *Very worried.*

"I think you ought to get into bed," he said.

"What? You mean for the rest of my pregnancy? But

how can I do that? What about my teaching? My students?" Probably I sounded a bit hysterical. I felt it.

"Look, you can't bury your head in the sand. You have an incompetent cervix. We have to get the weight of gravity off the suture or you'll deliver in a matter of weeks."

"Oh, no," I moaned.

Arnie put his face in his hands. We were frozen, numb, silent. "I don't understand," Arnie said after a while. "We know lots of women who have been sutured and they didn't have to stay in bed."

"Your wife has a short cervix," Morgan said, speaking directly to Arnie as though I weren't in the room. "There's practically no posterior lip."

"But no one ever told me my cervix was too short," I protested. Too short for what? I didn't know. But obviously too short to sustain a pregnancy.

"Well, maybe it hasn't always been this way. . . ." His voice trailed off as he turned back to the beginning of my chart. "I *still* don't understand why Bentley did a cervical biopsy when you never had a positive Pap test."

"You think he took off too much of the cervix?" I leaned forward in my chair, shuddering slightly at the thought.

Morgan rubbed his eyes behind his glasses. "I don't know. . . . Maybe."

"But if she stays in bed," Arnie interrupted, "will she carry to term?"

"I hope so—our chances are pretty good." He tapped his pen up and down on the desk a few times. "We'll start seeing you every week from now on," he said finally. "You can get out of bed to go to the bathroom, to shower, and to eat. The rest of the time, try to remain flat. Think of it as a sabbatical," he said, sounding a little lighter.

I forced a weak smile. Arnie and I bundled up and left the office. We walked to the car under a sky that looked as if it had been smudged with a dirty eraser. As soon as I sat down inside, my control gave way. Tears started streaming down my cheeks. I was so confused, so totally unprepared for this, so frightened.

I had to decide what I was going to do. How could I stop teaching? I had a contract, and my students counted on me. I'd worked with them the whole year, knew them, knew their intimacies, understood their strengths, weaknesses. I knew that Wendy had had an abortion, that Jena couldn't bear to speak in class, that Anita worked as a cleaning woman to earn money. I knew how all these things affected their studies. Seven months it had taken me to gain their confidence. How could I quit them now?

But the baby—could I risk losing it? No. There was absolutely no choice.

I put off calling the college all afternoon. But at three o'clock I knew I couldn't wait any longer. I picked up the phone and dialed so fast I got Claire's Cleaners instead of the school. The second time, I reached Sarah Lawrence. Dean Roberts listened sympathetically while I explained my situation and my offer to help any replacement they could find. He said he'd call back in a half-hour.

Twenty minutes later the phone rang. "If you're willing, we'll bus each of your seminars to your apartment once a week. We'd like to keep you on."

Jubilation! I couldn't believe their flexibility, their respect for my priorities. Oh, God, I was touched. And I knew that it would be good for me to have the teaching, to see my students, to follow their progress for the rest of the year. Yes, there was something to that Sarah Lawrence tradition after all. That night we ordered in Chinese food. I was starting to feel a little better.

On Saturday Arnie drove out to Long Island to see Laura. He went early, leaving lunch for me in the refrigerator. I looked at the clock—only two hours had passed. I'll never be able to do this. *Three and a half months in bed. It's impossible.* I began to cry.

Chapter 5

What gloom! For days it lasted. I couldn't shake it. I couldn't adjust. I hated being so restricted; it was anathema to me. I was bored and lonely, and angry. Yes. Angry that I should have to go through all this to have a baby when other women, women who didn't even want kids, did it so effortlessly.

So I wailed the plaintive wail from time out of mind. *"It's not fair!"*

Poor Arnie. He was getting the brunt of it. And he was trying so hard to make it tolerable for me. He whipped up tempting meals (restraining his culinary proclivities a bit for my sake), and even learned how to do needlepoint during his lunch hour so he could teach it to me, the bedridden.

He was patient at first, listening to me, reasoning with me. But after ten days he finally threw up his hands and stormed out of the room. "Okay then. Get out of bed. Do it and get it over with."

I became frightened at Arnie's challenge. He had called my bluff. I couldn't get out of bed. I knew I couldn't. As silly as I thought it was to lie there feeling so healthy and energetic, I trusted Morgan's judgment. It made sense to keep the weight off the cervix. And I couldn't— I *absolutely couldn't*—bear the thought of losing another baby. Do you hear that, God? I won't survive it!

81

So I had no choice. No choice at all. And with that came a certain calm and almost acceptance.

I threw myself into it and made it a project, experimenting with ways to make the time go faster. Three and a half months in bed was too long to imagine. So I tackled one week at a time. From one Wednesday "Living" section of *The New York Times* to the next Wednesday "Living" section; from one Friday appointment with Dr. Morgan to the next; from one episode of "Upstairs, Downstairs" to another. I read, knit, sewed, and prepared for my classes, which were going to start right after spring vacation.

I had been in bed about three weeks when Arnie had to leave for a meeting in Chattanooga; he wouldn't be back until the next day. "Are you sure you'll be okay alone tonight?" asked my mother. "How will you manage to get dressed? How will you make breakfast?"

"I'll be fine. It's just a question of logistics." That's Arnie's expression, really. I think he developed it after marrying into my family. I don't know how others use it, but for him it means *it can be done without the hysteria*.

A perfect example: getting my desk into the second bedroom of our new apartment. We were moving primarily so that I could have an office to work in. The new apartment was ideal, except for the minor detail that my desk wouldn't fit through the doorway of the study.

"Lady, you should have thought about this before you took the place," the movers yelled, dumping the desk right in the middle of the living room.

"Take it all out. Everything. We're not staying." I was already at the door.

Only Arnie remained calm. Methodically, piece by piece, he took the desk apart, carried the pieces into the study, and just as methodically reassembled them. Logistics. Plain and simple.

So that's what I thought about when I woke up the next morning. I'd coordinate my trip to the bathroom with going to the kitchen. I'd get some bread and juice and skip the coffee; it would take too long to make.

But as soon as I stood up, I felt an unfamiliar wetness. Probably just perspiration. I ignored it until I saw a round spot of blood on the toilet paper. I couldn't believe it. Bleeding? In my seventh month? I froze, then started to panic.

Logistics. I had to get to the office and I had to find a way of getting there. Lucy. I'd call Lucy. She'd leave her daughter with a neighbor and come right over. Then the office. Dr. Davis would be in at nine. "Count on him being a little late," the nurse said, "but come as soon as you can."

The nurse put me in examining room No. I. My least favorite room. I lay back on the table and tried to calm myself by counting the bulls in the wallpaper. Bulls in a gynecologist's office? I wonder what that means. . . .

"How's the professor doing?" boomed Dr. Davis, looking like the prototype for Peter Pan. Thin and agile, he perched on the counter reading my chart. He found no cause for the bleeding. "But you'd better restrict your activities even more. Urinate in a bedpan, don't get up for meals, and stop showering. Stay in bed, completely horizontal as much as humanly possible."

"We'll do it," Arnie reassured me later that day on the phone when he heard the news. "It's simply a matter of attending to the details. It's not that different from what you're already doing. And with Davis saying you'll save the pregnancy this way, I don't see that we have any choice."

"Maybe it's just a matter of details for you," I said accusingly, "but it's going to be awful for me. How can I use a bedpan with my students around? How will we manage washing my hair?" I would have gone on, but Arnie interrupted.

"I can't, I really can't go into it now. I just got in from the airport. Joe's waiting to see me, and I have a dozen phone messages. We'll talk when I get home." He clicked off.

I held on to the receiver for a few seconds, then slammed it down. Whenever Arnie got off the phone so abruptly I felt slightly rejected, but today even more so. I lay on the bed staring straight ahead for about twenty minutes. How would we manage? Would we?

I knew how resourceful Arnie was: If anyone could figure out how to live in a queen-size bed, he could. But would *I* be able to do it? Not getting up for meals? Using a bedpan? I am—or maybe *was* is a better word—a fairly inhibited person. I don't have much difficulty sharing ideas or feelings, but where my body is concerned, I generally opt for *enclosure* rather than *exposure*. Arnie still teases me for refusing to enter a coed sauna in Norway even though I didn't know any of the people inside.

"C'mon, don't be so modest," he teased.

"I'm *not* modest," said I, undoing the top few buttons of my blouse.

"Then why won't you go in?" Arnie started to open the door.

"I'm too modest."

Well, that was a while ago. It's hard to remain modest when the condition of your cervix is a subject of daily conversation with friends, colleagues, and doctors.

A bedpan, of course, was a little different. But if I could manage to use it when only Arnie was around . . . well, maybe I could do it. We'd have to buy one. I reached for a pad and pencil and started making lists of things to get. I was organizing, planning, directing. It made me feel better.

Arnie came home looking weary. He hadn't shaved closely, his tie was loosened, and his shirt collar undone. He threw his suitcase on the chair and sat down next to me.

"I wish you didn't have to travel anymore," I began as soon as I saw him. "I was so nervous this morning not being able to get in touch with you."

"But you reached Lucy."

"It's not the same," I protested. "And besides, if I'm really going to be so restricted, it'll be impossible for me to be alone overnight."

"What can I do?" asked Arnie. "If I have to go away again, maybe your parents can sleep here."

"Can't you tell Joe that you can't travel for the next three months?"

"It's not up to him. He doesn't tell me when to go. I'm in the midst of an important trial."

"And I'm in the midst of an important pregnancy," I snapped.

"Look," said Arnie, raising his voice a little, "it might not always be this way, but right now we're living on my salary. That's what's paying for the doctors and almost everything else."

Well, here it was—the typical male response. I hated when he did this. It didn't happen often, and always surprised me when it did.

Arnie is as far from being a male chauvinist as I am from being the total woman. I remember when we were first living together—I was working full-time and studying for my doctoral orals in the evenings, and Arnie was working full-time and cleaning and cooking for us in the evenings.

"I'm sorry you have to do all this," I would call from the living room, a disembodied voice floating above a stack of books and pads.

"Boy, do you ever need your consciousness raised," he would laugh. "Why is this any more your job than mine?"

And he believed it. So what was this your-baby-versus-my-job shit now?

"Look, I didn't mean it," Arnie began.

"But you *did* mean it, Arnie, and I think that's important. This whole thing's getting to be a bit much, isn't it?"

Arnie hesitated. We had both become so afraid to complain about what was happening with the pregnancy. Being pregnant and in bed was better than not being pregnant at all. "Well—yes, I guess it is a lot to contend with."

"It's impossible."

"It's terrible."

"It's the worst."

"It sucks."

We both breathed sighs of relief. We'd said it. No more pretending that we were enjoying it, or that it was easy. No more supercopers. It was the pits. But we had no choice, so we'd do it. Sometimes well, sometimes poorly, but without deception. At least not with each other.

We talked for about an hour. About the fears, frustrations, anxieties, and insecurities that this was calling forth. It was one of those special times, when neither tries to win or prove or show, and both just want to understand.

Our first step was to look for someone to clean the house. In the past, we had always split the work; and when I was bedridden, Arnie carried on alone. But now he had to spend more of his time doing things for me.

So we found Mamie. Every other Thursday Mamie arrived at eight o'clock, a large, sweet-faced woman. She didn't clean very well, but was pleasant company and often came into my room to chat. She'd lower herself slowly into the faded chair, a remnant from my first marriage, dustrag in one hand, cup of tea in the other, and talk about her children. She had ten. Most were "good children," but her oldest son had dropped out of school. That was the one who worried her.

The other days Arnie and I established our own routine. We'd wake up about an hour earlier each morning so Arnie could get everything done. He'd bring me my toothbrush, soap, and basin, and then dash into the kitchen to make breakfast. Then, while I was having my second cup of coffee, Arnie made lunch. He had purchased an insulated picnic basket so the food could stay by the bed until I was ready to eat. Every so often Arnie hid a note inside my lunch box: "To my own Sophia Loren, I'm so proud of you. We're going to make it this time."

Before he left for the day, he'd move a bench next to the bed with everything I needed to get through the next eight hours: books for teaching; books for relaxing;

pads; pencils; magazines; needlepoint; knitting; the telephone; an emery board; a bottle of astringent; cotton; a jar of Keri Lotion (to prevent bedsores); Wash'n Dries; powder; my comb; a hand mirror; and the bedpan, which I would use and then dump in a diaper pail nearby. My bedside table was a veritable notions counter.

Days passed. Slowly I began to adjust. I remember reading that women in concentration camps worried about what to do when they got their periods, but that in time their bodies took care of it: From the tension and malnutrition, they stopped menstruating.

So, too, bed rest created its own imperatives, its own rationale. The inactivity produced a lethargy that made even a walk around the block seem too strenuous. Amazing how quickly my muscles atrophied. We noticed it first in my legs; usually firm and strong from years of ballet classes inspired by the movie *The Red Shoes*, they now had become weak and flaccid.

"Do you think the same thing's happening to my mind?" I asked only half jokingly.

"I doubt it," Arnie said. But I didn't. It was tempting to fall into an invalid mentality, to identify with my physical condition and become totally passive. It was easier. Sometimes.

Although it was only April, New York City was having a brief flirtation with summer, and without the central air conditioning the apartment became stifling. The whole room seemed to perspire. The headboard became sticky, the plants drooped. I'd lie in bed pouring powder down the front of my nightgown and feeling sorry for myself. I was messy and stale. The air hung heavy and acrid with urine. I couldn't wait for Arnie to come home, bathe me, wash my hair, give me a clean nightgown.

It was 5:10. It wouldn't be long now. But a few minutes later the phone rang, and as soon as I heard Arnie's voice, I knew he'd be delayed.

"Some business people we're negotiating with are up from the South, and Joe's asked me to entertain them tonight. They're set on going to Regine's. I'll try not to be too late."

I felt my heart sink to my toes. "But what about my dinner?"

"Oh, damn. I forgot about that. Call Hickory Pit. They'll deliver. Nothing'll happen if you just go to answer the door."

"Never mind, I'll manage"—my voice crisp and taut. Of course I won't manage. I won't get out of bed to open the door. Arnie knows that. I just won't eat until he gets home. That'll . . . what? Show him?

The phone rang again. It was my neighbor, Florence. "Arnie just called and asked if I could bring you dinner. He didn't have time to call you back, but said to tell you that as soon as he hung up he realized that you wouldn't order in. I just made meatballs and spaghetti. I'll bring some over as soon as I get the twins to sleep."

"Are you sure you have enough?" I asked, only out of politeness. Florence always had *more* than enough. Her cooking was legendary in our building, as was her unfailing generosity.

Florence had the keys to our apartment, and in about twenty minutes I heard them jingling in the lock. She set a steaming platter on the bench next to me and refilled the Thermos I had drained hours earlier.

"How late will Arnie be?"

"I really don't know. He had an important meeting," I lied. Florence would never understand about Regine's.

I looked at the heaping plate beside me. A hot heavy meal was the last thing I felt like eating. Maybe later. I poured a cup of water and sipped it slowly. It was only seven o'clock. What would I do for the next four hours? I reached for *Gaudy Night*. Having read every Agatha Christie mystery, including some I don't think even she remembered writing, I had become a convert to Dorothy Sayers.

All my friends told me that I'd find the book engrossing, with its descriptions of Oxford University, the ethical questions it poses about the relative value of academic research. But I couldn't concentrate. I kept thinking of Arnie and felt uneasy. I wasn't annoyed—maybe just a little hurt at his "Oh, damn," like I was some kind of nuisance—but something, *something* wasn't sitting quite right.

Arnie at Regine's. Watching disco dancing. Disco seething with sexuality. Maybe he was trying it himself, whirling around some shapely thing who could dance, who could *walk*.

I felt threatened, really threatened. And why not? The new celibacy wasn't all it's cracked up to be. I didn't feel purer or more ethereal. I felt horny. *Very horny*.

And Arnie, what must he feel? Don't ask. Don't even think about it.

It was easier for me. It *had* to be. I was so worried about the baby that even the thought of sex was unthinkable. But Arnie didn't have the same physical prohibitions.

I grabbed for my hand mirror and winced at the reflection. My hair hung limply about my shoulders. My complextion—somewhere on the palette between beige and gray. Even my eyes were dull and lacking. Hardly the glow of pregnancy!

I slithered to the edge of my bed, reached for the knob of my dresser, and opened it. But I still couldn't quite grasp a nightgown. Taking a wire hanger from my bench, I fished around until I hooked a light blue cotton one.

Ah, logistics. I put it on, reveling in the way it felt against my body. Pathetic as it was, I felt proud of my accomplishment.

I combed my hair and pulled it on top of my head, fastening it with an elastic band. I almost never wore it this way, but knew Arnie had always liked this style on me. I picked up my makeup kit, first dabbing on a little rouge, then some lip gloss. I was like a child playing with her mother's things. I hunted inside and found an old white and gold container with the writing so rubbed off I could barely read the words "Mellow Midnight" on the label. This was what I was looking for, my eye shadow. It was years since I'd worn it. I had gotten rid of my eye shadow about the same time I got rid of my bra, when I started believing that women were okay the way they were.

I smeared the blue cream across my lid, but it was so dry it stood out in one ludicrous streak. It jarred me into thought. Why was I doing this? To look attractive? Sexy? I, who had always been so outspoken about women not being regarded as sex objects?

But it had been so long since we had made love. Feeling the baby kick had become our substitute. It was an intense experience, binding us together in many ways, but as father and mother, not as husband and wife. And even with Arnie's assurance that he loved the way I looked pregnant, he had to shave my legs for me, cut my toenails, dump my bedpan. It was hardly sexy, all this.

I thought I heard someone at the door. I strained to listen. "Who is it?" I called. Florence would have phoned first. I hoped she had locked the door properly. "Who is it?" I yelled again, becoming more agitated.

"It's me. Don't worry, it's me." Arnie's deep voice filled the apartment.

"God, you scared me. Is anything wrong? Why are you home so early?"

"I got some of the lawyers at Kaye, Scholer to take our guests to Regine's. I just had a quick drink with them first." Arnie, now standing at the bedroom door, was staring at me intently. "What in the world have you got on your eye?"

"On my eye? Oh—er—oh, shit, Arnie. I was feeling grubby and unattract—"

"See what I brought to eat," Arnie interrupted.

I recognized the green and orange bag in his hand as coming from Healthworks and knew without looking inside that he had stopped for frozen yogurt and fruit salad. "Oh, great!" I said enthusiastically. "I'm starving."

"Let me just get the tray and some utensils and we'll eat." Arnie set up my yellow plastic tray and moved his chair and stack table close to the bed. For a few minutes we concentrated on eating, Arnie without stopping, me pausing between mouthfuls to tell him how delicious it was.

"It's really amazing," Arnie said after a while. "You're worried that I'm ignoring you, and I'm worried that you're so caught up in the pregnancy you've forgotten about me."

"You are? Oh, Arnie-dwarmie. Why didn't you tell me?" I reached out and took his hand.

"I don't know, I guess I feel a little embarrassed about it," he said sheepishly.

"It's a good thing our insecurities blend so well," I said, still with my one iridescent eye.

Arnie gazed down at his now empty yogurt cup and looked hungrily at mine. "Hey, I'll trade you three grapes, four raisins, and a spoonful of your chocolate yogurt for a hair-wash."

"You drive a hard bargain," I said, "but my students are coming tomorrow and we haven't washed my hair since Saturday. If I throw in an extra grape, will you shave my legs, too?"

"You're on!" Arnie said, smiling widely.

Two nights a week my class came. Arnie would carry me to the sofa and I would lie with two pillows under my head, feeling much like the hostess of a French salon. The students assembled on the floor around me. We had no living-room carpet, so they sat on assorted large pillows with Indian designs, their books spread out in front of them.

The first time they came, I kept apologizing for their inconvenience. The bus ride took almost an hour each way, it was second semester, contracts would be due soon, term projects had to be completed. I knew how pressed for time even the most organized would be.

But it turned out that they enjoyed the new arrangement. Being in my living room added a special dimension to our conversations. All year I had tried to keep my classes as impersonal as possible, but the apartment intruded upon my resolve. Without meaning to, it revealed us. Arnie's photographs of Yosemite,

Norway, and Paris on the walls; my Doris Lessing
novels, the covers worn thin from so many readings; the
collage I had made of old snapshots, some taken before
we were married—Arnie without his beard, me with
teased hair and dark nail polish.

"God, you look different here!" exclaimed Sarah.
"When was this taken?"

"A lifetime ago," I replied.

We talked long after the class ended. The bus driver
would ring impatiently, anxious to get them back to
campus. One night, a few lingered behind, opting to
take the train back to school: Maureen, from the
Midwest, diffident at first among the worldly Westchest-
erites, but now an articulate A student; Wendy, a high-
school cheerleader with soft dark eyes and fragile
features, whose deliberately unkempt appearance
couldn't conceal her natural beauty; Miriam, who
couldn't make up her mind if she wanted to be a feminist
or socialist or both, the one I would have chosen for my
daughter. I loved talking to them, hearing their commit-
ments, their idealism, their demands for absolutes, their
refusal to compromise. Arnie joined us. They asked him
about law school, me about graduate school, swearing
that they'd never be co-opted by the system.

"How do you think the classes are going?" I asked.

"Great," said Miriam. "It's terrific being off campus."

"That place is a hole," interrupted Wendy. "It's so
isolating. Everyone's into herself. I don't know if I can
stand it for another year."

Arnie made coffee, we finished Laura's box of Oreos.
We talked until Miriam glanced at her watch and
realized they had only twenty-five minutes to make the
11:00 P.M. train.

The next week a few more stayed, then a few more.
It was becoming a ritual. Arnie and I discussed serving
some food. "After all," I reasoned, "we met during their
dinner hour, and most of them are on the meal plan. It's
bad enough they have to schlepp all the way here, I
think it's the least we could do."

"How many in each seminar?" Arnie asked.

"Fifteen in one, seventeen in another." I paused for a moment, trying to calculate the expense. "I guess it'll be too much," I finally said.

"Well, I think we ought to do it," Arnie said. "They're only kids, they'll eat anything."

They did eat anything, and *everything*. They were always starving, always searching for nibbles. I could hear the refrigerator door open and Jackie, one of the graduate students, start counting: "Eleven, twelve, thirteen . . . I don't believe this." She started laughing.

"What are you doing?" I called out, feeling like a stranger in my own apartment.

"Wait a minute . . . nineteen, twenty, twenty-one . . ." She came out of the kitchen. "You have twenty-two cans of tuna fish in your refrigerator," she announced. We all roared.

Every Saturday morning I would make up the shopping list for Arnie. I thought it was a little silly for me to do this, considering it had been over a month since I had seen the inside of my kitchen. But he claimed he wouldn't know what to buy.

"Why did you keep getting tuna fish if we weren't using it up?" I asked.

"I don't know. You kept putting it on the list, so I kept buying it."

Sometimes I really wonder about the wisdom of role reversal.

I looked forward to my classes all week. My students brought me my mail, gossip from campus, and one time a New York City coloring book with a note saying, "Some people will do anything to get out of the suburbs."

They had been coming to the apartment for about a month and we were up to Part III of the syllabus— Contemporary Feminism: Conflicts and Choices. I was excited about teaching this section. I hoped to help them to understand the class components of feminism, the limits of ideology; to realize that work, so desirable and liberating for a middle-class woman, was not necessarily so for her poorer sister. I had assigned tough, stimulating readings.

The class was eager; they loved the books, were anxious to talk about them, and for the first hour the discussion was impassioned. Louella, there on scholarship from the Bronx, spoke poignantly of the women she knew and their wasted, untapped lives, and wondered if the woman's movement had any value for blacks. Carol, from a wealthy suburb of Philadelphia, was trying to understand whether emotional deprivation was as bad as economic deprivation, or possibly worse.

"Are there any threads common to woman's experience that transcend class or race?" I asked enthusiastically.

"The ability to have children!" blurted out Donna, and everyone became deadly quiet.

I looked around. Miriam was fidgeting with her books, Wendy was busy taking notes. No one would make eye contact with me. Moments passed. Say something, I kept urging myself. I couldn't think of anything to say. The back of my neck under my hair grew damp. I knew they were waiting for me to move the discussion. I glanced down at the pile of books on the table next to me.

"What does Bernard have to say about the economics of motherhood?" I finally asked.

They picked up their books and leafed through them a little too intently. The conversation limped until the end of the class. No one stayed afterward.

"I have to talk to them," I told Arnie later that night. "I know they're worried that they've hurt my feelings."

"Did they?"

"Yes. No. Oh, I don't know. *They* didn't. It's the whole thing that does—the suture, the staying in bed. I'm embarrassed by the gestalt of my childbearing. Do you know that when they first started coming I was surprised that they were still taking notes, that they still thought I had anything worthwhile to say?"

Arnie looked at me curiously, sadly too, I think.

"But if I don't say anything, the class will be strained with"—I couldn't resist the pun—"*pregnant silences*. Besides, I'm worried that my experience is getting them nervous about the whole question of having children. In spite of their sophistication, they really are very young."

The next week passed quietly. The ritual morning phone calls, more Dorothy Sayers, the sweater that I was knitting for the baby, a pleasant weekend with Laura playing Monopoly and Authors on my bed. And through it all, I kept thinking of what I would say to my class.

I waited for them to get settled—it always took a few minutes for book bags to be emptied, shawls to be flung on chairs, coffee cups to be filled.

"There's something I've wanted to discuss with you for some time," I began nervously. They looked concerned, interested. "I guess . . . "—I hesitated slightly, deliberately taking a sip of my tea—"I guess I want you to know that you have the great honor of being taught by a very unusual obstetrical patient."

They laughed a little—tense, forced laughter—not quite sure how to respond. I knew that my attempt at humor had failed, but at least it committed me to continuing.

"Seriously, most women, the overwhelming majority in fact, have healthy, normal pregnancies."

Gail raised her hand. "I don't know if I should ask this or not." She looked at me questioningly. I nodded for her to continue. "But do you think you're having these problems because you postponed becoming pregnant until you were older? I mean, so you could have your career and everything," she added quickly.

"Not unless you're convinced God truly is a male chauvinist," I said.

This time they really laughed. The tension had been broken. I knew this was something they were worried about; they considered themselves feminists, most wanted to have careers.

"My problems relate to some surgical procedures I had years ago, it has nothing to do with age. Actually, women can have children well into their thirties—their forties, even—and more and more are doing it. If the last ten years has had any meaning, it should be that you young women are freer than ever before to do what you want with your lives. To have a career, a career and a family, or just a family if that's what you decide." Several heads were bobbing in agreement.

"But I don't want you to be afraid of having children because of what I'm going through. Because in spite of how it may appear, this is still the happiest time of my life, and your—your willingness to share it with me has made it even more special."

I glanced at Miriam. She looked a bit misty. So was I.

"Can we feel the baby kick?" asked Susan, changing the mood.

"Sure," I said proudly, pulling up my blue-and-white jersey top. I took her hand and placed it high on my abdomen. I felt the baby move and saw a smile spread across her face.

"So it went okay?" Arnie asked as he emerged from the bedroom where he had spent the last two hours. Often he sat in on the classes, but this time we thought his presence might be inhibiting.

I told him about it as I watched him put the chairs back around the dining-room table, pick up the pillows, and start collecting the plates, cups, and assorted papers strewn around the floor. Sometimes the students helped clean up, but tonight they hadn't.

"What should I defrost for tomorrow night's dinner?" he asked from the kitchen.

"How about lamb chops? Laura loves them."

"I hate to bring this up, bit I promised Laura that I'd do something special with her on Saturday. Maybe

I'll take her to see the New York Experience. What do you think?"

What could I say? I didn't want to be alone the whole day. I looked forward to their company. But if I asked them to stick around, I felt guilty, and it heightened Laura's resentment toward the baby.

Once, after a whole weekend in the apartment, she again told me she didn't want to share *her* room with the baby. Another time she balked at my request that she assist Arnie: "Why should I help with the dishes when all you're doing is lying in bed?"

She was usually so compliant and so good, probably even too good, that we knew immediately her anger was really fear. We tried to reassure her that we would continue to love her and see her every weekend after the baby came, but that didn't stop her comments about being confined with me. "This is so boring," she'd say, stretching the "so" out for a full second.

There'd always been a lot of guilt mixed in with our love for Laura. We felt somehow that we had to compensate her for the upheaval of the divorce, for the fact that her father lives with me. Now there was even more. We knew the baby *would* make a difference in our lives and in hers, that she *would* feel rejected, that we *wouldn't* have as much time for her.

Right after she found out I was pregnant she had tearfully protested: "But the new baby will get to know you so much better than I do." I'd held her close to me, her thin awkward frame trembling with emotion. I loved her; it was she who showed me how to mother; it was she who showed me that I wanted to be a mother.

"I think you ought to take her," I said at last, "and maybe out to Rumpelmayer's afterward."

With my assorted books on pregnancy within reach, I followed my baby's progression diligently. It was about three and a half pounds now, and fully formed. I watched with pleasure as it marked my body: the elongating brown line up my middle; the blue blood vessels on my torso, giving my body the appearance of a road map. The changes I had worried about last year, all welcomed as signs that things were going as ordered.

And I wept, wept unashamedly, as I read the birth-and-delivery section in Guttmacher. I didn't even take offense at his labeling it the triumphant moment in a woman's life. I closed my eyes and thought about it. Soon . . . soon. I was starting my eighth month. The cervix hadn't changed, the therapy was working.

I was thinking about the baby a lot. The crib, the changing table, the dresser we had ordered months before. Finding that I loved the delicate form inside me. I would lie for hours with my hands on my stomach.

"What've you been doing?" Arnie would ask when he called.

"Playing with the baby." And I really felt that I was.

We had a feeling it was a girl. I wanted to name her Rachel, after my great-aunt Rose. My mother had recently given me her memoirs, the story of her passage to America with her younger sister, my grandmother; their horror as they watched the fire at Triangle Shirt-waist factory, where they had worked only two weeks before; my aunt's subsequent commitment to unionism. A whole life recorded on crumbling paper. Rachel would be her namesake. Heir to her sense of justice and her belief in common humanity. I just *knew* the baby would be a girl. The heartbeat told me.

None of my doctors put any stock in it, but there is a theory that a fetal heart rate of 120-140 beats per minute is male and 140-160 is female. My baby's was 156. I counted it on Friday while Morgan was listening.

"You're really getting there. Only another six weeks to term."

"You're not going to let me go into labor, are you?"

"Not if we can help it. We'll induce you about a week before your due date."

"I know I can't attend the Lamaze class," I said, sitting down in a chair, "but I want to have natural childbirth. I think about the delivery all the time, and Arnie and I really want to watch this baby being born."

Morgan smiled. He took out the card of one of the

nurses who taught his patients. "I'm sure she'll come to your house to give you private lessons. You won't need more than a few. You can practice the breathing, but don't do any of the pushing exercises," he cautioned. "I'll see you next week."

It was a beautiful morning—just the hint of spring. Arnie was waiting outside in the car, always nervous until he heard what Morgan had to say.

As soon as I got home I stretched out on the sofa. No point in going into the bedroom. My women's history seminar was coming in about an hour; we had changed the time for our last class.

They arrived, and within minutes the living room was completely transformed. They were giving me a baby shower. Boxes covered with pastel paper, lilac and white ribbons on top. Cookies, a cake. I was wearing my yellow two-piece maternity pants outfit. "You look like an Easter bunny," one of them said.

"I thought I looked like a banana," I replied.

"No, more like a pineapple," Miriam decided. We all laughed.

They had gotten me an assortment of new-mommy things—booties, a warming dish, rattles, and the two volumes of *War and Peace,* guaranteed to take me to my due date. But best of all was a patchwork quilt they had made. Each student had embroidered a different patch: a covered wagon, a corset, a suffrage banner, a sister-hood-is-powerful symbol. It was a sampler of woman's history. I was overcome.

"I think you ought to name the baby Sarah," said Kathleen, "and if it's a boy, name him Lawrence."

"No, give it a composite name made up of all our initials." That was Joyce.

I took down their summer addresses, promised to let them know as soon as I delivered, and we kissed goodbye. I stayed in the living room deep in thought, about my students, about Rachel.

The next day Arnie, Laura, and my mother went to buy the layette. They kept trying to involve me in the decisions, calling from the stores. Which did I want more of, kimonos or stretchies? Saks only had towels with turquoise trim. Should they buy them or order the yellow ones?

They came home brimming with things to show me: a crib blanket, a musical lamb, the robe I would wear in the hospital—white with a high lace collar and lace cuffs, a bit more modest than Arnie's previous selection. It was the day before Mother's Day and the stores were jammed, but they had completed most of their assignments.

The next morning Arnie brought in my tray with a special breakfast and a batch of Mother's Day cards. For the first time Laura had forgotten. I wondered about it. But someone who signed its name with a "?" had remembered. My first gift from the new baby. I hung the card—"To the best Mommy ever"—on my bed, and planned to look at it whenever I felt low.

Arnie had to fly to Boston Tuesday morning. The weather had turned sharply cold again and thunderstorms were predicted. That worried me. And I was feeling vaguely uncomfortable, as though I had indigestion. I had trouble sleeping Monday night; I was restless, queasy. I woke up before the alarm. The indigestion was still there. No, not indigestion, more like . . . more like contractions. I went into the bathroom feeling shaky and nervous. There was a red smear on the paper. "Oh, no," I screamed out.

Arnie came rushing in. I leaned against him and tried to steady myself. Maybe it's nothing. Maybe just the start of labor. But the baby wouldn't be that premature. A month and a half to term. Not *that* premature. Maybe they could stop the labor. Sometimes they could.

We called the service. About five minutes later a sleepy Dr. Roth called back, telling us to go right over to the office, Dr. Morgan would be there at eight.

I called Roz and my parents. My mother wanted to come with us. Arnie helped me dress.

"What about Boston?" he said. He was packing already. Later I realized Arnie might have needed to get away from it, from the rushed trips to doctors' offices, from the anxiety, the waiting. But at the time I only knew that I needed him with me, couldn't get through it without him. "But I may be having the baby today. Please don't go," I pleaded.

He finished making his phone calls as my parents rang the bell. I got into the car gingerly, trying not to sit with my whole weight. We drove up a bleak Park Avenue in silence.

Morgan saw me immediately. "You're bleeding from the cervix. The contractions are causing the suture to tear slightly. It's not serious. I'm going to send you to Hillcrest. They'll give you something to stop the contractions."

"Not morphine," I reminded him. "It makes me vomit."

"No, they'll use Valium. Don't bother with Admitting, I want you to go right up to the second floor. We'll phone ahead."

Arnie embraced me as I came out of the office. My mother cried with relief. "Just premature contractions, thank God."

They were expecting me at Hillcrest. As soon as I got off the elevator, a nurse ushered me through the dingy halls into one of the labor rooms. She tossed a blue and white hospital gown on the bed and told me she'd be right back. I struggled out of my clothes and put on the gown, trying to decide whether it closed in the front or back.

Within a few minutes she returned to start administering Valium in an IV drip. I averted my eyes as she pushed the needle into my vein. In practically no time the contractions began to subside. I looked around. The room was crisp and bright. It was a cheerful place to be in labor. Through the window I could see the street. The day was dismal, but the trees had the thick lushness of spring.

A thin blonde nurse came in with a stethoscope to listen to the heartbeat. She moved the instrument from spot to spot, probing so deeply she left circular indentations all over. "Could this hurt the baby?" I started to ask her, but she quieted me with a finger on her lips. She listened intently, then moved over to listen again. Why was it taking so long? I was getting agitated.

"I have it," she said, beaming. I unclenched my hands. It was going to be all right.

Arnie finally came up from the parking lot. My mother came in too. Another nurse brought in the fetal monitor. "We have to check the heartbeat during the contractions," she told us.

She tried several places. "That's where the other nurse heard it," I said confidently, pointing to the left side of my stomach.

"Oh, you mean Gwen? The blonde one?" She moved the metal disk over the spot and looked at her watch. I could see her lips moving as she counted. I held my breath.

"That's *your* heartbeat. I can't seem to find the baby's."

Arnie's eyes locked on mine. They were filled with fear. *Oh, please, not again. I won't live through it*. My mother was off to the side of the room. I think she was praying. Her face was pale and taut—one of the few times I remember seeing her outside the house without makeup.

"I'm going to get Karen, the sonogram technician," the nurse said, running from the room.

I held on to Arnie's hand. No one spoke. Karen came in, brisk and efficient.

"I hear you've been a real trouper, spending all this time in bed," she said to me. And to the nurse: "You can't get a heartbeat with all that jelly. Give me a damp cloth. Let's clean her off."

So that was it. They were using too much Surgilube. I relaxed my grip on Arnie's hand.

Karen smeared a dot of the cold salve on my stomach and placed the receiver over it. Nothing. *Where is it?* Nothing. *Oh, please let her find it*. Nothing. *My Rachel*. Nothing. *Oh, God. God, not again*. Nothing.

Nothing. Nothing. Not even the wush-wush of the blood going through the placenta.

Karen shook her head slowly. A cry from deep inside escaped my lips. I lurched forward as if to throw myself off the bed. Arnie restrained me, holding me with his arms. We were shaking, sobbing, crying hysterically. The nurse had her arms around my mother, trying to comfort her. Only Karen stood above me, calm and composed.

Dr. Roth came rushing in. He took the monitor and tried. "I'm sorry," he said. "Dr. Morgan will come by after office hours to cut the suture and do the delivery."

"When will that be?" asked Karen.

"Some time after noon."

"Don't let them take my baby," I pleaded. "Oh, Arnie, please don't let them." I was wringing my hands, barely coherent.

Karen came over to the bed and took my hand firmly in hers. "You have to get hold of yourself," she said sternly. "You must *try* to relax." I stared at her uncomprehendingly. A minute or so passed, maybe more. I was numbed by shock and disbelief. I lay silently. The nurse stood on the other side of my bed, opposite Karen.

"How was your vacation?" the nurse asked her.

"Great. I would have stayed longer, but my cats really missed me."

"Do you have any pets?" she asked, directing her question to me.

"A cat," I mumbled.

"What kind is it?" the nurse asked, as if we were a group of friends at tea.

This attempt at small talk was unbearable. I wanted to scream, kick, yell, tell them they were wrong. It was my baby, they didn't know. I couldn't talk about cats, vacations.

"Please," I begged. "Please, I just want to be alone with my family."

The room became quiet again. The nurse collected her things and left, giving me a sad, reproachful look. Karen stood at my bedside a little longer. "I know you really wanted this baby. But these things happen. You must try to accept it and take care of yourself." She lingered as if she were trying to think of something else to say, but either couldn't or decided against it. I watched her regal figure retreat through the doorway.

It couldn't be true, what everyone was telling me. That my baby was dead. How could it be? Only Sunday night we had felt it kicking so strongly that we joked it must be a boy. To think that we had ever cared which sex it was. Friends used to say it didn't matter what they had, as long as it was a healthy baby. Now I understood them, really understood what they meant.

I saw a large mound drift across my stomach. "Look, it's moving!" I yelled. "Arnie, come here! Look, the baby's moving! Get the nurse quickly!"

My mother ran into the hall. She returned with a stout woman about her own age who spoke with a clipped British accent. She felt my stomach and said irritably, "That's a contraction. It's moving the body around. Next time you want something, use the button. Don't send your mother screaming out into the hall."

Her words came crashing down upon me, snuffing out my last brief hope. Her hideous, horrible, cruel words. "The body." No longer a baby. Just a body. When had it stopped moving on its own? When had it become a body? Sometime during the night while I lay tossing restlessly, it had died. Passing from life as quietly as it had begun, without knowledge, without permission. A life and death together. It had come full circle without ever having a breath. My arms ached with emptiness, my belly throbbed with the awareness that it held a tiny being I would never know.

Why had this happened? Had I let down my vigil? Had I stopped wanting it, wishing for it, even for a second? I sobbed and sobbed, hoarse choking noises. There was nothing but my grief. Minutes passed with excruciating slowness.

From the corridor came the sound of women being wheeled from the labor suite into the delivery room. Women crying out in pain. Be grateful for this agony of birth, I wanted to tell them. While others brought forth life, I seemed only to produce death.

I felt an uncontrollable frenzy. What can I do now without the baby? We had everything planned. "I want to go away. I can't go back to Sarah Lawrence." My thoughts came tumbling out frantic, random, unconnected.

"Did you tell Lucy?" I finally asked.

My mother nodded. "She's outside sitting with daddy."

Suddenly I wanted all my friends to know, to surround myself with them. To help me. "What about Susan, Roz?"

"I haven't called yet. Should I?" asked Arnie.

That morning while we were waiting for my parents to get to our apartment, I had made a list of all our friends' numbers in case the baby was born that day. Had that been only three hours ago? Arnie took out the piece of yellow paper and the tears rolled down his face. We held on to each other tightly, desperately. Only after he left did I realize how wet the front of my nightgown was. My mother moved quietly around the room, hanging my clothing in the closet, folding the blanket on my bed.

Arnie was gone a long time. When he came back, his eyes were red, his lids thick and swollen. He took my hand in his. I noticed four raised nail marks near his wrist. "That's where you were holding me when Karen was using the monitor," he said, his voice shaky. "My parents asked if we wanted them to come down."

"No, not yet."

Arnie pulled a chair next to the bed. His face was drawn, his forehead furrowed. Before we were married I called these his worry lines. I had promised to erase them, undo the pain of his first marriage, his separation from Laura. I couldn't bear to think about all that. I felt weak from crying, weary, spent, drained.

A dull heavy feeling took possession of my head. The Valium was starting to take effect. It was almost noon. "Did daddy eat anything?" I asked, suddenly worried about him.

"No."

"Why don't you all go have some lunch?"

"I'm not leaving you," said Arnie.

"Daddy and I will eat after Dr. Morgan comes."

We didn't have too much longer to wait. He arrived a little after 12:30, looking upset. He nodded compassionately at Arnie and took my hand. His were cold. "I really thought we had made it," he said. "I just couldn't believe it when I got the call. I thought you were a little small for thirty-four weeks, but the sonogram looked good."

"But what could have happened?" my mother asked.

He shook his head sadly. "It could be any number of things. We'll know a lot more after the delivery. I know how much this pregnancy meant to you, but there isn't anything else I can tell you about it now.

"I'm going to remove the suture. The nurse will give you something to make you drowsy," he said to me, still holding my hand.

"No, I want to be awake, I don't want anything," I said, surprised at how forceful I sounded.

Morgan sat down on the bed. He rubbed his eyes behind his glasses. "Labor is very painful. There's no reason for you to go through it. Also . . . look, I don't know, but the baby might be deformed. You shouldn't see it."

I had never really thought about having a deformed baby. I hesitated. "I need time," I said. "And I want Arnie to be with me."

"Okay. We'll see how it goes. I'm going to remove the suture now," he said to Arnie and my mother. "I'll have to ask you to leave."

A nurse came in bringing stirrups which attached to the end of the bed, and a tray with instruments. "I'm really disappointed. I thought we'd made it," he said again.

Disappointed? What a strange word to have used. He sat on a stool at the end of the bed, holding something that resembled a long scissors in one hand. I looked at him, waiting for him to begin. He paused. "This is murder," he said, his mouth pulled grim and tight.

I felt a snipping sensation, but no pain. For a moment my curiosity took over. I watched as he examined the suture. It looked just like a twisty from the plastic lunch bags.

"I'm going to rupture your membranes now." I closed my eyes.

"Did I hurt you?" he asked in a second.

"No, not really. I just want Arnie back here."

Morgan went out to get him.

"Can you get me a cigarette?" I begged as soon as I saw him. He already had a pack. We had stopped smoking after the miscarriage, but now . . . now this was turning into a hideous little two-step: We stop smoking, I lose a baby, we start again. The nurse told us that if we smoked in the room it would set off the alarm, so we dragged the IV pole into the bathroom. I leaned against Arnie, and both of us leaned against the wall. Neither of us spoke. We smoked with the door closed. Two children hiding from their parents. Two grownups hiding from their lives.

I smoked two cigarettes in a row. I felt dizzy and lightheaded when I returned to the bed. The nurse changed the bottle in my drip from Valium to Pitocin.

"This should bring on labor fairly soon," Morgan said. "It usually increases the intensity and frequency of contractions, but if it doesn't work, we'll have to try a saline solution. That could take as long as eight hours."

I shuddered.

"This should do it, though," he said, trying to sound reassuring.

I must have been very sensitive to the drug. The contractions started building almost immediately. I began doing the breathing exercises I remembered from my reading. Arnie started counting. For just a minute we were like any other couple going through labor together, except that there was no monitor thumping out the heartbeat.

The contractions were coming closer, stronger, closer, stronger. I bit on my lip so as not to cry out. I started to feel nauseated. "Arnie, I'm going to throw up," I yelled. "Quick, get me something."

While he was searching, Morgan came in. "This isn't right. You shouldn't go through this. I think we ought to put you to sleep."

I felt myself weakening. He was my doctor. He was trying to spare me. Suppose the baby really was hideously deformed. Would I be scarred for life by seeing it? I remembered that Arnie's aunt had given birth to a formless blob. It had lived for a year, but no one would let her see it. I became frightened. The contractions were so intense now, my whole body arched in submission. Closer Stronger Closer Stronger. Don't scream. Think of anything. Talk to me. Someone talk to me about anything. Morgan is my doctor. He knows best. But they'll take my baby. Arnie, talk to me. Say something. CloserStrongerCloserStronger.

"Please, Barbara, listen to Morgan," Arnie was begging me. "He wants what's best for you."

I nodded my assent. Arnie put his arms around me. "I love you. I'll be waiting just outside."

"Don't worry," I heard Morgan reassure him, "I'll stay with her."

The nurse came in and gave me an injection that burned slightly as it went through my skin. There was a metallic taste in my mouth. She talked to me until I felt too sleepy to talk anymore.

My head felt hazy, foggy. I faded in and out of sleep. A strong contraction. Morgan examining me.

"What's the activity?" I remember asking.

"You're seven centimeters dilated."

I succumbed to a confused, troubled sleep. How many hours that way? Four? Five? Then the pressure. That feeling that your whole body is pulling out from you.

"Get Morgan," I said. But he was already there. Dressed in his OR greens. They wheeled me to the delivery room and slid me onto the table.

"You can push," he said.

A relief. What the body supremely wants to do. The anesthesiologist came in. He talked to Morgan, then tried to put something over my mouth. I struggled to avoid him. . . .

My throat felt dry and it was too bright in the room. A woman lying next to me. Moaning. No sense of where I was or why. Only that my throat hurt. I wanted water. Wasn't there anyone who could bring me a drink?

Morgan came in wearing his suit. He stood over the bed, looking down at me. Morgan? Why was he here? Then I remembered a dream, a dream about a baby. Not a dream. *My baby*. What have they done with it? I started to ask, but the words caught in my throat. I looked at him with the question in my eyes. He touched my face lightly with his hand and left.

Arnie came over to the bed. He held my hand, moving his thumb slowly back and forth over it.

"Can you hear me, honey?"

I nodded.

"It was a girl, and she was—she was perfectly formed."

"Did you see her?" I asked, my voice quivering.

"No, but Morgan told me. They're all very upset."

A nurse jabbed me with a needle. "Something to dry up your milk."

Next came my mother. Her face was ashen. My beautiful mother. How much pain she had known! "Now daddy and I won't live to see your baby," she said.

I lay in the recovery room for what seemed a long time before they took me to another room on a different floor. Morgan was just outside, saying something about an autopsy. Did we want a funeral? "No," I heard myself saying.

My parents and Lucy were waiting for me. I couldn't face their anguish. I couldn't face Lucy's robust second pregnancy. They came into my room and seated themselves around the bed. I was drugged and sleepy; my eyelids felt heavy, leaden, they kept closing. I could hear my parents sighing audibly and Lucy shifting positions; she was already too big to be comfortable in the small, straight-backed chair. From time to time they hypothesized about the baby's death.

"Maybe it was toxoplasmosis," my mother was saying. "I kept urging her to be tested for it. With a cat around, you never know."

"But I think those babies *look* deformed," Lucy interrupted. "Didn't Arnie have a cold sore last week? I read that herpes virus can cause stillbirths."

"Even if Barbara didn't have it?"

"I don't know," Lucy answered.

An orderly came in with my dinner tray, but I couldn't eat. All I wanted was another cigarette. There seemed to be nothing to do but lie in bed and smoke. Nothing, nothing but that.

Finally, my family left. Arnie was going to spend the night. I was on a general-surgery floor, but the nurses knew why I was there and went out of their way to help us, getting Arnie a cot, extra sheets, and a blanket. I closed my eyes again.

Around ten Arnie shook me gently. "Honey?"

"Yes?"

"I'm going out to the hall phone to call Howie. Will you be okay until I get back?"

"Yes . . . I think so."

Howie is one of Arnie's few close friends. Like most men, Arnie has lots of business associates and colleagues, many men with whom he talks, but few with whom he shares.

Alone in the room, the day covered me like a shroud. I couldn't go through it again. I wouldn't go through it again. I had said that I wouldn't survive it, and I wouldn't. Pills. An overdose of sleeping pills, I decided, and fell back to sleep.

At 3:00 A.M. we were both awake. A momentary forgetfulness, then the crushing blow of recognition. "Please don't shut me out of your grief this time, the way you did after the miscarriage," Arnie was saying. "I feel it too, she was my baby also. . . ." Arnie's voice drifted off, echoing through the quiet halls. He lay down next to me on the narrow bed. I cradled him in my arms. He was my child, he was my father. We smoked in the dark, the two of us clinging together as though our lives depended on it. I cried until the tears stopped coming.

The senior resident came in around eight. He didn't even bother to knock. He pushed at my stomach to make sure the uterus was shrinking. "How do you feel?"

How could I answer? What words could I use? Hollow, numb, stricken. "Devastated," I finally replied.

"Well, what can you do? You can't knock your head against the wall," he said.

"That's just what I feel like doing."

"Well, that's not normal," he diagnosed, and walked out.

What was normal? I didn't even know anymore. To become pregnant and have a baby. *That* was normal. But losing two, one year after the other, how do you categorize that? And what of the grief, the anguish, the desperation? Wasn't *that* normal? Then why didn't someone tell me it was? I needed a resident, a nurse, a social worker, someone to tell me what I would feel, should feel, might expect to feel.

Morgan came in next, quietly, respectfully. He told us he couldn't stay long, he had a woman in labor. Hearing that gave me a sick feeling. He said he had given my "case" to one of the best fetal pathologists in the country. He had spoken to her at length about my history. I listened dumbly.

"I didn't notice any amniotic fluid when I ruptured your membranes. Maybe the baby had no kidneys," he speculated. "But we'll have an answer soon. At this point, I don't see any reason why you can't become pregnant again this summer. Call me Friday to let me know how you're doing," he said kindly. He squeezed my hand and left.

I sat in the room for a long time. Another pregnancy? As if this one were already gone and forgotten. As if there were no baby involved, nothing to mourn, no loss to endure.

But there *had* been a baby, hadn't there? I didn't know anymore. Pregnant and full and hopeful one day. Empty and fragmented the next. And with no real understanding or acceptance of what had happened in between.

Coming back to the apartment was more terrible than I had imagined. All the things for the baby were in the second bedroom, my bed still sported the Mother's Day card, the sweater I had finished over the weekend and decorated with a pink ribbon, my bench exactly the way I'd left it Tuesday morning.

"Let's get this over with," I said, frantically trying to put everything away.

"What should I do with the bedpan?" Arnie asked.

"Throw it out. Throw it all out. I'm never going through this again." I had to stop myself from smashing things against the wall. I was sobbing hysterically.

We closed the door to the other bedroom. I couldn't bear to go into it. It was the nursery. I knew where all the furniture was to have gone, where I was going to hang the needlepoint, the pictures my mother had saved from my own infancy.

Arnie helped me shower. We both wept as we looked at my empty, naked body, the blood vessels already lighter, the brown line stopped in its journey up my middle. Everything was cut short, unfulfilled, unfinished, and every part of me screamed for completion. Arnie took me in his arms. I could feel the heat radiating from his body like the burners of a stove. I held him close, inhaling the faint mix of nicotine, sweat, and yesterday's shaving cream. His darkly handsome face was contorted with pain. "This is too much," he was crying. "This is too much."

Later, my friends, none of them yet pregnant, came over to share my grief. My parents came also. Others phoned. "At least it wasn't the cervix. That's hopeful for the next time," they said. I couldn't think about the future. The past was still my present. I smoked one cigarette after the other.

"You have to eat something," my mother said.

"I'm not hungry."

"You haven't eaten anything for twenty-four hours. You'll get sick."

"So I'll get sick. What difference does it make? I'm not pregnant anymore."

My mother looked helplessly at my friend Nina.

Around eight o'clock Arnie ordered some dinner. Susan and my parents had gone. I couldn't eat, but joined Arnie, Nina, and Roz at the table. We talked quietly, as though the lowness of our voices would keep our words from penetrating. I felt—I don't know—angry at Dr. Morgan for insisting I be asleep.

"He didn't really insist," protested Arnie. "He thought it was better for you, and I did too. I still don't understand why you wanted to be awake."

I stared at my tea bag for a long time. I didn't understand either. "I don't know. Maybe because when they put me to sleep I knew that it was over—that I had no more control. . . ." I couldn't finish. Nina reached over and took my hand. Her eyes were wet.

Arnie and I sat in the living room long after our friends left. It was the only place I felt safe. I dreaded going into the bedroom with its vivid memories.

"It's nearly midnight. I think we'd better get some sleep," Arnie finally said.

I followed him into our room and put on my nightgown. Tired, drained of emotion, I got into bed and lay on my back out of habit. For months I had been afraid to lie on my stomach. Morgan had laughed when I asked him about it, but still I had been afraid. Now, I rolled over and put my arms around the pillow like a child hugging a stuffed animal. My stomach felt so different against the mattress—flatter, softer, wasted. I cried until I fell asleep.

On Friday I went to see Morgan. He was running late. The waiting room was filled with pregnant women, some with their toddlers. "I'm going out for a while. I'll be back later," I told the secretary.

Walking was hard. My legs felt weak, shaky. I had forgotten about all the time in bed.

Lunchtime on a Friday in May. Mothers were picking up their children at school, groups were heading toward Central Park. *I'll never get over this. Never.*

When I got back, Morgan was ready. I walked into the large office with the crescent-shaped antique desk and chose the chair facing the window. I kept my eyes off the large color photographs of the developing fetus that adorned the walls.

"The gross pathology was normal," he said as soon as I sat down. "We'll have the complete autopsy report in about four weeks."

"I would rather she had been deformed," I blurted out without even knowing I was saying or thinking this.

There was a heavy, deadly silence. Then Morgan spoke. "It's better this way. Maybe not right now, but in the long run. Birth defects sometimes repeat themselves. If I had to guess the cause, I'd say it was some kind of infection—either an ascending one from the suture, or a descending one. Were you sick at all?"

"No. I felt terrific."

He sighed sadly. "I couldn't go home afterward. I sat downstairs for about an hour."

"Why were *you* so upset?" I asked.

He paused. "Usually we deliver babies or we deliver *things*. This was a beautifully formed baby, almost four pounds. Everyone gasped when they saw her. And she was—well—she was—I really hadn't intended to tell you this, but she was very pretty."

I felt myself choking for air. I couldn't trust myself to speak. I pushed the chair back, nodded to Morgan, and rushed past the women in the waiting room with their bellies and their babies. Only outside did I weep, leaning against a parked car and crying as I never had before.

My galleys arrived from the publisher the next week. Friends urged me to get busy. They told me I'd feel better if I worked. But I did nothing. I was in mourning.

Arnie told Laura what had happened as he drove her into the city that Friday, choosing his words carefully. He told her too, that we wouldn't be doing much over the weekend and maybe not for a while because mommy and daddy were feeling so unhappy. It was better, we had thought, to tell her of our grief. We had made a mistake the year before. Sorrow was an honest, natural response to death. It would help her to value life. We hoped she would express some concern, ask some questions. She did, but not the ones we were hoping for. "Now can you come to my dance recital?" she wanted to know.

It was too soon for me, too painful to have to respond to a daughter who wasn't mine. I wanted a child of my own, to know that complete responsibility, that extravagant love, to feel that innocent trust, that sweet, warm flesh against mine. I wanted to be a mother, not just a stepmother.

"Look, mommy, I have long legs just like you," she said that first weekend as she sat on the floor playing jacks.

Her words cut through me.

Time passed thickly, reluctantly, dragging me with it. I had no will to lighten it or use it. No will at all. No appetites, no interests.

I heard Arnie talking to my mother on the bedroom phone. "I'm really starting to worry about her. Last year at least she got busy immediately, went right back to the Graduate Center, saw people. Now if I suggest a movie or a visit with some friends, she gets annoyed, accuses me of being callous. It's been three weeks, and all she does is sit in the living room and smoke."

Arnie was silent for a while, then I heard him look around for some paper. "Okay, I'll suggest it, but I don't know if she'll go," he said skeptically.

Later that evening as I was getting out of my maternity jeans, Arnie came into the bedroom. He glanced at me briefly, then averted his eyes uncomfortably, the way people do when witnessing a scene of desecration or great misfortune. Since the stillbirth, it seemed, neither of us could bear to look at me naked. We didn't discuss it, but it worried me. Oh, Arnie, it worried me. Would we ever walk around with the same casual, comfortable nudity? Would we ever be the same?

"I was talking to your mom before," he began, sitting on the tired blue chair. "And she suggested that maybe you ought to see your father's old colleague, Dr. Herder. She's done a lot of work on the psychology of pregnancy, and maybe she can help you."

I remembered the name Louisa Herder from when I was a kid. "She must be pretty old by now. Is she still in practice?"

Arnie nodded. "She's up on Central Park West and Eighty-seventh Street."

She was with someone when I got to her office. I looked around the waiting room. A square Oriental rug covered the center of the floor: mauve flowers against a pale blue background. The walls were painted a slightly deeper shade of blue, giving the room the appearance of dawn. A Victorian étagère displayed Greek art: terracotta jugs, serpentine bowls. Business must be good. I sat down and leafed through a copy of *Architectural Digest*. I continued reading as her patient walked past me to the coat closet, but looked up when I heard the office door open again.

A short woman in a narrowly cut gray suit stood before me, retying the bow of her lavender silk blouse. Her thin, wispy hair caught carelessly in a knot on the top of her head and her sharp blue eyes gave her a birdlike appearance. She spoke with a thick German accent and punctuated each remark with "You understand?"

I followed her into her office and sat on the edge of the chair as though I might be leaving any minute. After all, I wasn't there as a patient, more like someone doing research into a particular topic.

She began by asking about my father. She smiled, remembering something from their past, a smile that spread to her eyes, even her temples. I slipped off my shoes, pulled my feet up under me, leaned back, and started to tell her everything, all my thoughts.

". . . And the worst part of this whole thing," I was saying, "is not the grief or the depression—I expected that—but that I—that I—I feel like I lost a baby that I had held and fed. I keep picturing her in the crib, in the carriage."

"Did you actually see the baby?" Herder wanted to know.

I shook my head. "No one even suggested it. I don't know if I would have wanted to. But now I think it would have been better if I had."

Herder leaned forward. "The loss of a baby at any time in a pregnancy is hard, very hard. But after the mother feels life? Ah, then it is as if she knew that baby, had actually taken care of her. You understand? It *would* have been better to see the baby. But we are here still in the Dark Ages. People think to deny it, to pretend it didn't happen, then it will be better. But it is like all other grief, you understand?"

I nodded, reaching for the tissue box.

"If a woman loses her mother or her husband, no one thinks it strange if she mourns for a year, maybe even more. And the same thing is true now."

I wiped my eyes.

"Don't rush through the mourning period, but each day try to do a little more, something that has nothing to do with the baby and the pregnancy, you understand? Slowly you will rebuild your life."

I left the office feeling stronger than I had since the stillbirth. I walked all the way home thinking about the conversation. She was right, I had to do a little more. I was still clinging to too much of the past, with all the baby things in the other room. I'd get rid of them as soon as I got home. I'd pack them up and send them back to the stores.

I marched into the apartment and threw open the

door to the second bedroom. A ghost room: boxes of bright toys; piles of clothing; satiny quilts, coverlets; sweet-faced animals waiting, waiting in stark and empty welcome.

I stood staring for a while, then grabbed at things blindly, furiously folding them, stuffing them back into their boxes. I was doing it. Not thinking about it, just doing it. Pressing down the lid of one of the boxes that wouldn't quite close. From deep inside came the sound of the musical lamb playing "Rockabye Baby," softly, sweetly. "Rockabye baby."

I ran from the room sobbing.

Two weeks later, Morgan's office called. The autopsy report was in. I made an appointment to see Morgan that Monday evening, his late night with patients.

He seemed upset as he handed me an official-looking paper and left the room.

NAME: BERG-SCHLANGER, FEMALE FETUS

CAUSE OF DEATH: Asphyxia and shock, cause not anatomically determined (see comment)

COMMENT

There is *insufficient evidence* of systemic infection notwithstanding the presence of chrioamnionitis. . . . One may have to consider chronic transplacental blood loss which could account for . . . increased nucleated red cells in the fetal blood. . . . The immediate cause of death is not known. . . .

"What does this mean?" I asked as soon as Morgan returned.

"It means they don't know. The lung culture was negative, but it could have been a nonfilterable virus. Or maybe some nonspecific placental failure; possibly the baby's blood flowed back into yours, causing anemia.

. . . But this is all guesswork. They really couldn't come up with anything."

"But something caused her death," I protested, leaning forward in my seat. You die of *something*, right? Kidney failure, pneumonia, heart disease. You don't die of insufficient evidence.

Morgan moved a paper clip back and forth between his fingers. "There are about twenty stillbirths for every one thousand infants born; and in a large portion of these, there's no obvious explanation. I still think it was an infection."

"Could it have come from my cat? From using the bedpan? From one of my students?" I was firing questions like a shotgun.

Morgan's shoulders hunched under his white coat; he turned the palms of his hands upward. "I don't know," he said, shaking his head slightly. "You're a very difficult obstetrical case, you have to be realistic about it. But I still think you ought to give it another try."

How could I give it another try unless I knew what had happened this time? What would they check? What would they monitor? How could I go through it again, put Arnie through it again, without some assurance, some hope? And how could I ever accept Rachel's death without knowing why she died, how she died?

I burrowed inside of my grief like a mole.

Chapter 6

The weeks were stubborn, they refused to move. And my grief stayed also, binding itself to me like a thick, pernicious glue. I talked it, walked it, dreamed it. I was saturated with death and dying, but it would not let go.

Finally, I gave in to reading the galleys of my book. What a shock it was to see what I had written four years ago. "Women have an identity apart from motherhood and the other *incidental relations* of their lives."

The words jumped off the page and assaulted me. I crossed out the phrase with such vehemence that my pencil made a rip in the paper. How could I have written that? I felt disassociated from the book and its insidious put-down of motherhood.

And yet, in that happier time, I had been so sure of what I believed, so sure of my purpose. Now my whole life seemed an arena of defeat. Nothing seemed real, nothing worthwile, except a few friends and family. These brave souls tolerated me, visited me, and listened to me talk about Rachel and the possible causes of her death as if they were hearing these soliloquies for the first time.

Roz. We had known each other since college, but our real friendship started afterward, when she was a not-so-swinging single, and I a not-so-happy newlywed. As we tried to break through the shibboleths of our situations, we reached out to each other for understanding and support. We were closest friends, caring deeply for one another long before the women's movement told us we should. I know I once let her down, but I don't think she's ever failed me.

One day in early June, she was visiting me. I watched her take a long sip of her coffee and swirl it around in her mouth a little before swallowing, her long honey-colored hair falling softly about her face. With her free hand, she pulled the restless strands back and kept them at the nape of her neck. It's her gesture. Others do it, too, but it always makes me think of Roz.

"So we've decided to take the apartment," she said, putting down her mug. "There's a swimming pool downstairs and it'll be great for Bob's kids."

"That's wonderful," I forced myself to say. I didn't sound too convincing in my good wishes for her new relationship.

"We'll still see each other just as often," Roz promised quickly. "I'll be in the city every day and we can meet for dinner. And we won't worry about the phone calls. I told Bob already, we're just going to consider it part of the rent." She glanced at her watch. "I'd better go. He'll be here any minute, and I told him I'd wait downstairs."

I walked Roz to the door, and as soon as she left, I burst into tears. What a response. I should have been happy, delighted. Roz and Bob were taking an apartment together. It was what *we* wanted. What *we* wanted for her. A good, loving man. But *New Jersey*. She could have told me Bangkok, it sounded so far away.

Everyone was leaving me, abandoning me. First the baby, now Roz. Would Arnie be next? Would he find some young thing who could give him kids, easily, simply? No fanfare, no Cecil B. DeMille production. The way it should be done.

Every time he took a business trip, even if it was just for the day, I felt that gnawing emptiness. And once when it was for a week, a desperate anxiety.

I dreamed torturously of the baby. I watched her being taken away. "Please don't do it," I begged. "Let her stay with me, just for a minute. I want to see her, hold her. Please don't take her. She'll be so frightened of the dark. She'll be scared without her mommy." I'd wake up shaking and lie in bed and smoke.

Arnie knew. He could see that I was getting too thin, see the purple circles under my eyes, see the crumpled tissues stuffed into the pocket of my faded work shirt, see the ashtrays overflowing with cigarette butts.

"We've got to get beyond this," he said, taking off his glasses and brushing back his hair with his fingers. "It's like quicksand, pulling us down."

I sat next to him, as close as possible. "I'm trying, Arnie, I'm *really trying*."

"Do you think it'll help if we get away for a while? I was planning to take a couple of weeks off in July anyway."

"I know." My voice had a hollow sound to it. A few weeks off in July to spend time with the baby. To play with her, get to know her, push her proudly in the elegant blue pram my mother had insisted on buying for us, Arnie straight and spare, and me loose and sticky and seeping.

"What do you think?"

I started. "What? I'm sorry, I wasn't really listening."

"About going away. Do you think we ought to make reservations somewhere?"

I shrugged.

Laura's summer camp was right near Tanglewood. We decided to make a combined visit. Camp Rah Me Wah is paved with pine needles, and a recent rain had made them soft and spongy under our feet. I walked holding on to Arnie, my high-heeled sandals sinking into the ground. I felt over-dressed in my red chenille top and white draw-string pants among so many jeans and sweat shirts, and I worried that Laura would think so too.

As we waited for her to reach the head counselor's

building, I felt uneasy. How would she respond to me? How would I feel about seeing her again?

There had been an unacknowledged tension between us in the weeks before she left, each of us holding back, confused about how the other was feeling. Arnie had persuaded me to go to her dance recital. "It means so much to her," he had argued, and I knew that it did.

But it was the end of June, two weeks before my due date, and I was feeling Rachel's loss keenly. Watching scores of little girls in frilly, satiny costumes drove the nail in deeper. Which one would she have been like? That one over there with the ponytail and the skinny straight legs? Or that one with the Shirley Temple ringlets? . . . No, more like that one off to the side, the dark one with the large brooding eyes, thoughtful, mysterious.

It happened to me all the time. When I was on Third Avenue, or in the subway, or walking past a school, I kept looking for Rachel, *searching* for her, scanning faces. Was it that one? That one? God. Why am I doing this to myself?

But I couldn't stop. I saw her everyplace. And no place. No, not in this stuffy gymnasium. She wasn't here. She was too little. She couldn't be out this late.

I'd started to breathe quickly. I felt sweaty, clammy. "I'm going out for a cigarette," I told Arnie, and rushed to the side exit.

When it was over, Laura had run out to greet us. Exuberant, high. "Did you like it? Wasn't it great? Listen, instead of going out for ice cream with you, is it all right if I go out with Jennie and *her* mother? She said I could."

"It's not all right. Daddy and I spent an hour driving out here to see you. We haven't even had dinner yet. And we'd like to spend some time with you," I snapped.

Immediately I regretted my words. Laura turned her large hurt eyes to me. "That's okay, I'll go with you."

For the rest of the evening Arnie and I had made conversation over a too-sweet sundae while Laura looked longingly at her friends. I didn't like myself that night at all.

But if Laura hadn't forgotten it, at least she had forgiven. She ran breathlessly up the hill and threw herself into my arms. "You look terrific," she beamed. And she looked . . . was it possible? Taller and older in just three weeks.

"C'mon," she said, taking our hands and practically pulling us back down the hill. "I want you to meet my counselors and see my bunk before they all go to general swim." This, of course, was not the regular visiting day. Charlotte and her new husband, Murray, were coming up then.

The bunks were set in a semicircle on a slight ridge in the land: mock log cabins, each brightly decorated with assorted wooden plaques immortalizing the names of the campers who had summered there. Bunk Six was right in the middle, and as we approached we were met by an assortment of Band-Aids, elbows, and knees that coalesced into little girls.

"Is that Laura's ex-father?" one of her bunkmates whispered, and Arnie and I nudged each other and exchanged amused winks.

"You have to wait outside until everyone changes," Laura instructed Arnie, but she tugged at my hand and pulled me into a dark, poorly ventilated room.

"This is my mom," she said without hesitation, and in a minute I was surrounded by her friends looking at me curiously.

Someone brought out jacks, and before I knew it, white pants and all, I was down on the floor flipping for first.

"Wait a sec," called Laura. She dusted the wooden planks with some talcum powder. "So you won't get splinters."

"That's something new," I said. "We didn't have that in my day."

"Did you go here?" one of the campers asked.

"No. Actually, I didn't go to camp at all when I was your age."

"Really?" they gasped, as if I were confessing an unheard-of sin.

Until I was nine years old my family spent their summers at Oak Mountain Camp on the Vermont side of Lake Champlain. Every July we closed up the apartment for two months and started off on our long journey. For the first few years we went by train. Lucy and I loved that trip, falling asleep in the protected bunk beds and waking up to the tall green grass and gentle mountains and breakfast in the dining car where the waiter only filled the milk glass halfway so it wouldn't spill. I was sorry when we finally got a car and could drive to Vermont as most of the other twelve families did.

It was the same group every year. New York City schoolteachers, principals, and college professors, all with two months' summer vacation and many with liberal or leftist politics. We lived in small green-and-white cottages with kerosene stoves and large old-fashioned iceboxes instead of refrigerators. We picked berries, made our own jams, baked our own breads and cakes, went on nature walks up Oak Mountain, and had evening campfires right at the water's edge. The parents shopped for one another, cooked for one another, and held each other's crying children.

It was a carefree, young, sharing time. The summers stretched long, most families staying well into September to avoid the polio epidemics back home. By then the evening chill would tingle our faces and we would wear heavy sweaters and roast marshmallows huddled around a fire. During the day we watched stately Oak Mountain become garish with color, and we knew that our vacation was ending.

When I was a child, I thought that we would always spend our summers in Vermont, but then the era of McCarthyism struck and Oak Mountain Camp fell victim. We all returned a few years more, even the one or two families where jobs had been lost, but we were no longer a community. Rumor, innuendo separated us. And one by one we stopped going.

I was so warmed to see the easy way Laura played

with her new bunkmates; she seemed as happy in her summer as I had been once in mine. We had gotten permission to take her out of camp for lunch, and we drove a short way to a small local restaurant, sort of a cross between a McDonald's and a coffee shop. But Laura ordered as though she were at the Plaza. "The food at Rah Me Wah is the pits," she said between bites of her cheeseburger.

It must have been if Laura, who could live on Captain Crunch and Bubble Yum, was complaining about it.

"Aside from the food, how is everything going?"

Laura paused for a minute. "Well, I guess I'm having a pretty good time. The kids in the bunk are a little babyish, except for Ricky. She's my closest friend, but she's really homesick."

"Is this her first time at camp?" Arnie interjected.

"No."

"Then why do you think she's so unhappy?"

"I dunno. Maybe because her parents said they might be separating during the summer. At least *I* don't have to worry about *that* one," Laura added philosophically.

I tried to suppress my smile. I was always amazed at Laura's sense of irony. "You can be helpful to her," I said, knowing that Laura and I share the bridge-over-troubled-waters syndrome.

"I'm trying to be. I told her it's not so bad. In fact, it's kind of neat," she said, squeezing my hand.

Kind of neat? It really was. How many women were lucky enough to have such a great stepdaughter? But that was the problem. That forbidden word that Laura and I never used. *Step.* *Step*daughter, *step*mother. Pretending for the world it wasn't there. And for ourselves, too.

But I couldn't deny it any longer. Her presence seemed a taunt. Here she was: a daughter who wanted hugs and kisses, who needed her hair washed and her bows tied, but who disappeared from my house every Sunday. My daughter/not-my-daughter. I was supposed to love her and treat her as I would my own, knowing all the time that she wasn't.

After two more sweltering weeks in Manhattan, we were ready to get away again. We decided to spend some time in the Hamptons. Neither Arnie nor I had ever been to that part of Long Island before, but on the advice of those who had, we chose a hotel in Southampton, near to our friends in Westhampton and Bridgehampton, and far from the family populations of Montauk and Amagansett.

They must have run out of money while they were building the Hampton Court Inn. That was the only explanation we could come up with. They were short on everything: furniture, soundproofing, sheets, and towels. Each morning I would hunt after the linen cart, trying to swipe what I could and hide the extras in the closet. But my squirreling was always discovered. "This is the only place I know where you bring a towel and the hotel steals it," Arnie quipped.

But still it wasn't too bad. There were tennis courts surrounded by fresh sweet grass, a large pool, and the ocean nearby. There were only a few children around. The bulk of the guests were single and divorced, and everyone was very friendly. We'd sit around the pool talking and sipping gin and tonics while the sun daubed streaks of fuchsia in the sky.

I still needed to talk about the baby. I found myself hoping always to be asked if we had children, looking for an opportunity to bring it up—and this was to people who were really strangers. It was a drive accompanied by a forlorn hope that maybe one of them had heard of a similar story, possibly of someone it had happened to, who now had two children. I was always looking for encouragement, for some shred of hope.

We didn't know what to do. Should I become pregnant again? It was easier here, on vacation, to think about a life without children. Surrounded by adults who talked of other things, who asked me about my work;

men who admired my suntan ardently. Everything seemed free and breezy in this world of grown-ups.

Could it ever be the way it had been before? Arnie and I talked about it constantly, but kept colliding with the same questions, the same doubts, the same yearnings.

"Let's shelve it until after the vacation," Arnie suggested. "We won't talk about it, and let's try not to think about it either."

"Okay, I'll give it a try," I said, looking in the mirror at the brown line still halfway up my middle.

So we banished the topic of another pregnancy from our conversation for about six days, until Arnie came down with a violent stomach virus that lasted more than the usual twenty-four hours. He is an absolute five-year-old when it comes to taking medicine, so we tried to get him food that might help. I remembered my niece used to eat bananas when she was sick. Unfortunately, I didn't think of this until around seven o'clock Saturday evening. All the stores were closed, but we were sure that the coffee shops would sell us a few. We were wrong. They wouldn't hear of it. "We need them for tomorrow's breakfast. People like them with their cereal."

The ice cream parlors needed theirs for banana splits. "Suppose we paid for a banana split?" No deal. I was beginning to think we'd stolen this scene from *Five Easy Pieces*.

"I can't believe we can't get one lousy banana on the whole damn island," Arnie grumbled.

It was now turning into a challenge for us. But I knew we could do it. I had just thought of a way. I walked into the Southampton Ice Cream Shoppe.

"My baby is sick and the doctor said to give her mashed bananas."

"Sure, how many do you need?"

"Two ought to do it."

He gave me three. "Hope she's better," the freckled kid at the counter grinned. "And if not," he whispered, "come in tomorrow and I'll give you some more."

"Thanks," I said, and burst into tears.

"Gee, I'm sorry," the boy said. "Is she *that* sick?"

"No. She'll be okay," I muttered. This was getting to be too much for me. Why had I started this charade? To prove to Arnie, to prove to myself, how universal children were? How much a part of the total life experience? How much I wanted them? Oh, God, I wanted them. How could I pretend I didn't?

I'd lie in bed again, I'd take Sarah Lawrence up on their offer to give me a year's leave. I'd do *anything*, if only someone would tell me I could *have* my baby.

As soon as we got back from the Hamptons, I made an appointment to see Dr. Davis, Morgan's associate. I wanted another opinion on the autopsy report and my chances for a successful pregnancy.

The office was pleasantly air-conditioned, the tan-and-lime decor a welcome relief from the sultry yellow day. A few women were there ahead of me, maternity sundresses in straight-backed chairs, lean women looking through magazines. Some of them were discussing the doctors, exchanging stories about them, deciding which of the three was their favorite.

I listened with amusement and interest. Why do obstetricians engender so much speculation and fantasy? I couldn't, for example, imagine women sitting around discussing the marriages of their dermatologists.

The conversation was so lively, I hardly noticed that almost an hour had passed before the nurse called me into the consultation room. She asked me how I was doing, plopped my chart on the desk, and left. As soon as she was out the door, I pulled over my folder and leafed through it. It is a habit of mine to read my medical records whenever I get a chance. But these I knew by heart.

I wandered around the room and stopped in front of the rosewood bookcases. I took out a frayed copy of the *Journal of Obstetrics and Gynecology* and looked for an interesting article.

Just then, Dr. Davis poked his head in. "Sorry you've been waiting so long, but I've had an emergency."

Those words sent an electric shock down my spine.

"Want some tea while you're waiting?" he asked.

The nurse brought in two cups of chamomile tea, and I took that as a sign that he'd be in soon.

"Boy, am I tired," he said, returning shortly and sinking into the red leather chair behind his desk. "I really hit the jackpot. Two deliveries last night, and Ronald [he always referred to Dr. Morgan by his first name] is off somewhere in the south of France."

There was something about Dr. Davis that always made me feel comfortable. Perhaps it was his slightly irreverent manner. It dispelled some of the "Herr Doctor" mystique that other physicians tried so hard to cultivate.

"What is it you want to discuss?" he asked, reaching over for his tea.

"How familiar are you with my case?"

"Probably not as familiar as I should be. Let me spend a few minutes reading it through."

I sipped my tea while he read, trying to decipher the expression on his face.

"How long did Ronald say the baby was dead before delivery?"

"About twelve hours."

"Did you notice any cessation of movement before Tuesday morning?"

"Well, the baby was kicking a lot over the weekend, but Dr. Morgan said that what I thought was the baby moving on Monday may have been the start of contractions."

Davis nodded, knowingly.

"I'm feeling pretty anxious about the whole thing," I said for no special reason.

"Of course you are. You'll feel anxious until you have a baby. It sounds to me like it was some kind of placental failure."

I must have looked distraught, because he quickly added, "We can check how well the placenta is functioning through weekly blood tests. We're going to throw the book at you next time around. But you'll have your baby. I've seen it happen time and time again."

The contagion of his optimism lifted my spirits. Maybe it *would* work. Arnie and I had already agreed that we would do anything to make it work. But suppose—suppose it didn't? Could we put ourselves through it again, endure nine months of waiting, knowing that at any moment the baby might stop moving. Could I accept the aching, screaming emptiness, my breasts still dripping milk, my uterus contracting? Could I accept it and survive? Could I accept death as a part of life, coming together at birth in one vast inscrutable moment?

Arnie and I lay naked together in bed, touching softly. From the stereo the muted sounds of song:

With one blue sky above us, one ocean lapping at our
*   shores,*
One earth so rich and round, who could ask for more?
And because I love you, I'll give it one more try,
To show our rainbow race, It's too soon to die,
It's too soon to die.

I reached between my legs, pulled out my diaphragm, and tossed it off the bed.

"Now, Arnie," I whispered. "Now."

Chapter 7

We called upon every bit of magical thinking and every good luck charm we could think of to assure conception and a healthy pregnancy. One friend put a note in the Wailing Wall for us. Another lit candles at Saint Peter's Cathedral. Arnie and I would have worshiped graven images if it would have helped us have a baby.

We talked about a possible pregnancy throughout that first month. When would I be due? When would I be sutured? Should I start taking it easy? I even started believing that I had conceived. Were my breasts a little fuller? Was I getting a little tired?

We had done such a good job of convincing ourselves I was pregnant that when I did get my period, it hit like the thud of a dead, heavy branch. It was more than depression, it was that sense of loss again—being pregnant, then not being pregnant.

We were in Woodstock, visiting Nina and her husband, Peter, at their summer house. It was our last day there, and I threw myself into it with a vengeance. I had refrained from playing tennis or running, but now I did it all, playing almost angrily, and running faster and farther than I should have. I was punishing my body, making it do penance.

We drove back to the city in silence. I wore my thoughts like a burlap veil. The summer was over, Laura was returning from camp, Arnie was going back to work,

132

and with my leave approved, I faced a year of . . .
what? Nothingness.

That night, far too wakeful for the hour, I lay in bed
thinking. *Nothing. I have nothing to do. Nothing to do
meant I was nothing. Nobody. No one would love me.*
Arnie slept peacefully beside me. I reached over to
touch his arm. I needed that body contact, proof that he
was still there. He moaned and rolled over. I quickly
withdrew my hand.

No one will love me. I'll be alone. I suddenly felt
afraid and very small. I tried to lie still, but a volcano of
anguish was erupting in my mind. I couldn't stay in bed.
I walked to the sofa and sat there in the dark.

"What's wrong?" asked Arnie, waking after a while
and following me into the living room. He was rubbing
his eyes like a child. "It's three o'clock. Are you feeling
okay?"

"I can't sleep. I feel as jumpy as if I'd drunk ten cups
of coffee."

"Why don't you take a Valium?"

"I'm afraid to. Suppose I become pregnant this
month?"

"But you just got your period. One Valium wouldn't
hurt."

"No. I hate the idea of being dependent on drugs."

Arnie shrugged. "Okay then, I'm going back to
sleep. I have to be in early tomorrow."

I watched Arnie walk away and felt an urge to rush
after him and throw myself into his arms. I didn't want to
stay alone in the dark. I walked around the quiet
apartment and looked out the window. A few lights were
on in the building across the street. I lit a cigarette and
smoked it down to the filter, and then lit another. I felt
charged with energy. I went back into the bedroom,
purposely noisy.

Arnie woke up again. "What's happening to me?" I
asked. "I never felt this way before."

"It sounds like you're being a little anxious."

"But I feel so frightened and I don't even know why.
Will you always love me?" I asked miserably.

"Of course I love you."

"I know you do, but will you always, even if we don't have children?" I think I was holding his hand, pleading with him.

"We'll have children," said Arnie wearily.

"But suppose we don't? Will you love me then?"

"Yes. I've already told you. I don't care about having children if only you could be happy without them."

"How can we be happy without them? We're different people now than we were four years ago. We've been through two terrible tragedies. We can't pretend they're not part of our history—"

"But they *are* history," Arnie interrupted, sitting up now and taking one of my cigarettes. "They're in the past. We have to go on with our lives. We have each other and we have Laura, that's the present. We can't destroy it."

"I don't want to destroy it. I'm trying to get through this. Believe me, I want to sleep. Maybe I'm just not tired tonight."

We talked until 6:30, got up and showered, and went out for breakfast. My mouth felt scorched from all the cigarettes. Nothing tasted good, but I ate anyway. Morning was calming, fresh, new, an unwritten day. I walked Arnie to the subway station, watching the city wake up around us, and I felt a little better.

But as soon as he left I started to get edgy again. I stood on Lexington Avenue and Seventy-seventh Street absolutely transfixed. Where should I go? What should I do? Everyone I knew was busy, either with work or with children. I had neither. I fit nowhere.

A wave of nervousness swept over me. I willed myself to stay calm. I bought a newspaper, counting out the change with great deliberateness, and found a coffee shop where I could read it. I drank my coffee slowly, trying to decide what to do. I couldn't go back to the empty apartment.

Suddenly, I thought of something: I'd go to the library. I took the Lexington Avenue subway to Forty-second Street and headed for the New York Public

Library. Over the past five years it had become a second home, but at the same time it never lost its aura of majesty for me. I approached it with the kind of respect one has for an ancient cathedral.

I'd felt this way about the library from my first days in graduate school. Then the chance to work there was the best thing about getting a doctorate. Nina and I were the first women to penetrate the male-monopolized Ph.D. history program at our school. In those isolating, lonely days, fellow students looked at us suspiciously. "What's a girl like you doing in a place like this?" they joked. But it didn't turn out to be very funny. There was a difference and I noticed it. Noticed that my papers weren't taken quite as seriously in seminar, noticed that I wasn't asked to join the best study groups.

And Nina? Well, we hadn't exactly started up our own chapter of NOW. In fact, we kind of ignored each other. Like new immigrants anxious for acceptance, we tried to prove our commitment, not to each other but to those already Americanized.

"What's a girl like you doing in a place like this?"

"One thing's for sure, I'm not avoiding the draft," I finally retorted.

Nina smiled. I smiled back. We had coffee together. I had an ally, a friend. Graduate school was going to be okay after all.

I walked up the large marble steps, decorated with squares of sunlight from the casement windows, and went straight to the card catalog. Maybe I would write an article for a journal. I didn't know, I just needed something to keep me busy. I thought about doing something on nineteenth-century women novelists, a topic I'd become interested in while writing my dissertation. I started filling out call slips.

Seeing the familiar names, holding the dusty old books with their elegant embossed titles, their extravagant dedications, brought me back to a secure time in my life. For about two hours I read so intently that I didn't notice how hot it had become. Then I realized that the room was stifling. I went to the phone booth and, on an impulse, called my parents. "I think I'll stop over," I said casually.

They had recently moved to Manhattan, my mother separating from the old apartment with difficulty. No matter that most of her neighbors had already left, or that the familiar, chatty shopkeepers had long closed their stores, or that muggings were an increasing occurrence, to her it was the home of our youth and she left it in mourning.

I hadn't planned to tell my parents how panicky I felt, but as soon as I saw them I blurted it out. Maybe I was looking to curl up into the lap of my childhood for a while. My mother put down the cup she was holding. My father looked helpless and shaken.

"I'll be all right," I said quickly. "Everyone has trouble sleeping now and then."

"Look at Belle's sister-in-law," said my mother, sounding more upbeat than I'm sure she felt. "She had two hydrocephalic babies and even her doctors told her to quit. But she wouldn't listen to them, and now she has three beautiful children, two in college and one in law school."

I had heard this before, of course, as it was one of those little happy-ending tales that my family had had all too many occasions to invoke. Still, it gave me hope. I felt a little better as I walked home.

Back in my apartment I busied myself with making dinner, talking on the phone, and watching the six o'clock news. But after we ate I started feeling nervous again.

"What's on TV?" I asked. "I don't want to watch anything scary or violent." I seemed to have lost my ability to tolerate any bloodshed. Anything about death or dying was a personal threat.

"That probably eliminates everything," said Arnie, looking through the paper. "Listen, Barb, I don't think you ought to worry about whether or not you'll sleep. It's probably better not to focus on it."

I tried to follow his advice. I took a novel into the

bathtub with me and propped it up while I let the water run in warm and full. I read until I became limp and lazy.

But as soon as I got into bed I was wide awake. My whole body felt jumpy. "I can't sleep," I said desperately, after about an hour.

"You'll fall asleep. I'll stay up with you until you do," said Arnie, turning toward me.

"Don't be silly, you have to go to work," I replied.

Arnie mumbled something, and in a few minutes I heard the heavy, even sound of his breathing.

I felt hyperactive, like a tape recorder was playing and I couldn't turn it off. *Will I ever have a baby? What will I do all year with no baby and no work? Arnie will get tired of me. I'll be alone.* I felt terrified. I didn't want to think these things. I didn't even believe them, but I couldn't stop thinking them.

I rolled my body against Arnie, needing to feel his protection. He woke and held me.

"I can feel your heart pounding. Are you all right?"

"I don't know. I feel so scared."

"Of what?"

"I'm not sure. That you'll leave me. That we'll never have children. I don't know why I feel this way."

Again we talked and smoked. Then I slept a few hours and watched the room lighten with day. My eyes burned, but I got dressed and went to the library.

Two more days and nights passed. I hardly noticed. I'd get out of bed with Arnie, we'd have breakfast, and I'd go to Forty-second Street. I'd try to work for a few hours, usually quitting before two o'clock, when the heat of the day made even the lightest clothing seem unbearable. The scared me, the sleepless me, was hidden from view. But as soon as I got out of the subway near my apartment, the feeling of separateness returned. The Upper East Side of Manhattan, with its elegant boutiques, its expensive restaurants, was so sure of itself, so smug. What did it know of wanting? What did it care?

I'd enter the apartment and immediately start making phone calls: Lucy, Roz, Susan, Nina. I needed to connect. I am Barbara. I have friends. People care about me. There's a center to my life, a structure.

But there didn't seem to be any structure. Things that once seemed so important to me now seemed meaningless; and things that I had taken for granted—like having children, or sleeping at night—had become crucial and unattainable.

"Can't you just relax and try to convince yourself you'll be able to sleep?" Arnie asked one night.

"I tell myself that all the time. I guess I just don't believe me," I said lightly.

Arnie didn't seem to appreciate my humor. "Well, you can't go on this way. *We* can't. I'm exhausted too."

"I know you are."

"Would you consider going back to Dr. Weissman for a while?"

"I don't know. I haven't really thought about it."

I had been in therapy with Dr. Weissman for a time when I was trying to get out of my first marriage. At that time I recognized that I needed help. My marriage was lousy. I was bored and lonely. So why was I staying in it? This was something different. What was Weissman going to do? Tell me it hadn't happened? Promise me that it couldn't happen again?

But at 3:00 A.M. as I rolled my body heavily against Arnie's, frantic and frustrated that I still hadn't slept, Arnie suggested again that I call Weissman, and I agreed reluctantly.

I phoned from the library. He had just had a cancellation and suggested I take the hour.

The bus crept slowly up Eighth Avenue like a large wounded beast. I sat near the window, hoping to get a little breeze. The streets looked tired. An Indian summer is hard on a city. Vacations are over, the air conditioning is off, the summer clothing is wilted. I was glad when we turned into Central Park West.

There was something regressive about being back in Weissman's office. The waiting room, the *New Yorker* magazines, the monochromatic painting, the obligatory fan were all too familiar, but also comforting.

I heard some doors slide in the other part of the apartment, where Weissman and his family lived, and knew from experience that this was a signal my session would be beginning. Within seconds the door opened and Dr. Weissman extended his hand in greeting. He looked much as I remembered him—the same old-fashioned glasses, the same careless clothing, and maybe a little more gray in his hair and beard. "It's nice to see you again," he said, following me into the office.

"I wish I could say the same," I joked, sitting in a soft armchair, bought since I'd been here last. "I mean, I'd rather not have any reason to be here," I added, hoping to make my meaning clear.

"Of course."

I started telling him about my last few nights, but quickly began talking about the last few months. He said nothing until I stopped.

"Perhaps you felt that the baby abandoned you. Aren't you good enough to be a mother? Do you need to punish yourself by not sleeping?"

I decided to continue seeing him, but the insomnia continued anyway. I'd lie in bed watching the digital clock—2:25, 2:26, 2:27 . . . I'd move to the sofa, to Laura's convertible in the study. Sometimes I managed a few hours of uninterrupted sleep, but there were nights when I never closed my eyes at all.

The days were a blur. Physically painful from the fatigue. Even my trips to the library brought no respite. The stories I was researching were maudlin, filled with infants' deaths, celebrations of motherhood. Sorrow pursued me relentlessly.

Weissman: "Are you perhaps subconsciously trying to prevent conception by your anxieties? Maybe you're afraid to become pregnant—and who could blame you if you were? Maybe you should start using your diaphragm for a few months."

I wouldn't hear of it. I wanted to become pregnant. Throughout the insomnia, the fears, the anxieties, we were trying. September drew to a close. I got my period and with it I felt hope seep from my body, leaving me dry, unleavened.

Weissman: "What does it mean to you, being pregnant? Why is it so important? Will you be less of a woman? Less of a person?"

I watched the clock—3:18, 3:19, 3:20 . . . "A childless woman is a monstrosity" (Balzac) . . . 4:41, 4:42, 4:43 . . . "I have no child and it seems the want of it must paralyze me" (Margaret Fuller) . . . 5:12, 5:13, 5:14 . . . I longed to sleep, but the more I wanted to, the less I could. The less I could sleep, the more nervous I was. The more nervous I was, the less I slept. And so on and so forth, for a month.

I started reading about insomnia. When in doubt, do research! It was reassuring—somewhat. Nothing terrible happens to you from lack of sleep. And certain foods are supposed to help you sleep, though none of them worked for me.

But one article, which I copied and read and reread, linked sleep problems to a recent and intimate experience with death.

How much more intimate could death be than the death of one's baby? A death that occurred inside you. What death could be closer, other than your own?

But it might take months before I adjusted to Rachel's death. I couldn't wait that long to start sleeping.

Then I remembered that a colleague at Sarah Lawrence had stopped smoking after three sessions with a hypnotist. Until hearing her story, I had always rated hypnosis as being somewhere between witchcraft and phrenology in the scientific order, but seeing Anne, a longtime heavy smoker miraculously cured, made me a believer.

I raised the subject with my internist.

"They're doing wonderful things with it these days," he said. "I was just reading a journal article about teaching hemophiliacs to control their bleeding through the use of hypnosis."

"Maybe that was the 'magic' Rasputin used on the czar's son."

"Could be," he said, handing me a piece of paper with his referral on it. "She's a Ph.D., not an M.D., but many of my patients have used her and been pleased with the results. Take care of yourself and let me know if it works. Sometimes I think the people who are chosen for these hardships are those who are best able to take it," he added, sounding more like a Talmudic scholar than the scientist he is.

I got an appointment quickly and put all my hopes in it. I was dreading October, my sister Lucy's ninth month, knowing it would be a tough time for me even if I *were* sleeping well.

As I rode downtown to her office, I kept trying to imagine what a hypnotist would look like. A small and spooky person, like the ones who so delighted us on the "Ed Sullivan Show" was all I could conjure up. But Dr. Hazel Alligood was slim and tall with long black hair and so attractive she might have stepped out of the pages of *Vogue* magazine. She was in her thirties or forties, with a deep, no-nonsense voice that added years.

"Do you see shapes in clouds?" "Do you day-dream?" "Do you perceive a person's presence in the room after he is gone?" I was taking a test to see if I would be a good subject. The scale was one to five. I scored a four. Alligood thought we'd be successful.

That first day was fascinating. We talked a little about the things Arnie and I used to enjoy doing together. Then Alligood, speaking in soft, measured tones, said, "I want you to raise your eyes to the ceiling and bring down your lids. Take a deep breath and let the air out. Picture a large television screen in front of you. On it is a picture of you and your husband in Norway. You are walking slowly in the mountains. It is very quiet. The sky is blue and the water is aqua. We will call this scene 'Crystal Lake.' Whenever you hear those words, I want you to picture this scene and relax. Imagine that your body is being lifted, you are floating, being carried away."

All the tension left my body. My mind drifted into calm and peaceful coves. Alligood picked up my arm. I was aware of its thumping loosely back down on the arm of the chair.

She continued, still using the same lulling voice. "You must sleep at night. Your body needs sleep to be healthy. It's good for you to take care of your body. Tonight when you get into bed you will think of Crystal Lake and you will be able to sleep. When I count to three, you will open your eyes. One, two, three."

I raised my lids slowly and saw her peering into my face with a quizzical look. "How do you feel?" she asked.

"Good and *very* relaxed. I remember hearing everything you said, but I heard it in a dreamy way."

She nodded. "Now, tonight when you get into bed, I want you to do the same thing."

We ran through it once again, and I left, making an appointment for the following week.

I put off getting into bed that night until almost midnight, to be really exhausted. Then I began going through the steps I had practiced that day, and was immediately aware of Arnie's eyes on me. I turned my head and saw him up on one elbow, watching. "Please don't look," I begged. "It makes me too self-conscious."

I thought of Crystal Lake and imagined myself floating. I was the red balloon being carried above the rooftops by all the balloons of Paris. That image evoked a distant day, when Laura and I saw the movie *The Red Balloon* in a large tent in Central Park, feeling warm and protected from the tinsel rain outside. Tranquil thoughts, happy thoughts. I gave in to sleep.

When I opened my eyes it was 2:30 A.M. I went to the bathroom and got right back into bed with no cigarettes, no thinking, and no conversation. I tried the technique again. It was much like the yoga relaxation exercises I'd been doing for years. I drifted off again until five. This was a definite improvement! I looked forward to my next session.

Dr. Alligood had on her business voice. "I've spoken to Dr. Weissman, and we thought you should continue here with me for a while. You know, it's sort of like having a mother and a father."

I already *have* a mother and a father. What I need is a baby.

"Well, okay, I'll try it." I'll try anything that works.

"So how did you sleep during the week?"

"Better."

"Good. You know, I was thinking about your wish for a child and I'm not sure I understand why it's so important to you. After all, you've accomplished so much already. Many women would be glad to have your credentials. I know a lot of professional women who are sorry they have children. You won't be able to accomplish so much, you know, once you're tied down."

Was she talking about me or her?

"You can't have everything in life, you know," she said, as if she were reprimanding a spoiled child. "You have a lot to be grateful for. You have your husband, you have your health. You should be happy."

Should I count my blessings instead of sheep?

"Well, now, why don't you move over to the chair near the window so we can try the hypnotism again." She switched into a soft, low tone. I found it hard to adjust to the two voices: one harsh and critical, the other warm and comforting.

Will the real Hazel Alligood please stand up?

Weissman: "Why don't you tell Dr. Alligood that you are angry? A lot of the success of hypnosis depends upon your trust in the hypnotist. Are you angry at Alligood, or at Lucy for having a second baby?"

The truth was I was angry at both of them. Lucy had started using Dr. Morgan shortly after I did, and her baby would be born at Hillcrest. Because she knew that she was having a cesarean delivery, the date was planned weeks ahead of time.

As her time drew nearer, I became more agitated. There she was in the same hospital, the same delivery room where only six months before I had lost Rachel. My memories were still so vivid, so intense.

My mother called with the news. "It's a boy and they named him Jonathan."

I was relieved. Seeing an infant girl, watching her grow, would have been an ever-present reminder of Rachel.

"I don't think you ought to come to the hospital. Lucy will understand. Her room is right next to the newborn nursery. You'll have to pass it to see her."

When my mother had given birth to Lucy, her aunt, my great-aunt Rose, who never married, hadn't come to the hospital to visit. This was considered a *shanda*—a shame, a story told in whispers.

Should I stay away, shielding myself? Or should I go, screaming inside, "This hurts, this hurts like hell, but I'm going to do it anyway"?

As it turned out, I had no choice. Lucy was running a slight fever and couldn't leave Hillcrest. So the *bris*, a religious circumcision, was to be held at the hospital, and of course I had to be there. At least *I* felt I had to be there. Arnie disagreed. "You're too damned concerned about doing the right thing, being the good girl. No one will care if you're not there, believe me."

But *I* cared. My sister's son. My own nephew. How could I not go? If I didn't go, it would be . . . oh, Christ, it would be a *shanda*.

Arnie went to California on business. At home, the night before the *bris*, I roamed the empty apartment, smoking and watching the clock. I had a whole night to get through. I picked up a book, flipped on the TV, but nothing satisfied. Nothing could lessen the dread of the next day.

I felt raw and scraped with cold and fatigue. And again the plaintive wail: It's not fair. Not fair that Lucy should have two children and I should have none. God, are you hearing this? *It's not fair*. I hated the self-pity and the wailing and the whining. And I knew that there were worse things, far worse things, in life than not being able to have children. But I couldn't think of any. *Not one*.

I dressed early the next morning, in a sweater and

kilt that hung limp and loose from my waist. I pulled it tighter with safety pins.

At Hillcrest my parents and I went right down to the ceremonial circumcision room. Everyone was there, but I felt absolutely cut off. A *bris*. A joyous event. But for me it was a time for renewed mourning.

The nurse brought Jonathan out and asked me to hold him until the rabbi got ready. I started to refuse, but the words stuck in my throat. The baby was beautiful—soft, healthy, and *alive*. I averted my eyes and kept my arms stiff. It took all my effort to maintain my composure.

Everyone became silent as the rabbi started his prayers. Tears rolled down my father's face.

Afterward, we drank wine and ate bits of challah and cinnamon pastry. My mother sat down next to me, her pale blue woolen dress almost matching the color of her eyes. "Did you see daddy crying?" she asked.

I nodded.

"He was crying because he feels so miserable for you. Please, darling," she said, her own eyes filling with tears. "Daddy and I are so worried about you. If there's anything we can do for you and Arnie, please let us. There's a specialist in Philadelphia who deals with problem pregnancies. I saw him on television. If you want to go to him for a consultation, daddy and I will pay."

"Thank you," I said, bending over and kissing her cheek. "I don't think so."

I was sick with shame. How could I do this to my family? It was intolerable.

That afternoon, at my appointment with Dr. Alligood, my feelings came spilling out like an overturned bucket.

"So, you're jealous of your sister because she has children and you've been barren," she said, looking directly at me.

Barren? Devoid, lacking, nonproductive.

"It's hard for you to imagine, but there may be a time when you wouldn't want children."

"You're right. I can't imagine it. I'm not sorry I got my degree or wrote my book, but none of that seems to matter as much as having a baby now."

"Well, still, you never know. Your husband might decide to leave you and *then* you wouldn't want children," she said. A self-satisfied grin spread across her face.

Had she said what I thought she said? Yes, she had said it. Now what are you going to say? Oh, come on, Barbara, say *something*. But I just mumbled that I didn't think Arnie would leave me, and then walked out of the office.

Weissman: "You must speak to her about your feelings. Why is it so difficult for you to show anger?"

"Arnie, this is getting ridiculous." I complained that evening. "All my sessions with Dr. Weissman are spent discussing Dr. Alligood."

"But I thought you weren't going to see her anymore."

"I'm not, but Weissman wants to explore why I didn't assert myself with her."

"Well, that's important, isn't it? You're not exactly the world's most aggressive person."

"If I want to be more assertive, I'll take an assertiveness training course. What I need now is a course in how to become pregnant."

"It seems to me you know how—perfectly well."

"Well, then, what's wrong? What's wrong with my body? Why isn't it doing what it's supposed to be doing? What every thirteen-year-old kid's is doing." I threw up my hands.

"Oh, stop it already," Arnie said impatiently. "So it'll take you *five* months to become pregnant. It'll happen."

If I just could have believed that, I would have been all right. But the stillbirth seemed to have totally destroyed my confidence in the goodness and rightness of life. Losing a baby that way had been positively my deepest and worst fear. Every time a few hours had passed and I didn't feel life, every time the doctors had listened for the heartbeat, every time I'd felt cramps, I'd worried.

It was my greatest nightmare. And still it had happened. Not to someone else. But to me. Barbara. And if that could happen, so could anything else.

We were taking Laura to Washington, D.C., for her tenth birthday. I was glad we were going. Being with Laura was one of the few things that made me happy and took me out of myself a little.

Arnie had some business meetings during the day, so Laura and I spent our afternoons together like any other mother and daughter. I was born in Washington and had done research at the Library of Congress, so I knew the city well. We went to the FBI Building, the Ford's Theater, and the house where Lincoln had died. "Boy, that's creepy," Laura said, looking at his bed, but she listened with rapt attention to my stories of his presidency and the Civil War.

This is good, I kept saying to myself as we walked holding hands in front of the White House. Even if I never have children of my own, I have Laura. I've helped to raise her. I felt closer to her than I had in years.

On Saturday night the three of us went to the Jean Pierre for dinner. Laura and I had dressed together in the hotel bathroom, she in a raspberry velvet pantsuit and me in a gray and blue peasant dress. We'd giggled over silly jokes as we combed our hair, and Laura sat on the toilet seat watching me put on makeup as she always did at home.

The restaurant was dim and elegant, and Arnie and I looked on with pride as Laura ordered for herself from the heavy cream-colored menu. She sat next to me on the banquette and held my hand until she had to release it to eat. She was telling Arnie about the lab at the FBI Building where they matched blood and skin samples.

"And they used microscopes and slides and everything," she said, her girlish voice full of excitement. "You know, mommy," she said, turning to me, suddenly serious, "I think I want to be a doctor. You'd like that, wouldn't you?"

I didn't answer for a moment, but rumpled her hair instead. What was it parents were supposed to say on such occasions? "I want you to be whatever will make you happy." I managed some version of that, but secretly I felt elated. In the ridiculous games that divorced parents play for the loyalty of their children, Laura's interest in education and learning had become associated with our side. We were the city parents, the museum parents. I couldn't pretend I was neutral about what she did with her life.

"Laura needs you so much," Arnie whispered later that evening as we sat in the dark hotel room, Laura sleeping in the cot bed near ours. "She's really enjoying all the time alone with you."

"She's not the only one."

The afterglow of Saturday night still warmed me the next morning at breakfast. We ate in a small coffee shop near the hotel.

"Look, they have their Thanksgiving decorations up already." I pointed to the large cardboard cutouts of turkeys and cornucopias on the walls. "Have you learned about the pilgrims yet?"

"Yep. When is Thanksgiving anyway?"

"In about three and a half weeks."

"Well, I don't think I'm coming to you then. We've just spent *so much time* together now. I should be with my mother."

There it was again. I was just filling in. I'm sorry but your time is up. I felt like a woman spending a night with her lover and waking up to an empty bed.

"Nothing I do makes any difference to her," I told Arnie later that day when we were back in the apartment.

"How can you say that? She tells everyone that she looks like you, she copies all your expressions and your mannerisms. It's just that when she spends time with us and has so much fun, she feels guilty about Charlotte. You understand. . . ."

"Sure, I understand. She has another mother and I wish she didn't. I guess it's that I want to have a child so much that I try to make Laura into something she can never be."

"You'll have a child," Arnie said, the tedium in his voice reflecting the countless times he had told me the same thing. "But you've got to try to stop doing this to yourself, to us. All the joy, the spontaneity, has gone out of our lives. I used to love to come home to talk to you, to see you, and now . . ."

"And now?" His words stung.

"And now, all you talk about is babies."

"That's all I think about."

"I know." Arnie sighed heavily.

Oh, Arnie, please don't talk of joy and spontaneity. I don't feel joyous. I don't feel spontaneous. I am still grieving. It's not the same for you. It can't be. You have a child. Someone who looks at you with that special pride and adoration and says, "That's *my* daddy." Someone who loves you in that pure, undiluted way forever lost to adults.

And the inadequacy, the insecurity. It couldn't be the same for you. Why should it? Your body worked. Did what it was supposed to. And it doesn't matter that I'm not supposed to believe in all this. In fact, I don't believe it. But I *feel* it. And that's a hell of a lot worse.

Chapter 8

An advance copy of my book finally arrived from the publisher. "It's so small," I exclaimed. Print had reduced six hundred manuscript pages to a slim little volume. And I wanted, *needed*, something substantial, to look like four years of work, to convince me that it had been worth the effort, the time, the postponement of a family.

I glanced through the book halfheartedly and tossed it up on the shelf.

"C'mon, Barb, don't you want to leave it out, display it?"

I shrugged.

"Well, I'm taking it to my office. I'm proud of it even if you're not."

Proud? What's to be proud of? It wasn't like a painting or other work of art that you go back to time and time again. It was finished, done, completed. No fun in that. It didn't age well, or please your senses like a sculpture, or a concerto, or even a good glass of wine. Pages and print, dry and dull. And certainly it was nothing to comfort you in your old age.

Weissman: "Don't you like anything you do? What does it mean to you that your book is too small? Are you really talking about your uterus? Are you really dissatisfied with your body?"

My therapy was going nowhere. I didn't want to talk about penis envy, I wanted to get pregnant. I was obsessed with it. But month after month I got my period, and I went crazy. Crazy with frustration, with anger, with despair.

"Maybe you could talk to her, mom," I heard Arnie whisper into the phone one day. He was recommending a mother/daughter chat. I was game.

So we planned a lunch out. A real grown-up ladies' luncheon at the Carlyle. We both wore suits.

A magic mirror of seventeen years before. Again both of us in suits, taking the train for my first college interview. It was a far cry from Flatbush, Smith College, that bastion of solid gold circle pins. I'd been wearing my Best & Co. navy blue interview outfit, and my mother had on a herringbone classic with a velvet collar. We looked pretty spiffy. I think we were even wearing white gloves. Yes, we were. Had to show we were proper, had breeding. We had talked about exactly how to act.

But I didn't quite catch the name when I was introduced to the woman who was to interview me.

"Excuse me, but what is your name?"

"Miss Humphrididumph."

"Excuse me?"

"Miss Humphrididumph."

How many times could you ask without them thinking you were either an idiot or hard-of-hearing?

So I spent the entire interview scanning her desk for a letterhead, an envelope, *something* to reveal her name. Dreading, positively dreading, the moment when I'd have to introduce her to my mother.

When we walked out of the room together, I thought for a moment that she might take the initiative herself. But, no, she stood there waiting for me, watching how I conducted myself.

"This—this is my mother," I muttered gracelessly, wishing with all my heart that the floor would open up and swallow me. I worried about it for weeks.

How mindless, how impossibly silly it all seemed now. Everything was too frivolous: this restaurant, the lovely ladies picking at their shrimp salads. But my mother wasn't lighthearted. She was trying to help.

"You know, when you first told us you and Hank were getting divorced, it was hard for us. We were fond of him, so accustomed to seeing you as a couple. But Arnie's become—well, you know, like a real son to us."

I smiled.

"And he's so concerned about you. He'd turn the world upside down if it would make you happy. You have to try a little for his sake."

"But I *am* trying."

My mother looked at me sadly. "Think of daddy, being sick with Parkinson's disease for so long. Did you ever wonder why he goes on, knowing what lies ahead of him?"

Yes, yes, I'd wondered. More in this last year than ever before. A once-powerful athlete who now needed help walking, a brilliant lecturer whose voice now was barely audible.

"He goes on for our sake. He told me that once. 'If it weren't for you and the children, I'd just give up.'"

"I know, mommy, I know about daddy. But it really doesn't help. It's just like my friend Sylvia. Every time I talk to her she tells me about one friend who had a radical mastectomy at thirty-eight, about another who developed Hodgkin's disease at forty. Sure, it could be worse. But there's no guarantee that these things aren't going to happen to me also. I'm not sure someone's keeping track and saying, 'Oh, yeah, Barbara Berg, she lost two babies two years running. Let's pass her by for infantile paralysis.'"

"You know what I mean," said my mother, resisting a smile.

And I did. In the beginning it was important for me to experience my grief, not to deny it with my characteristic black sense of humor, or to intellectualize it, or to make it into something creative. But that was seven months ago. It was time to heal.

So I worked at healing, made a project of it. Met Arnie for lunch on the spur of the moment, visited with my sister, shopped at Bloomingdale's—anything to break the pattern of indifference. I went to theater with friends, started redecorating our apartment, and even bought an outrageously extravagant Oriental rug for our living room.

"Are you sure you want one with a white field?" the saleswoman asked.

"Yes, sure."

"But in a New York City apartment with kids running around . . ."

"Oh, we may not have kids." Very cool and casual. And inside I was dying. *Absolutely dying*.

Being infertile was the worst of it all. The bottom of the Ob/Gyn problem barrel. It was humiliating, degrading, isolating. Women would rather admit to adultery than infertility, I discovered. A miscarrige you could mention, a stillbirth you could talk about, but infertility—that was the great silencer.

To whom could you tell what it did to you? How it made you feel inadequate, unwomanly, and definitely unsexy: checking the ol' cervical mucus, to see if it was thick and gloppy or thin and watery; ever so casually lying in bed after lovemaking, with my feet pointing up to the ceiling to keep the sperm in—*hoping Arnie wouldn't notice*.

Who could understand these things? Not your doctors; stories like these made them fiddle with their paper clips. Not your husband; he'd heard enough already. Only another infertile woman. And she was as unlikely to admit her problem as you.

Jeanne is the wife of one of Arnie's old chums. We had always been friendly, but never close. She knew about my losses, of course, but I knew little about her that was intimate. She worked as an acquisitions editor at a prestigious publishing house, and her husband, Ted, was a banker. They had a lovely old co-op on the West Side and a summer place. Their lives seemed perfect.

In early November, Jeanne asked me if I wanted to meet for lunch. We sat in a booth and ordered while talking. Away from our husbands, the conversation flowed. Our education . . . feminism . . . publishing. I sipped my white wine and ate my omelet *aux fines herbes* slowly. I was savoring the meal and the sense of a new friend.

Loosened by the talk and the drink, I asked a question I usually consider forbidden.

"What are you and Ted planning to do about a family?"

"It's not up to me." Jeanne looked down at her plate.

"Who is it up to—Ted?"

"No, it's up to—I don't know—I guess it's up to God!"

"Oh, Jeanne, I'm sorry. I really had no idea," I quickly apologized. "But if you're having problems, make sure you get the best medical advice available."

"I *have* been getting good care, supposedly, for the last *five years*." Her voice had a tinge of bitterness.

I let my breath out and drew patterns with the parsley on my plate, silently cursing my big mouth and my insensitivity. But Jeanne kept talking.

"I've been to all the specialists. I could write a Michelin guide to infertility doctors." She was impassioned.

"Do they know what the problem is?"

She made a disgusted face. "Mostly, they act as though it's my fault. It's as if they are saying: 'Why aren't you getting pregnant like a good girl and letting me play the great healer?'"

"I know just what you mean." I shook my head.

"The whole thing's surrounded by a kind of social taboo. Women's movement and all, children are still *the* badge of achievement. No one asks how many books you're responsible for bringing to life, they ask how many children you have."

"I know," I agreed. "Nothing has ever affected me like this. I'm jealous of every pregnant woman I see, every supermarket cart loaded with Pampers. I can't stand to see my friends with children or hear about my sister's babies. And I *hate* myself for feeling this way."

"The therapist I was seeing described a woman's

unfulfilled wish for a child as cosmic. She didn't think that anything in the male psyche approached it."

"I didn't know you were in therapy."

"I've stopped now. I've finally come to terms with my inability to have a child."

"How did you do it?" I leaned foward, ready to digest some formula, grasp some magical key.

Jeanne paused. "I don't *really* think I have," she said sadly. "It's just something I tell myself."

"Five months of trying isn't really *that* long," Dr. Morgan said as he assembled his instruments for the Rubin test.

He had said that on the phone, too. But I didn't care. I wanted the whole infertility work-up from A to Z. So we were beginning with tubal insufflation to make sure that no mucus was blocking my tubes.

He was shooting small bits of air through the cervix and uterus into the fallopin tubes. He would hear if it went through, and I'd be able to tell also by the pain in my shoulder.

"It went in better on the left side than the right, but that shouldn't matter. You can become pregnant even if one of your tubes is blocked," he said afterward.

My shoulders felt burning with fever. "What other things might be preventing—" I caught myself. I had vowed never to do this, never to hold a conversation with a doctor while still in the stirrups.

"Can I talk to you in the office?" I corrected.

As soon as Morgan settled behind the desk, I repeated my question.

"Well, the cervical mucus might have become inhospitable to your husband's sperm. It's easy enough to adjust and we can check it with a simple test."

I gestured for him to go on.

"On the fourteenth or fifteenth day of your cycle, have intercourse about five hours before you come to the office. We'll examine a smear from the cervix under the microscope. If the pH is good, there should be a lot of live sperm."

"Can I have the test this month?"

"Sure, but why are you putting so much pressure on yourself to become pregnant?" Paper clip in hand.

"Well . . . for one thing, I only have one year's leave from Sarah Lawrence and it's unfair to go back knowing I'm still trying, because I'll probably have to stop if I do conceive." For another thing, I want a child so much it's tearing me to pieces. For another thing, I seem to need to prove that I can do what every other woman can do. For another thing, it's driving Arnie crazy and maybe away from me. For another thing—oh, what's the use? The paper clip was already moving with Sarah Lawrence.

I made an appointment for a postcoital and left.

Arnie was irritable the morning of the test. We set our alarm clock early, but when I turned toward him he stayed closed and stiff.

"I hate having to do this on schedule. Besides, I have to be at work early."

"This is the first time you've been asked to do anything. Think of all that *I've* been through!" I stormed out of bed, pulled my robe from the closet, and sat sulking in the living room.

Oh, terrific! I could just imagine if we really had to get into infertility studies—screwing on schedule, peeing into jars, keeping time charts and temperature charts. How would we deal with it?

Arnie came in. I sat glaring at him. Hell hath no fury . . .

"It isn't true that I've done nothing. Think about all the things I did when you were in bed, all the nights I didn't sleep when you were anxious. . . ."

"Okay, okay," I said, wrapping the robe around me. "You're right. But this is no time to get into that. If you don't feel like making love, we can wait until tomorrow, or I can take the test next month. But it's not *so* late and you can always take a cab to work. Just don't act as though I'm asking you to do something awful!"

Arnie's face softened immediately. "Did I say anything about awful?" He pulled me toward him and led me to the bedroom.

"Hey, take a look at that," Dr. Davis said when he put my specimen under the microscope. "See all the sperm swimming around?"

I dragged myself off the table, keeping the white sheet wrapped around me like a toga, and shuffled over to the counter. Shadowy dots moved on my slide.

"So far so good. I'd like to make sure you ovulate. Do you take your temperature?"

Here it goes. . . . "I really don't want to start that. It'll make me too nervous to know when the right time is."

Davis nodded. "We can always do an endometrial biopsy. It'll show us the same thing. But let's give it another month or so. Give me a call after the holidays to let me know how you're doing."

So I'd passed the test, but I felt worse than before. All along I'd kept hoping they'd come up with some simple, correctable problem. But of course, deep down I also had my own ideas. I still wasn't sleeping and I was losing weight and feeling anxious most of the time— hardly the ideal conditions for conception. I suspected this, but I didn't say it. Why? Because I imagined my doctors were already thinking it. Female anxiety is the conventional explanation of infertility. *Just tell her to relax. Have a glass of wine*. Our fault. As if it were something we had control over.

One thing I did have control over was my therapy. I felt that my sessions with Dr. Weissman weren't helping much. I put off discussing it with him for weeks, but finally forced myself to tell him I wanted to stop.

If he was surprised, he didn't show it. We agreed that I should continue coming for a few more weeks, and then he would refer me to one of his colleagues.

I took the name, but postponed calling. I was tired of doctors. Sick of going over my story again. Sick of being asked, "Why is it so important to you to have children?"

I hated that question, with its implication that the wish was neurotic, something to be worked out. Having children was expanding, fulfilling, life-affirming, tying you to the past and the present, forcing you beyond yourself to enter another life in the richest, deepest way possible.

If I never have children . . . if I never have children . . . I will die without knowing the most *profound human experience*.

When did I start thinking about adoption? I'm not really sure. Certainly right after the stillbirth, friends mentioned it. But then adoption meant admitting that I couldn't have children, that I was a failure, that I was inadequate. How could I give up, accept that I might never be pregnant again? The thought was excruciating. But it was far more painful to think that I'd never hold a sleepy baby in my arms, never feel that innocent warm flesh against mine, that I'd never be a mother. Oh, yes, that's worse—far, far worse.

I discussed it with Jeanne one evening over dinner. "Have you and Ted ever thought about adopting?"

"Sure, we've thought about it, but it's awfully hard to get a baby these days. And besides, I'd worry how intelligent it would be, what it would look like. I know it's silly, but . . ."

Was I worried about these things? I honestly didn't think so. But maybe I was just denying. I started testing myself, by looking at children on the street. Oriental children, interracial children, blond children. Children who didn't resemble me. Children whose ancestors didn't come from Russia, whose grandma and Aunt Rose didn't study nights with damp cloths wrapped around their heads to extinguish the candle they read by in case they fell asleep.

Could I love that one? Could I love that one?

Did it really matter what your children looked like? And how important *was* my family heritage? Background? Surely I wasn't so thrilled with our medical history that I felt compelled to pass it on to our offspring.

And what did flesh of my flesh and bones of my bones mean anyway? Wasn't it really just another form of proprietorship—men of their women, women of their children?

Could I love that one? That one?

Yes, yes, *yes!*

"What do you think about adoption?" I asked Arnie casually one night.

"You mean in general, or for us?"

"Both." I was surprised at how nervous I was, waiting for his response.

"Well, I have nothing against it. I think it's terrific for some people."

"What about for us?" I held my breath.

"Maybe. But I think it's premature to give up on having our own." Arnie looked at me directly. "Besides, I thought *you* were the one who was so anxious to give birth, to have another pregnancy."

"I was—I am. But I'm trying to be realistic. It isn't happening. It may not happen." The truth may make you free, but it will also make you miserable.

Arnie thought for a few minutes, scratching his beard. "But with adoption, there's no guarantee—"

I shrugged. "There's no guarantee in anything."

Arnie nodded his head slightly. Agreeing?

So I launched my campaign. And I am nothing if not persistent. "Why don't you talk to your cousin about it? C'mon, Arnie, ask her how she feels about her kids, whether she feels any different because one is adopted." Or I'd say: "You know, Laura's not my own child and I love her." This last one was effective. I think Arnie sometimes forgot, as I did, that I hadn't given birth to Laura. "And believe me, I don't love her because half her genes are yours, and certainly not because half her genes are Charlotte's! I love her because I've helped to raise her and nurture her and because she has ripped out a piece of my heart and I a piece of hers."

It was funny how our positions were reversed in this

process. Arnie, who usually embraced things immediately, hung back; and I, the cautious one, bounded on ahead. I realized there were uncertainties in adoption. But there were uncertainties in raising any children. I saw it in my friends' kids. This one had terrible temper tantrums, that one had sleep problems, this one had a stutter. And not one of them adopted.

So what did it mean? There are no guarantees, Arnie. None at all. If we're looking for guarantees, we should be thinking about buying a washing machine, not becoming parents.

What do you think, Arnie? Should we wait and try to reproduce our birthmarks and long legs, or should we *produce* life, inexorably bound to it, and sharing forever its fate?

"I can love any child," Arnie finally said as he was packing to go to California. "But I think we ought to wait a few months more."

"But we've been waiting so long already. And it could take *years* to adopt."

"I don't think it'll take years." Arnie, my perennial optimist! "And besides," he said, walking over and kissing the top of my head, "you might already be pregnant."

My period was two days late. I tried not to think about it. Okay, that was impossible. I tried not to think about it *all the time*. And I even started to do a little research on a biography I wanted to write. I'd leave the library early so I could walk for a while along Fifth Avenue enjoying the Christmas windows, the smell of hot chestnuts, and the songs of the Salvation Army volunteers before boarding the Madison Avenue bus uptown.

It was my favorite time of the year. The first week in December, the stores still not too crowded but the glow and excitement of the holidays already illuminating the streets.

Arnie would call every evening from California. "What's new?"

"Nothing."

We'd both laugh. We were bad for each other. Each saying we shouldn't get our hopes up and doing it anyway. Six days late. It had never happened before.

But on the morning of the seventh day I woke up to severe cramps and bleeding. A late period? An early miscarriage? It didn't matter. I wasn't pregnant, and the thought was too much to bear.

I wanted to phone Arnie, but it was too early. There was no one to call, no one to tell. I sat in the house and smoked.

Finally Arnie called. "You'll get pregnant," he insisted, struggling to keep the disappointment out of his voice, but we were both wondering if I ever would.

I stayed in the apartment, shielding myself from the Christmas shoppers and holiday season, once again feeling lost, desperate, and hopeless.

Motherhood is an option, not a necessity. Women can be as satisfied with their careers as with their families. Biology is not destiny.

I had written these words, argued them, and taught them. And, yes, in spite of everything, I still believed in their truth.

But I knew that for me there was another kind of reality also, a reality that had nothing to do with rhetoric or reason, one that was basic, even primitive, and haunting.

Arnie came home with a small, slim present. I ripped off the paper and into my hands fell *The Little Engine That Could*. "Let's adopt a baby," he had written on the first page. "I THINK WE CAN, I THINK WE CAN, *I KNOW WE CAN!*"

Chapter 9

I began with "Arnie and I are *talking* about adopting a baby," warmed up to "Arnie and I are *thinking* about adopting a baby," and finally got to "Arnie and I are *trying* to adopt a baby."

We told everyone, and we heard good news and bad. The good news was that every adoptive family we spoke to endorsed the idea enthusiastically. The bad news was that there were no healthy infants available. There were two-to-four-year waits at agencies, black-market lawyers who charged upwards of $15,000, and an uncertain stream of sickly babies from Latin America.

Gone were the days when college kids "got into trouble," gone were the days when Austrian and German mothers came to the United States to have and relinquish their newborns in return for payment of medical expenses and anonymity. Gone, too, it seemed, were the kingpins of adoption whose slick operations were under investigation.

Adoption was the most wonderful thing in the world—and it was also the most impossible.

We responded to this news true to our old form, with me becoming discouraged and despairing and Arnie refusing to. But we both were discouraged about the prospect of the upcoming Christmas and New Year's holidays. Jeanne and Ted had invited us to their home in

East Hampton—they, too, wanted to flee from the gifts and the gaiety—but we were uncertain about accepting.

"Do you think it might turn into an orgy of self-pity?" Arnie wanted to know.

"It might."

Ever since Jeanne and I had discovered our bond, our childlessness insinuated itself into nearly every conversation.

But what the hell? Empathy was better than indifference. We decided to go.

Arnie took Friday off from work and we left the city early, planning to spend the whole day in the Hamptons before Jeanne and Ted arrived that evening. Ted had offered Arnie the key to their house, but he refused, sure that sightseeing and shopping would occupy our afternoon.

The morning was vivid, staccato clouds on a sky saturated with blue. Everything looked clean and crisp and sharply drawn. But by 1:00 P.M. the sun had wearied and the day turned bleak and desolate. We wandered aimlessly up Main Street peering into closed stores. The street was transformed in winter to smalltown U.S.A., with a supermarket, a drugstore, a luncheonette, and a five-and-dime the only stores open.

"Let's go back to the car to warm up," Arnie finally suggested.

I opened all the heater vents. "What time is it?"

"Two."

"And we're not meeting Jeanne and Ted until eight? I wish you had taken the key."

Arnie gave me *a look*, then softened. "Hey, I know. How about a drink at Gurney's Inn?"

"Great," I said, rubbing my hands together. "Maybe we can even get a room for a few hours so we can shower and rest before going to dinner."

We entered the wood-paneled cocktail lounge and immediately gravitated to one of the two booths next to the fire. We ordered drinks, and, while waiting for them to come, Arnie went off to see about finding a room.

From the booth behind me came muffled, troubled

voices. I glanced back quickly over my shoulder. A dark-haired woman, her tiredly pretty face wet with tears, was talking to a thickly built, balding man she called Ray.

He won't leave his wife, I concluded, and turned back to watch the fire. My drink came, but Arnie still hadn't returned. He had been gone a long time. I looked at my watch. Only ten minutes, but it seemed more. I started to listen to the conversation behind me. I wasn't really eavesdropping. They weren't exactly talking in whispers, and it *was very interesting*.

Ray: We'll get her home, I promise you. Then we'll be able to take care of this whole mess.

Woman: (Between sobs) I can't believe that this has happened. She's so young. My mother would turn over in her grave if she knew.

Arnie came back to the table, half amused, half annoyed. The clerk had become incensed at the idea of renting a room for a few hours. "Gurney's clients are respectable people," he'd informed Arnie righteously. Nothing short of producing a marriage license with our photographs would have convinced him of our purpose.

"Hey, are you listening to me?" Arnie suddenly asked.

I motioned with my head and rolled my eyes to the booth behind ours. Then leaning over I whispered, "They know a girl in some kind of trouble."

Arnie knit his eyebrows and made a disbelieving face. "Barbara, you're impossible."

I put my finger over my lips. I wanted to listen more.

For a while there were no clues. Then I heard Ray ask "Well, how far along is she?"

I waited for the next question. It came quickly. "Has she been to the doctor yet?"

My heart started to pound. Perspiration ran in icy streams down my arms. I waved Arnie forward with my hand.

"They know someone who's pregnant. Should I say something?"

"How can you?" he asked in amazement.

I hesitated for a moment. It would be so rude, so obviously intrusive. Coins clicked down on the table behind me.

"Excuse me," I said, turning around slightly. "I couldn't help overhearing your conversation." Arnie almost choked on his olive. "Do you know someone who's—er—er—in trouble?"

"My daughter," the woman replied without the slightest hesitation. "She's three months pregnant, but we're Catholics, we don't believe in abortion."

Oh wonderful. *Wonderful.* "Gee, I'm awfully sorry."

"She goes to college in Florida. And she's only eighteen." She started to cry again.

"What does she want to do?"

"I don't know. I don't think *she* knows. The father's married. He's some fancy executive or something. I'd like her to give the baby up for adoption, but she says she's just too confused now to make any decision." She wiped her face with a cocktail napkin.

I couldn't believe what I was hearing. It was too strange. Too crazy, too staged. Should I say something?

"We're—my husband and I are very much interested in adopting a baby."

The woman smiled. "I thought perhaps you were. My name is Marissa." She held out a thin, almost transparent hand, as delicately veined as a butterfly's wing.

Arnie and I introduced ourselves also. He had come to join me on my bench.

Ray stirred restlessly. Evidently *he* disapproved of our intrusion. But Marissa seized upon us, wanted to keep talking, asking us about ourselves, telling us again and again about how smart her daughter was, how pretty.

She's trying to sell us, I thought. But I don't need convincing. I'm already convinced.

"When do you expect to hear from your daughter?" Arnie wanted to know.

"I'm not sure. I'm trying to get her to come home so she can have a chance to think about things."

"Yeah. We don't want to pressure her," Ray said pointedly.

Arnie nudged me under the table. "Oh, of course not. She has to make up her own mind," I said quickly.

Ray was starting to stand up.

"Why don't we exchange phone numbers," Arnie suggested to Marissa, "and we'll call you in . . . let's say about three or four weeks."

"Oh, yes. That'll be wonderful. As soon as I go home I'm going to call my daughter and tell her all about you." She practically kissed us goodbye.

It was unbelievable, except it was true.

That episode sustained us through an otherwise depressing three days. None of us dwelled on our childlessness—we didn't have to; it permeated the air of our weekend. But whenever Arnie and I were off on our own, hope simmered.

"There just *have* to be more women like Marissa's daughter." Arnie was certain.

"The most incredible part to me was that she acted as though we'd be saving her daughter's life. When it would be the other way around."

Arnie thought for a moment. "Well, it's really true both ways. Her daughter has a terrible problem. And we're the ones who could solve it, simply and with a minimum of guilt."

"Why with a minimum of guilt? If I were giving up a baby for adoption, I'd feel guilty as hell."

"I'm sure she must. But at least they know how much we want a child and how much we would love it. You told Marissa that about a hundred times."

"Well, I meant it. I can't wait until we can call her."

But once back home, Arnie was insistent that we not put too much hope in our "Gurney's connection." "She's only one woman. If we met her so easily, think about how many other women there must be," he said as we sat in the living room one evening.

"But this was a one-in-a-million coincidence," I protested.

"I know. And by the way, isn't it a good thing I *didn't* take Ted's key?" Arnie gave me a roguish smile.

I grinned back. "So, superhero, tell me how we're going to find out about other pregnant women? I can't exactly accost every middle-aged woman on Third Avenue and say, 'Excuse me, I'm interested in adopting a baby. Do you by any chance have a pregnant daughter?'"

"I wouldn't put it past you."

"Be serious."

"I *am* being serious. We have to tell everyone." *Logistics again*.

"We *have* told everyone," I said, going into the kitchen and putting the light under the kettle.

"We've told everyone we know. We have to tell everyone we don't know."

I looked at him skeptically while measuring spoonfuls of coffee.

He ignored me. "Who would know about a pregnant woman?"

"The man who got her that way, some of the time. And, of course, her doctor."

"That's it." Arnie smiled broadly. "Her doctor, and, if she's thinking of giving up the baby, her lawyer. We'll have to get in touch with doctors and lawyers outside of the Greater Metropolitan Area and tell them a little about ourselves and that we're interested in adopting."

So that's how it started, the marketing approach. With Arnie exuberant and me cautious, but both of us wanting to give it a try. I researched the problem. The South, Southwest, and Far West were the best areas for adoption. We decided to concentrate on those: getting in touch with anyone we knew living there—old roommates, Arnie's former fraternity brothers, colleagues, friends of friends—asking them if they would contact their (or their wives') gynecologists, their lawyers, or anyone else who might know about an available baby for us.

We felt a little awkward calling upon people we

hadn't seen in years or didn't know very well, but everyone was sympathetic, and most promised to help. A few questioned us about the legality of our method, but we were prepared for this, Arnie having checked it out carefully. Private adoption is *completely* legal. What is *not* legal is the solicitation of a child from its biological mother by any means and the payment of fees, other than for professional services at reasonable rates, to anyone involved in the adoption process.

We established about thirty or so contacts within a few weeks. It was good being in control at last of becoming parents. "We are not putting all our eggs in one basket," as Arnie punned to my groans.

Actually, I was against counting on any one approach. Marissa's daughter was still undecided about whether to have the baby, and I wanted to have as many options available as possible.

I made an appointment at the Louise Wise Adoption Agency. Neither Arnie nor I had any special feeling about adopting a Jewish child, but we knew we wouldn't be considered at the other agencies.

The first meeting was a group get-together. "Just for information, not an interview. We have too many applicants to see each couple separately at this early stage."

"Of course," I said in my sweetest telephone voice. (You don't want to start out with any strikes against you. *Curt and argumentative over the phone. Not fit for motherhood.*)

We were escorted into a spacious conference room where a small woman with short straight hair and a heavily powdered face was talking to several earnest-looking couples. In a honeyed voice she told us the discouraging news: "The majority of waiting youngsters are older children who have been in foster care or residential homes for many years, many with special physical or emotional handicaps."

Arnie and I exchanged glances, trying to keep the disappointment out of our faces. An older child. How old? Seven? Thirteen? Could a child that old ever relate to you as a mother? Or would she be constantly comparing you to the foster mother, the other mother, the way Laura did when she was younger? "My mommy Charlotte sings better than you do," she'd say, or "My mommy Barbara reads better stories."

In a flush of adult maturity generally absent from our interaction, Charlotte and I had talked this over and agreed upon a course of action. The next time Laura pulled her "My mommy Barbara cooks better eggs than you do" line, Charlotte simply said: "Well, Barbara may cook better eggs, but maybe I cook other things better." To which Laura replied, "Yeah, mom, you're pretty good at frozen peas."

I didn't want to be the frozen-peas mommy. I wanted to be the *compleat mommy*, the *everything mommy*. I felt on the verge of tears.

"Of course," the social worker continued, peering into the group over the top of her glasses, "we do place some ten to fifteen babies and toddlers a year, but for each of those we have about twenty applicants. All the babies have Jewish mothers, but the fathers, of course, can be any religion, and some are nonwhite. These we place with interracial couples."

Someone raised his hand. "Isn't it possible for a white couple to adopt an interracial child?"

"Not from this agency. We try to avoid it whenever possible."

Arnie and I hadn't really talked about adopting an interracial child, but I had thought about it from time to time. Once when we were walking past the Foundling Hospital, several small black children were out in front, chaperoned by large white women who discharged their responsibilities without passion or interest. One little boy kept begging for a pretzel from the corner vendor.

"Is it all right if I buy it for him?" Arnie asked reaching into his pocket.

The boy pleaded. The volunteer nodded.

"Thank you, man," he said, turning toward Arnie and giving him the biggest, most buck-toothed grin I've ever seen.

Could I love that one? Yes. Yes.

"How much does the adoptive couple know about the baby's background?" asked a man wearing a black felt hat and a long cloth coat.

"Most of the babies come through the city. We can testify to their health because they usually spend up to six months in foster care before being released for adoption. But we try not to give out too much information. We must observe strict anonymity."

He turned to his wife, a rosy-faced woman, and spoke to her in Hebrew, then stroked his long, curly beard and started again.

"Jewish law prohibits the marriage of close relatives. How can we ever be sure our child won't marry a sibling?"

The small woman's face became even whiter. It was clear she had no ready answer.

"Well, perhaps at that time they can come to the agency and we can tell them if they are related. But that's many years away," she said, her voice tight, perhaps angry. "Why don't you worry about that *after* you've adopted a child?"

Composed and professional again, she ran through the list of regulations. No one older than thirty-eight would be considered, no one who already had children, and no one whose doctor would not confirm in writing that they could not have children of their own.

Would Morgan write this? No one had ever said I definitely couldn't have childen. In fact, Morgan—and Davis, too—had urged me to try again. And even if they were willing to say what we wanted, would Arnie and I pass the home visits that are part of agency adoption?

We had heard stories about these. Many couples refused to subject themselves to them. One lawyer who worked with Arnie said, "I'll be damned if I'm going to let some snip of a twenty-year-old determine if I'd be a good mother." And another friend told us that the social worker had looked in their medicine chest to see what drugs they took and had asked questions about sexual intimacy.

"And what about Laura? You see her *every* week-end?" . . . Hmm, a bit of unresolved guilt there. "You were both married before?" . . . Maybe a touch of instability. "And, oh, you wrote a book on the origins of feminism. How terribly interesting!" . . . *Conflict over the mothering role. Scratch this one entirely.*

I began to feel frantic. We're never going to be able to adopt a baby—unless . . . unless . . .

"Arnie, what do you think about adopting a baby from Latin America?" I was ready with my list of people who had, in case I needed backup.

Silence. Arnie said nothing for a while.

"Did you hear me?"

"Yes. You asked me what I thougght about it. I'm *thinking*. . . ."

For me there was nothing more to think about. I'd done that a few months ago. I'd adopt *any* healthy infant. Older children, those who'd been in foster care, those with special problems—that would take some adjusting to. But I didn't rule it out. At least not completely.

"I'm not opposed," Arnie finally said. "But we'd be kidding ourselves if we thought there were no problems involved."

I sprang into action. "Well, Paula's sister's baby is from Colombia, and the whole family is crazy about him."

"Sure. But the son of the sister of your cousin's wife is not quite the same as a grandson. Your mother would have a stroke."

"Maybe at the idea, but not when she saw the baby," I retorted.

"I know, but when is the last time you did something that you knew your mother was opposed to?"

"That's ridiculous." I thought for a moment. "When I divorced Hank."

"Barbara, *that was eight years ago*."

I gave him what I hoped was a disdainful look.

"Look, honey, I think you're right about your mother, but that's only part of it. *We* have to be sure. It's a big responsibility. You can't alienate a child from his culture."

"So we won't. We'd learn all about Colombia or wherever the baby was from and make it part of our lives." I was already picturing the three of us looking through large books with colorful stories about fiestas.

"I just think we ought to find out more about what's involved."

On the worst, positively the worst, night of the year, with thick wet snow falling alternately with pellets of hail, Arnie and I were driving to the far reaches of Brooklyn to attend a workshop on South American adoption. We got lost several times on the way and reached the meeting late. We walked in quietly and sat on the floor of a sparsely furnished apartment. I put my coat over my shoulders and listened to Toby Metzger, who had adopted a daughter from Costa Rica and a son from Colombia, talk to the eight couples in her living room.

When she finished, a tall woman with a fashion-model look raised her hand. She told of friends who had flown to Nicaragua only to receive a sickly baby. Others in the group quickly told of hearing similar stories. I felt my body trembling, and gathered my coat around me more tightly.

Toby admitted that her son had been small and thin when she adopted him at five months. But he had thrived with proper medical attention. She invited anyone who wished to take a look at him sleeping in his crib. No one stirred, but I was *dying* to go into the bedroom.

"It's true," she said, "that the prenatal care these children receive isn't the best; they're undersize compared to American babies, and those that are adopted after six months may be developmentally slow at first. But the orphanage where he was—Casa de la Madre y el Niño—was clean and the children were dressed in stretchies and kept in bassinets. It is not the sterile, institutional atmosphere you think of."

I was starting to feel a little warmer. I raised my hand. "I thought it was possible to adopt these babies at birth."

Hal Metzger answered. "Well, what that means is that you are sent a picture of a newborn and you agree to take that child. But it probably won't find its way into your home for four or five months. There are a number of papers to be processed, and many bureaucratic delays. It all takes time. These countries are not known for their efficiency."

I left the meeting soggy all over. It was frightening to think of spending all that money and flying to South America to receive a sick child. What would you do then?

I didn't talk on the ride home. The driving was hazardous, and I think I wasn't up to hearing Arnie's reactions to the meeting. Later we decided to talk to a lawyer about South American adoption. The Metzgers had said it wasn't necessary, but we wanted a baby as young and as healthy as possible and hoped a lawyer could help accomplish that. We made an appointment.

His office was what Arnie and I call early tacky: vinyl chairs, suede wallpaper, piped-in music. But he was sincere and empathetic, and the pictures of his two robust Colombian children put us at ease. He couldn't promise us a newborn, but he would try.

"You can specify sex, however."

"Girl," we both blurted out.

"And shade."

"Shade?" we asked.

"Well, you know, the children are all Colombian, but some are of Caucasian stock and others are Indian or a mixture of the two. Their skin tones range considerably."

So do Arnie's and mine. I tend to be pale-skinned with bluish eyes, while Arnie's hair and eyes are almost coal, and his skin tawny.

"Any color is all right," we said, as though we were discussing the icing of a cake.

We left saying we needed more time to think about it and would be in touch.

Then I had an idea that at first seemed like a good one. If babies from agencies are placed in foster homes first, and if foster parents usually get the first shot at an adoption, why not become foster parents?

I called the Jewish Child Care Association of New York. The woman I spoke to told me that they don't accept applications from people solely interested in adopting, but that they do have children in foster care for whom there's a good likelihood parental rights will be terminated by the courts. A few are babies.

Maybe we'd be among the lucky ones. I kept urging Arnie to at least go to the group meeting. But he was vehemently opposed. He felt that to care for and love a child only to have it taken away would be unbearable.

We had covered a lot of ground over the last month. Our "Adoption" folder was thick and frayed. But still we had nothing for sure and the pain of the spring had diminished only a little. Like a migraine headache, it cast a painful aura over everything. My instinct for survival told me that I had to find some kind of work for second semester.

Most part-time or adjunct teaching positions become available at the last minute, but I decided to start calling early. The chairman at City College told me that there would probably be an opening and to call back in a week. I did. "It's too soon to know," he said. "Give me a ring next week." I did. This continued for a full month. I didn't know if he liked the feeling of power or just liked receiving phone calls. Finally, the first semester was drawing to a close. He asked me to come in for an interview.

I wasn't nervous as I sloshed through the deep snow to take the uptown bus. Actually, I had a rare moment of confidence. Even *I* believed I was qualified for the position and that the meeting with Professor Nader was just a formality.

But as soon as the secretary escorted me into the

office, I realized that this was going to be a serious interview. Nader sat behind his desk looking through his mail as I walked in. He didn't acknowledge my presence at first, and I stood off to the side, waiting uncomfortably like a child for the principal. When he finally did look up, he made no attempt to stand or move to greet me. If hands were going to be shaken, I'd have to walk to him.

He was a large man, with a bit too much flesh for his bone structure, thick white hair, and heavy dark eyebrows that seemed to curl over the tops of his glasses. He motioned me to take a seat in front of him, and immediately began asking questions. What was my doctoral thesis on? Who was my adviser? How would I teach the Navigation Acts? How well grounded was I in British history? What grade had I received in my British-history seminar?

Had I heard him correctly? What grade did I get in a graduate-school course? All this for a job with a salary of $900 a section? I couldn't wait to tell Nina about this one.

"Well, that sounds very good, very good indeed," said Nader. "If the job becomes available, I'll surely let you know," he said, taking an envelope in one hand and the letter opener in the other. "This has been quite interesting."

I took this as a sign that the interview was over. "Yes," I said, trying to gather up my coat, sweater, hat, gloves, and scarf, all of which I had kept on my lap while talking. "This has been *very interesting* for me, too." I tried to sound dignified and a bit annoyed, but my scarf got caught in my legs, tripping me as I stood up.

A week later, the head of the Humanities Division at Marymount Manhattan College called and offered me a position teaching a course on women's biographies. The course met twice a week, and there was conference work as well. I took it immediately.

Then came the terrible news. Marissa's daughter had had an abortion. I was devastated, desolate, weepy.

"For God's sake, Barbara," Arnie finally said, "wouldn't you have done the same thing?"

"Sure, but—" Wait a minute. Hold everything. Would I have? Four or five years ago I might have. Abortion is a key feminist issue. Women *have* to have control over their bodies or the whole thing is a sham. I had signed petitions for abortion, had worked for it. But, now, for the first time, I knew what *Adoption, Not Abortion* meant. I floundered on my contradictions. I didn't understand myself at all.

And if one woman had had an abortion, why wouldn't other women? Of course they would. All those private obstetricians and lawyers we'd contacted. What a waste! I started to pressure Arnie to get in touch with a black-market lawyer. We had received the names of a few from the couples we had spoken to. One in particular, from Georgia, sounded good. He had helped three families we knew, and all had been very pleased. He was a professional with a very smooth operation.

After an initial telephone contact, the couple would send a deposit of $1500 for the doctors' fees, along with a picture of themselves. The lawyer said it would take about a year, but each of the couples had been contacted within five months with the news that *their baby had been born*. Next was a flight to Georgia with an additional $15,000 *in cash*, a visit to the hospital to take custody, and then home with the baby. It was simple and easy. *And definite.*

We didn't have the money, but we knew that our parents would help us. After all, how can you put a price tag on an infant? I hated the term "black-market baby." A baby can't be illegal. Once it was in our home, how it got there would be of little consequence.

Arnie didn't agree. "You have to sign an affidavit about how much you paid in legal services. It means perjuring yourself. Suppose there is an investigation? The whole adoption might be overturned. Besides, how can we trust any information he gives us about the baby's background or health?"

There was something to Arnie's reservations, but not enough to deter me. I continued to look for ways to bring up the topic, at least once a day. I still wasn't pregnant, and we didn't know of any child available for adoption.

"You'll have a baby by next year," Arnie had promised me on New Year's Eve, but I didn't see how. And I didn't see how I could live my life without one.

Chapter 10

I was teaching biographies of women: Margaret Fuller, Edith Wharton, Judy Garland, Marilyn Monroe. I had to hand it to our sex, we sure suffered in style. But we were survivors also. We took our pain and shaped it, gave it meaning, charged it with purpose, and made it work for us. That was the woman I had discovered in my study of history—the woman shackled by chains, shackled by poverty, shackled by ignorance, shackled by convention; inarticulate, unnoticed, yet always striving.

I worked to make her alive for my students, to teach them, to touch them. I felt good about how it was going. And after class, as I picked up my books to leave, several students gathered around eager with questions, a sign they were feeling good about it too. Slowly, the room emptied and became quiet. I turned toward the door and focused on Arnie's familiar shape.

"What's wrong?" I asked immediately. Seeing him gave me the same panicky sensation as a 2:00 A.M. phone call. It was the middle of the afternoon.

"Nothing. I had a meeting uptown. It didn't take as long as I thought. Feel like having a cup of coffee?"

I always feel like having a cup of coffee, so we walked the two or three blocks to our local coffee shop and sat down at a small table near the back.

Arnie had a sort of tense, anticipatory look.

"Are you *sure* no one is sick?" I asked again.

"Positive"—the corners of his mouth twitching into a grin. Then, without waiting: "I don't think we ought to get our hopes up, but we may have a baby."

My adrenaline started flowing. I couldn't get the words out fast enough. I was ravenous for information. "What? Tell me, tell me!"

"Right before lunch I spoke to Ron Corwin."

I looked puzzled.

"You know, he's the lawyer from Syracuse who helped Rebecca and Jerry Dorn adopt their son."

It was starting to come back to me. Rebecca and Arnie knew each other from college. He had called her as part of our network/marketing effort. About seven years ago, she had lost a baby in her ninth month, but Ron had known of a college student—Phi Beta Kappa, no less—who was pregnant. It was all arranged quickly and legally. We had called Rebecca and her husband a month earlier, and Arnie had tried to get in touch with Corwin, but he and his family were on a vacation. He was just one name out of many, but Arnie kept calling.

The waitress came over to take our orders, but we hadn't even looked at the menus.

"It's the most unbelievable coincidence," Arnie was continuing. "Corwin told me he hadn't handled an adoption in about five years, but when I called he was just putting on his coat to meet a woman who wants to give up her baby. He almost didn't bother to take the call, except that the secretary told him I was a friend of Rebecca's."

"But what about the baby, the woman?" I was sitting on the edge of my seat, leaning toward Arnie.

"All I know is that she's in her fifth month and she's a medical secretary—works at the office of one of Corwin's friends. I told him a lot about us and he's going to call us at home later. I thought we should talk to him together."

"But the fifth month—it's not too late for her to have an abortion." I was already disbelieving.

"No. She won't. She's worked in a children's hospital and says she's seen too much to even consider it."

I was so excited I couldn't stay still. "Let's go right home. He might be trying us now."

We hurriedly gathered up our things, leaving a bewildered and slightly miffed waitress.

Once inside the apartment, I made Arnie repeat everything he had told me in the restaurant. I was so restless. I paced from one room to the other, picking things up, putting them down.

"I think I'll do a laundry," I said at last. "There's no point in just sitting here."

But as I was gathering up the sheets, the phone rang again. I stayed inside the bedroom until I heard Arnie call, "Honey, it's Ron, pick up."

He had just come back from his meeting with the mother-to-be and was very impressed. The woman was intelligent and sensitive, thirty-two years old, had been married before, and had a five-year-old son from that marriage, he reported. Both she and the father of the child she was carrying were college-educated.

I couldn't resist. "What does she look like?"

"She's about five-six, with red hair and large brown eyes. She's a beauty. The father is also supposed to be nice-looking, and very athletic."

"But is she sure about this? She won't change her mind?"

Ron's voice became firm. "She has the right to change her mind at any point along the way, even after the baby's been born. But if I'm any judge of character, she won't. Her son is sickly—nothing genetic; he had scarlet fever two years ago and it left him with heart damage. The medical costs are enormous. She has to continue working and can't see raising the child on her own."

"But what about the father?" Arnie asked. "Any chance of a reconciliation?"

"No. He's not even in Syracuse anymore. She doesn't want anything to do with him. She's very concerned about the welfare of the baby, though. The only thing that really interested her about you is how much you wanted a child. She's even thinking of talking to you. I would arrange the call, of course. She doesn't know your identity."

"Anything she wants," I said quickly.

"Well, there is one thing she wants."

Here it goes. The bribe. I'll relinquish the baby if you pay my son's medical bills.

"She does want me to come down and meet you. After all, I couldn't tell her *I* knew you personally."

I'm sure Ron heard my sigh of relief.

"Oh, sure. Of course."

"The only obstacle is telling her son. He knows she's pregnant. She hasn't encouraged talk about a new brother or sister, but she hasn't said anything about giving the baby up for adoption. She plans to tell him this weekend. I'll be in touch as soon as I hear from her."

Arnie and I put down our phones simultaneously and rushed to each other so fast we almost collided in the hall. We hugged and laughed.

"Didn't I tell you? Didn't I tell you?" Arnie said, scooping me up in his arms and spinning me around.

But I was being more cautious. "Let's wait until Monday before we celebrate."

We reveled in our excitement all weekend, and shared it only with our parents, Lucy, Roz, and Susan. No one else. It was too soon, and I was too superstitious.

Ron called Arnie Monday afternoon. "We're on," he said.

Arnie told me later that he couldn't talk for a moment, he was so choked with emotion. Ron answered all the questions we had compiled over the weekend. "So far the pregnancy is uneventful. She's gained twelve pounds. She sees her doctor every three weeks. I'll let you know when her next appointment is so you can feel involved in the pregnancy," he added.

I already did. I thought about a baby with soft red curls and felt suffused with the warmth of gestation. Energy pulsated through me. I started cleaning the apartment, making curtains, taking lampshades to be fixed, getting the place ready for the baby, and for Ron Corwin's trip to New York.

Ron told us to find an attorney to represent us in the adoption before his visit. We didn't have much trouble. Only a handful of New York attorneys practice adoption law on any consistent basis. Most of these have adopted children of their own, and this transforms the traditional lawyer-client relationship into a close bond.

Marty Ganz was of indeterminate age, his suits slightly too tight for his pillowed body, his gray hair settling in tufts around his ears. He had a soft and easy manner, which contrasted with Arnie's intense approach to life and law. They were the perfect foils for each other.

We met Marty for the first time over lunch at the Oyster Bar in Grand Central Station, an oasis surrounded by congested commotion.

"Most adoptions work," he said, buttering a soft muffin that reminded me of the kind I used to have at Lundy's restaurant in Brooklyn. "I've only handled one or two where the mother backed out at the last minute, and in these there were signs of difficulty all along."

The waiter put down our platters of bluefish, but my stomach seemed sealed with the anticipation.

Most adoptions work. I hugged those words. I was hardly listening to Marty now, though he was telling us how he'd felt so much more involved in the adoption of his son than in his wife's pregnancies. I had seen it happen with Arnie: At first, he had responded mainly to my suggestions and prodding, but, over the last few weeks he had become so enthusiastic and caught up in the process that he was constantly thinking of new people to call and new possibilities to explore.

The waiter put the dessert menu in our hands. Arnie and I declined, but Marty ordered a creamy-looking cheesecake. "I really shouldn't," he said, patting his stomach as if to make sure it was still there. "I have to fit into the suit I bought for Jason's bar mitzvah pretty soon."

"So, you really think she'll go through with it?" Arnie asked.

Marty nodded. "It's a good idea, though, to get Ron to have her sign an Intent form. It's not in any way binding, but if she refuses, we may have an indication of some resistance."

She signed willingly, and Ron was bringing the form to New York with him. We were all meeting at Arnie's office at 9:30, but Arnie and I were up hours in advance with last-minute jitters. We were so concerned that everything be perfect, we even dropped my cat off at my mother's on our way downtown. For all we knew, Ron hated cats or disapproved of their being around new-borns.

We were just going over our list of things to discuss with him when Arnie's secretary announced that Mr. Corwin had arrived. Hearts pounding uncontrollably, we went out to meet him, pacing ourselves so as not to appear too anxious.

Ron didn't look as we expected. He was Yves Saint Laurent clothed and incredibly sophisticated. Moments later Marty arrived, breathless, disheveled. No one would have been able to tell which was the upstate attorney and which the New York practitioner.

Arnie and I sat next to each other on a small love seat, Ron and Marty at right angles to us on chairs facing each other. Throughout the morning conversation Arnie and I held hands, partly for support and partly so that we could give each other a little nudge or tap, if necessary. We ate pastry and drank papery-tasting coffee from containers while we chatted about inconsequential things.

Slowly, the talk turned to adoption, Ron setting the tone with little anecdotes about the adoption of his daughter. So he really isn't here to grill us or be judgmental, I realized with relief. He's just trying to get a sense of the kind of people we are.

I had been sitting very tight and closed up, but now began to loosen, letting myself occupy more of the sofa, letting the back of my head touch Arnie's shoulder.

After about two hours spent covering all the details and questions, Marty went back to his office and Ron headed uptown with us to see our apartment. Everything was ready—the wood floors freshly waxed, my desktop clear of papers, and an azalea plant on the coffee table. Not the way it usually looked, of course, but this was not the time to make a statement about my disinclination to clean.

We talked a little longer, then Ron left, promising to keep us posted.

I couldn't make the time go by fast enough. As the weeks passed, her baby/our baby was becoming wonderfully real. We chose a bright cold Sunday in March and headed for the Lower East Side for a brunch of blueberry blintzes at Ratner's and then to Ben's for Kids. The store practically has landmark status, adorned with photographs of happy, dimpled babies attesting to thirty years of service. A visit there would make even the most hardened soul weak with longing for storybook illustrations of childhood. There were mobiles with pink and blue angels hanging from the ceiling; cribs painted with Little Bo Peeps; play pens filled with soft, cuddly things; Pooh Bears, Raggedy Anns, and embroidered coverlets. I felt a surge of emotion as soon as I walked in.

"Are you sure we ought to do this?" I whispered.

Arnie put down the musical lamb he was holding and turned to me. Never have I seen his face such a confusion of emotion. His eyes, deep and dark, were full of pain, but the lines around them crinkled with expectation. "Yes, I'm sure."

We wandered through the store, touching this, holding that. Everything we bought was completely different from what we had selected for Rachel. The owner, remembering us from the year before and Arnie's wrenching cancellation of our order, refused to take a deposit.

"Just give me eighteen dollars, *chai*."

The number is Hebrew for "life."

And that's just what it meant to us. For ten months I had merely inhabited my life, but now I was beginning to live it once more, excited, vivid, full of energy. I started running again, the wind rough against my face, burning, invigorating. Every time I thought of the baby, I felt explosions of joy.

I was involved with my students, teaching hard, hoping to untie their imaginations. And my period was late again. But even the unmistakable cramps that always preceded it brought only disappointment, not the despair of the month before. I kept going to the toilet to check. I had all the body feelings that lead one woman to tell another with instant understanding, "I'm getting my period." But still it dawdled. Four days passed. Five. I denied the possibility of a pregnancy. I wasn't going to be masochistic, setting myself up for a huge disappointment. The drawing sensation in my legs stopped, the cramps subsided. Ten days. Twelve days. Two weeks.

"Don't you think you ought to have a pregnancy test?" Arnie asked.

I went back to the Women's Center. The receptionist took my carefully wrapped specimen and told me to wait inside. I sat down on one of the modern square pieces that was supposed to serve as a sofa. A few magazines were sloppily spread out on another block that was a coffee table. I started looking through them, but most were several months old.

A young woman came into the room, her hair a halo of frizz, a loose-fitting blouse tucked into a long colorful skirt that swayed around her boots as she paced back and forth. She lit a cigarette and smoked it nervously. I hadn't had a cigarette in months, and, as the stale smell of hers filled the room, a wave of nausea overcame me. Gagging back a bitter taste, I rushed to the ladies' room, hung my head over the toilet and retched until I felt better.

I combed my hair, took out a tissue, patted the beads of perspiration on my forehead, and went outside. The receptionist was waiting for me. "It's positive," she whispered, and handed me a piece of paper confirming the report in writing.

I dashed to the phone booths to call Arnie. He was taking a noon flight to San Francisco, and I wanted to

catch him before he left the office. My heart was dancing
wildly as I heard his voice.

"Guess what?" I sked coyly.

"You're pregnant! I can't believe it. Oh, Barb, I'm so
happy. That's just wonderful."

We were like two children, laughing, delighted,
self-satisfied. We kissed each other through the phone
and said we'd talk that evening. It was more than I'd
ever hoped for. *Two babies.*

Months before, Arnie and I had decided that even if
I became pregnant, we would go ahead with our plans to
adopt. We had both become so excited about the idea—
reading about it, talking about it, attending adoptive
parents' workshops—so committed to the thought of
sharing our lives with another that nothing, *nothing*,
could change it.

And, of course, we knew, although we didn't talk
about it then, that a pregnancy in no way assured a baby.

Later that evening, Arnie called as he had promised. His voice sounded dull and flat. "I don't think we
have anything to worry about . . ." he began.

This particular phrase always makes me extremely
worried. It usually goes: "I don't think we have anything
to worry about, but your mother was just in a car
accident. . . ." Or, "I don't think we have anything to
worry about, but the typist mislaid the first one hundred
pages of your manuscript. . . ."

So what was it now that I shouldn't worry about
which would probably make me absolutely frantic?

". . . but Ron called me before I left to tell me the
woman has been having some premature labor pains."

I gasped, almost dropping the phone.

"I don't want you to get upset," Arnie went on. "If
she gets them again, she's going to have them checked."

"But what's she waiting for?" I knew, of course.
Premature labor meant bed rest or some curtailment of
activities. Even women desperate for children resent the
restrictions. I sure did. What about one with more than
the usual ambivalence? One who absolutely *had* to

work? Would she do the necessary things? Would I in her place?

I called Susan. I don't think I realized it then, but, in the complex interaction of my friendships, I looked to each of my closest friends for different things: Roz for commiseration, Nina for honesty, and Susan for cheering up. I had met Susan shortly after my divorce. She was a free spirit who wanted to grab handfuls of life and swallow them whole, who saw the ridiculous, the absurd, and refused to be daunted.

But even she couldn't cheer me now. I walked back and forth in the apartment, finally settling down with an apple and the TV. It was only nine o'clock, but I felt very tired. I watched some improbable murder on "Hawaii Five-O" and drifted into a light sleep. The phone rang. I fumbled for it.

"Long distance calling for Arnold Schlanger."

"He's not in," I mumbled.

"Not in, Los Angeles," I heard the operator say.

Why were they calling here? Didn't his associates know he was already on the Coast? I thought irritably.

"I'll speak to Mrs. Schlanger," I heard a male voice say. I sat up and tried to waken fully.

"I'm Jack Greenberg. I spoke to your husband about a month ago in connection with adopting a baby. I didn't know of any available, but one of my tennis partners just called and he has a woman who wants to give up her baby."

"Oh, we already know of a baby," I blurted out, and immediately regretted it. There was a pause at the other end of the line.

"Then you're not interested?" Disappointment was evident in his voice.

"Well, yes, we are interested—uh—I mean—I mean the other situation is only tentative," I stammered. "When is this woman due?"

"She's in labor now."

What? In labor now? Did you say she was in labor now? You mean she's *having* the baby? Someone in this country is actually *having* a baby. I sat completely straight and held the phone tightly. "My husband's in San Francisco now," I said.

"That's fine. He can fly here, see the baby, and talk to the doctors before he comes home. I haven't met the woman, of course, but I'm going to the hospital now to find out what I can. Let me give you my number. I'll be in later. Ask Arnold to call any time after eleven."

I had to look at the clock three or four times before I remembered that California time was three hours earlier. I felt trembly with excitement as I started to dial Information for Arnie's hotel. Then I remembered he'd told me he was changing hotels. I had no idea where to reach him. Maybe our friends or his business associates on the Coast would know. One was out; a few lines were busy; others hadn't heard from him.

My parents called. They always did when Arnie ws out of town, to make sure I ate dinner, to find out if everything was all right. I told them my news. They were cautious. "What about the other woman upstate? Aren't you committed to her?"

Oh, damn it! Why couldn't I reach Arnie?

After almost an hour of trying, he called me. "Who have you been talking to? You've been busy for so long."

"I was trying to reach *you*," I said, and immediately told him why.

"What? Tell me again," he said.

I could picture him sitting down and listening with the phone against one ear and the other resting on his hand, that intense expression on his face, his worry lines deep, although he would not really be worrying, just concentrating. I repeated the whole conversation, slowly, exactly as I remembered it.

"God. That's incredible. What do you think we should do?"

"I don't know. I really don't. Look, why don't I call Marty Ganz? Let's see if he has any point of view on this. Give me about thirty minutes and call me again."

When Arnie did call back, I told him what Marty had said, "The rule of thumb in adoption is that you take the first healthy, available baby." It made sense. Even if the Syracuse woman's pregnancy was successful, she could always change her mind at the last minute. But we felt so close to her, attached to her. . . . We talked until midnight, New York time, and finally decided that if this baby's background matched the other's and if it was healthy, we would adopt it.

I took a long bath and tried to relax, but my head was spinning like a top. Were we doing the right thing? Would I be able to fly to California to take custody? Would the Syracuse woman feel betrayed? I knew it would be easy to find parents for a baby like that. Maybe Jeanne and Ted . . . I'd have to discuss it with Arnie in the morning.

I'll never forget the sound of Arnie's voice at the other end of the phone the next morning. No hello, no preliminaries at all when I picked up, just "It's a girl!"

I sat right down on the bed as though someone had pulled my feet from under me.

"Arnie! She's born? She's a girl! Oh, Arnie!"

I'm not sure whether it was her sex or that she was already here waiting for us. But from that moment we knew, in the most absolute way of knowing, that this would be our baby.

Arnie had spoken to Jack late Wednesday night and again Thursday morning. The baby was born at 10:00 P.M. California time. Her background was good and the delivery uncomplicated. Before calling me, Arnie had spoken to the pediatrician at Los Angeles Memorial Hospital, who had assured him that the six-pound, eight-ounce infant was in fine health and spirits. He promised to meet Arnie at the newborn nursery later that day.

"We have to arrange for a home study," Arnie was saying, "and all the legal work has to be done before Monday. . . ."

I was hardly listening. The magnitude of the event was settling upon me. Only twelve hours earlier I had despaired of ever being a mother, and now an infant—the daughter we had wanted so desperately—would soon be ours. It was scary and strange and marvelous all at once.

". . . And a layette . . ."

I snapped back to reality. "I'd better jot this all down," I said, putting down the phone and running into the other room for a pad and pencil.

"We need a name for the birth certificate," Arnie continued. "What about Johanna?" he suggested.

"I like Alison," I said. "Alison and Gail for Grandma Gertrude. What do you think?"

"Fine. It sounds great. Alison with one or two *l*'s?"

I wrote out her whole name both ways. "One *l*, there are too many *l*'s already."

A birth certificate, a layette. Every part of my body was smiling.

"What are you going to do about Roz's shower?" Arnie asked.

"Make it, of course." I had been imagining making Roz a bridal shower long before she and Bob had decided to marry. Now it never occurred to me not to, although it was planned for that Saturday.

I looked at the list I'd made, and added the questions I wanted to ask Dr. Morgan that morning. My appointment was for 11:30, and it was almost 11:00 now. I put on a pair of blue pants and a matching plaid shirt, tossed the bedspread over the bed, and went into the kitchen. The cat purred at my legs. I picked her up and stroked her coat. "Poor Oliver," I said. "You're the only one who isn't going to be thrilled with the new baby."

Almost as if she understood, she licked my face with her sandpaper tongue. I opened a can of fishy-smelling cat food and put it down for her. I started putting the filter in the glass coffeepot, then caught myself: Better make instant. It tasted weak and lukewarm—I hadn't let the water boil long enough. I drank only about half the cup and spilled the rest into the sink. I knew I'd have a wait at the office, and I didn't want to get out too late.

"Congratulations," Morgan called out as he came into the examining room. He already knew that I was pregnant. My chart, in a glass envelope outside the door, listed me as an obstetrical patient. This was a new procedure, leaving the chart outside after the nurse took your weight and blood pressure. I guess they had discovered more patients like me who read their charts at every opportunity.

"Feels like a good pregnancy," he said, pressing on the uterus. "Let's talk in my office."

I dressed and went inside.

"I see you got pregnant a few months after the Rubin's test."

"I think it was the running that did it," I said, only half joking.

Morgan laughed. "I hope you've stopped running now."

I nodded. I took out my yellow sheet of paper with the questions. "Paper napkins, paper plates, Tab . . ." whoops, wrong list. After a bit of hunting, I finally found the right one.

He thought it would be okay for me to fly out to California, but advised me to get someone to help with the baby. "She's only six pounds, eight ounces now, but soon she'll be sixteen pounds. We're going to try to get a good tight suture in, so maybe you'll be able to remain mobile during this pregnancy, but I don't want you to do much lifting or carrying."

I left the office feeling so expansive I wanted to reach up and make love to the sky. Nothing could harden my mood, not the crowded Lexington Avenue bus and not even the new checker at D'Agostino's who had to ask the price of every other item before ringing it up.

"It's okay," I chimed, "no problem at all, sure, take your time."

I had a quick lunch, then sat down with list in hand to start making my calls. It wasn't easy to find a social worker who would do a home study on a Sunday morning. I must have tried a half-dozen and mostly got their answering services. I was feeling discouraged when I thought of calling a few hospitals to see if their social-services divisions could recommend anyone. Lenox Hill was able to, and I soon had an appointment for nine o'clock Sunday morning. I arranged for the baby furniture to be delivered, got a baby nurse, spoke to Marty several times, and then tried to keep the line free for Arnie's call.

When it came, his voice quivered with emotion. "I've just seen her, and she's beautiful, absolutely beautiful. We have to come back and get her soon."

"What does she look like?"

"She doesn't have much hair, hardly any at all, and her features are small and perfect. You'll see for yourself. She's all alone here, just waiting for us. We have to come soon," he said again.

Was he crying? "Are you all right?"

"Yes, fine. I love you."

"I love you too," I said, and put down the phone.

I hardly remember Saturday. If it weren't for the photographs confirming my presence, I wouldn't believe I really made Roz's shower. I was in a daze, talking, smiling, laughing, but everything focused on Alison. I couldn't wait for Arnie to get home.

Finally he did, around 6:00 P.M. All the guests had left; my parents were still helping me put things away. He looked tired, his suitcase heavy, his shirt wrinkled, the top two buttons undone so that I could see the dark hair from his chest curling into the opening.

How many times had he come home like this from business trips? Weary, drained. Both of us filled with our different worlds. Often colliding. Always a space to be crossed. Taking us a day or so to coalesce.

But not now. We flew to each other. Hugging, kissing, whispering. "Oh, Arnie-dwarmie . . . Do you think it will work? Tell me again what she looks like."

And each time he described her, *each time*, tears rolled down his face. It wasn't that he was sad, it was just that he loved her. As crazy and incredible as it sounds, *he already loved her*.

We got up early on Sunday and busily neatened the house in anticipation of the home study. But the social worker was more interested in us than in the apartment.

We sat around the dining-room table talking over Arnie's delicious coffee and leftover pastry from Roz's shower. The social worker was plump and cheerful and bright and took her job seriously, asking questions gently, but to the point. After about an hour, she congratulated us and said that she would send a copy of her report to Albany and give us another copy on Monday morning to take with us to Los Angeles.

We hoped to be on a 4:00 P.M. flight, but could only make it if we got all the legal work done that afternoon. Arnie cajoled his secretary into meeting us at his office, and Marty and his wife were coming too. There was no heat in the building, so we worked with our coats on. It was a marathon of details: phone calls to California, forms to be filled out, cold coffee, endless copies to be made on a stubborn Xerox machine, lunch ordered in from the local deli, more cold coffee, more calls to Jack, more forms, more calls. . . .

I was so tired and frazzled by 7:00 P.M. that I urged Arnie to stop even if it meant postponing our trip until Tuesday.

"Only about another half-hour," he promised. "We have to be done by then—that's the latest we can stall the delivery service." We had decided to have all the documents hand-delivered to Los Angeles so Greenberg could go through them in advance of our arrival.

As soon as we got home, Arnie took our suitcases down from the closet and I packed a bunch of warm-weather things. We had no idea how long we'd have to be away. I had arranged for my classes to be covered, and Arnie was going to try to work from our hotel as best as he could. My parents came over with more sand-wiches from another local deli, and all kinds of questions.

"What are you going to do about the bedroom?" my mother asked. Neither of us had given any thought to it. The apartment had become kind of shabby over the past year, and that room especially. I used it for my study, and there were piles of books and pads everywhere, no room for a crib or any of the other baby furniture.

My mother suggested that if my brother-in-law, Bob, came over and gave Arnie a hand taking the desk out, she and Lucy would try to get the room painted while we were gone.

"It'll be impossible to find a painter on such short notice," I said. But I knew that my mother, like my husband, refused to acknowledge the existence of the word "impossible." "Call Bob if you want," I said.

As I watched my brother-in-law and Arnie take the desk out of the second bedroom, I remembered how upset I had been when the movers couldn't get it through the door. So much had happened in the four years since then.

Early Monday, I met my parents and Lucy to buy the layette, and then went home to finish packing. Alison had her own suitcase, filled with stretchies, receiving blankets, and kimonos. Pinks, blues, yellows, and whites —it looked like a box of bonbons.

"I don't believe how much we're taking," said Arnie when he got home. "We're not going to Outer Mongolia, you know. Don't you think we'll be able to get everything we need once we're there?"

"Probably, but I feel better having it all with me, just in case." Just in case what? I'm not really sure. I think it was part of the disaster mentality I'd developed over the last few years. Just in case the stores are out of Pampers, just in case there's a national Similac strike, just in case . . .

"This is the last time we'll be in the apartment without a baby," we kept saying. "This is the last time the room will be so empty." We were so consumed with the meaning of our trip, so busy with last-minute arrangements, that I wasn't even nervous about the flight.

Jack and his wife, Katie, met us at the airport. As they helped us load everything into their car, Jack told us about the hotel he had gotten for us. "It's really more like a motel, but it has an efficiency, so you will be able to sterilize and keep things refrigerated, and it's close to our home in case you need anything."

"I hope it's okay," added Katie cautiously. "It's kind of old, but they've done some remodeling over the last few years."

But we weren't going right to the hotel. The hospital had given Jack permission to bring us up to the newborn nursery. *We were going directly to see Alison.*

As we reached the imposing entrance of Los Angeles Memorial, my heart was beating so loudly I was sure the others in the car would hear it. Jack went in before us and in a few minutes returned, motioning us to follow him. It was only seven o'clock, but the halls were quiet except for a few hushed voices from the nurses' station.

I held tightly to Arnie's hand. He was beaming like a flashlight, walking slightly ahead of me. "Just wait until you see her," he said proudly. After all, *he* had already held her, *he* was already her father.

My stomach was churning. I think my pulse was probably up to three hundred beats per minute. I couldn't wait.

But I paused. Glued to those freshly waxed floors, I stood a few feet from the window, waiting. I was not afraid, not nervous, but just savoring a moment that would stand by itself throughout my entire life.

Then I leaned forward, looked inside, and a smile automatically spread across my face. Alison was lying on her back in the front row. She was small and smooth, with just a little golden fuzz on her round head. One of the most beautiful babies I'd ever seen. *The* most beautiful baby I'd ever seen.

As she slept, she moved her hands slightly. I longed to put my finger in her hand, to feel it curl over in a delicate little fist, but I knew we couldn't stay. Jack had promised we would only be a few minutes.

"You'll be back around ten tomorrow morning?" the head nurse asked, signaling the end of our visit.

"Yes," Jack answered, hastily turning away from the window.

"You'll take good care of her, won't you?" I asked. The nurse smiled patronizingly.

It was almost dark when we left the hospital. The car lights on the freeway looked like yellow streamers. Arnie and I were anxious to unpack and get settled and be alone, but the Greenbergs insisted that we stop by their house for a drink. After we'd visited for a while, Jack drove Arnie to pick up a car for us to use while we were there and dropped me off at the hotel on the way.

I walked into the room and my spirits took a nose dive. The blue paint was peeling off the walls, and up near the ceiling there was a large, white-gray scar that looked as though it had been made by leaking water. The room was damp and smelled from mildew. The bedspreads were stained and about three shades lighter than the limp curtain they were supposed to match. There were melon seeds in the sink, and the pots were burned.

"We can't stay here," I said as soon as Arnie came in.

He looked around and agreed. "I don't know where we'll find a hotel with a vacancy this late," he wondered out loud. "The only place I can think of is the Beverly Wilshire. Maybe they'll give us a room because I stay there so often when I'm here on business."

He pulled the phone over to him and dialed. As he spoke to the manager, he looked up and nodded yes. I already had my coat on.

"They had a last-minute cancellation," Arnie explained to me in the car. "One of their better rooms on a high floor. That means it's going to be very expensive. I hope we don't have to stay there long."

I had been to the Wilshire many years before, and, like a good wine, it had aged well. The lobby was decorated in rich, subdued velvets, burgundy and blues. Even the elevators had atmosphere, still attended by thin young women, their dark dresses brightened only by one red rose.

The rooms on each floor were decorated in the style of a different country. Ours was French, with candy-striped chairs, a matching heavy bedspread, thick carpet, and curtains. The room was large and L-shaped so that the convertible sofa and table and chair were separated from the king-size bed. In the center of the dresser was a large basket of fruit, a small bottle of wine, and some wedges of Gruyère and Camembert cheese, all wrapped in yellow cellophane with a card stapled on, addressed to a Mr. Akinson with compliments of the hotel.

"Do you think we ought to eat it?"

"Sure," said Arnie with a mischievous grin.

I hadn't realized how hungry I was until I saw the food. It was 11:50, California time, almost 3:00 A.M. for us. But I wasn't tired any longer.

While Arnie unpacked, I washed my hair. Wrapping it in a towel, I sat down beside him and watched as he spread some cheese on a cracker. For a few minutes we ate in silence.

"I can't stop thinking about Alison," I said at last.

"I know, neither can I. Didn't I tell you she was beautiful?"

I nodded.

But more than just that. She was our baby, our child, our daughter. And we were her father and mother. Her parents. Incredible, a dream, awesome and wonderful.

We cut an apple into sections and drank a little wine, each with our own thoughts.

"We'd better get to sleep," Arnie said after a while, pulling the bedspread off while I dried my hair. "Do you think we ought to have the hotel wake us up?"

"Sure," I answered as I cuddled up next to him. "Have them call at eight."

But we were up way before. How could we sleep? We were tingling with excitement. At seven, I started packing the bag to take with us—formula, Pampers, undershirt, white stretchie, white-and-blue sweater, and the blue woolen bunting that Lucy and her children and I had all worn home from the hospital.

I dressed in a loose-fitting dirndl skirt and blouse. I was only eight weeks pregnant, but my body was thickening faster this time. I tossed a shawl around my shoulders and waited for Arnie to finish taking pictures of the morning.

The breakfast room was just as I remembered it, cheerful and sunny, with waitresses in colorful Mexican costumes pouring coffee so dark it almost stained the cup. We had just ordered when Arnie was paged to the phone.

"Nothing serious," he said as soon as he returned, seeing my concerned expression. "Jack will be a little late. He'll pick us up around eleven."

Not for another three hours? I was greedy for Alison.

We wandered around the lobby, waiting for some of the stores to open. We bought Laura a doll for her collection, Alison a large stuffed kangaroo with a baby in its pouch, and me a small pair of silver-and-turquoise earrings which I would never wear without thinking about that day. We walked on Rodeo Drive, proud and elegant in the morning sun, and took more pictures for our album until it was time to meet the Greenbergs.

Alison was awake and ready for us when we arrived at the hospital. The nurse brought her into one of the empty rooms so she could be dressed. "Do you want me to do it? Or would you like to try?" she asked.

Try? "Oh, I'll do it."

"All right, if you think you *can*."

"Come on, sweetheart. Mommy's going to dress you now." First the undershirt. That's not bad. Now the stretchie. One arm into one sleeve, then the other arm into the other. How do you get the other arm in? Sorry, honey, I didn't mean to hurt you. Mmmm, can't quite seem to find all the snaps. Oh. I see. There are the same number on each side. That's good to know. Oops. Where'd her feet go?

Oh, Alison honey, you don't really want to spit up over everything. Oh. You *do* want to spit up over everything. A helpless look at the nurse. You mean I'm *really* going to have to start all over again?

Dressing a baby isn't quite as simple as I thought. When I finally finished, the nurse showed me how to swab the umbilical cord and how to use an aspirator in case she choked on her formula. A volunteer gave me gifts from the hospital—formula, baby shampoo, Pampers, all the accouterments of motherhood. I was all set!

When we were ready to leave, I took out the blue bunting and slid her into it. She was so little she almost disappeared. It was doubtful that she really needed it. Lucy had been born in February, her children also when it was cold, and I had been born in November. Quite different from a hazy April morning in Los Angeles. But tradition is tradition, and I'm the last to interfere with it. So it was a very warm baby who slept in my arms on the way back to the hotel.

We had brought a folding carriage bed with us from New York, and had assembled it on the sofa before leaving that morning. As I tried to put her in it, she awoke and started to cry.

"Maybe she's hungry," Arnie suggested, opening one of the nursettes and handing it to me. She began drinking, but almost immediately started to hiccup.

"Hand me the aspirator, quick," I said nervously.

"She's okay, newborn babies always get the hiccups."

All of a sudden I felt very insecure. I was three thousand miles away from home, in a city where I hardly knew a soul. No doctor, no refrigerator, no way of sterilizing, with a newborn baby totally dependent upon me. For the first time since Alison was born, I worried about how well I'd manage. Other women "in waiting" worried about how well they'd cope with formula and schedules and croup. I hadn't. I had only worried about whether or not I'd have anyone to worry about. Now that I did, I worried about what everyone else worried about. Oh, it was rich.

Just then Lucy called. Still holding Alison in my arms, I sat on the bed and talked, cradling the receiver between my shoulder and ear. "She has the hiccups," I cried out in the same tone I would have said she had whooping cough.

"That's nothing," Lucy answered. "Didn't you bring a copy of Dr. Spock?"

Lucy was calling from my apartment, where she and my mother were supervising the painting of the bedroom. My mother picked up the extension. "Tell me everything about her," she urged breathlessly, and I did.

"When will you be home?" Lucy asked.

"I'm not sure. We have to wait until our papers from Albany arrive here."

"But with the way the mail is, that can take a week!" my mother interjected, sounding agitated.

"Well, we're hoping the head of the social-service division in Albany is going to send a telegram, so it might not be more than a day or two."

While I was talking, Alison fell asleep in my arms. Arnie took the receiver from me and arranged the pillows behind my back. I slid down, holding Alison on my breast. We were breathing together. Slow, easy. I could feel the warmth of her sweet milk breath against my neck, her fragile bones and vertebrae, her soft silk baby flesh. I closed my eyes. There was nothing but the rythm of our bodies together, together. . . .

I stayed that way while Arnie went down to buy a Dr. Spock and to look for more formula. Since we had no way of keeping an open bottle cold, we had to throw out anything she didn't take at each feeding. We were wasting a lot, and, worse, we'd run out within two days.

"I've been all over," Arnie said when he finally got back. "They don't have Similac with Iron anywhere. I must have gone to ten drugstores and supermarkets."

"Let's call the hospital," I suggested. "Maybe we can buy some from them."

They wouldn't sell it, but would gladly give us some extra bottles. He started out the door again, then turned back and came over to the bed. "Almost forgot this," he said, handing me a paper bag. I reached my arms over Alison and pulled out a copy of *Baby's Magazine*. "Now that you're a mommy, I thought you might find this interesting." He grinned and was out the door.

That night we had a celebration dinner in the room,

and toasted our newborn baby sleeping quietly beside us. After we finished, we called Arnie's parents to tell them our doubly happy news. We could feel their excitement through the phone.

We turned off the light around ten o'clock and got into bed, happy, intimate, talking softly about the day, about Alison. She was in my dreams—peaceful, satisfied dreams. I kept getting up to check her. I'd put my ear to her head to listen for her breathing and my hand on her back just to make sure. I couldn't wait for her to wake up. When she finally did, Arnie got out of bed too, and we fed her together. We both sat there, our arms around each other, long after she fell back to sleep.

A loud, insistent buzz filled the room. Sleepily, instinctively, I reached for the telephone, knocking the receiver off the hook as I did. Marty's voice was thick and gruff on the other end. "That gal in Albany's refusing to send a telegram. She insisted on sending your papers through the regular mail."

"What's wrong?" Arnie asked. I handed him the phone.

"But that's awful," he said, sitting up and pushing the blankets off. "It might take over a week for it to arrive. We don't have enough formula, we can't sterilize the nipples. Didn't you tell her we have a tiny baby here? We *have* to get her home."

The commotion awakened Alison. She started to whimper, but, sensing our agitation, she began screaming loudly.

"Listen, Marty, I've got to go," Arnie said. "Let me see what I can do from here. I'll call you back." He went over to pick up Alison, and I went into the bathroom to get washed.

When I came out, Arnie was feeding Alison. I stood in the doorway watching them: Arnie, dark and rumpled with sleep, holding that pink and golden bit of life in his arms. How many times had I looked at fathers feeding their babies, or at mothers walking proudly, their toddlers stringing after them like a row of young chicks, and envied their lives, knowing nothing else about them except that they had children? "You never know," Arnie would say, "maybe they lost three babies first or it took them years to conceive."

But none of that helped. They had children, and that's what counted. And now as I listened to Alison making contented gurgling sounds and saw Arnie's face smiling above her, I felt the same. We had a child, and that's what counted.

Then I remembered Marty's call. "What are we going to do about getting out of here? We're going to run out of formula and clean clothing for her. And I don't think we ought to continue to let Room Service in, or the cleaning woman."

"Why on earth not?"

"Well, I don't know what germs they're carrying— maybe they have young children who are sick."

Arnie gave me one of his you're-starting-to-sound-like-your-mother looks.

"When Lucy had Nancy, she didn't want Laura to visit, or anyone with young children," I pointed out.

Nervousness ballooned. Something might go wrong. Some paper not signed. Nothing was final yet. Every knock on the door, every ring of the phone, sent a shudder down my spine.

"I just want to get her home," I finally said.

"*Nothing* can ever take Alison from us," Arnie said, as if reading my fears. "We'll find a way. It just . . ."

I know, Arnie, it's just a matter of logistics.

Our breakfast arrived and we sat down, still talking about what to do.

"Suppose we called the woman in Albany ourselves and begged her to send a telegram, appealed to her sympathy. After all, we're not doing anything illegal. We just want to protect a tiny baby. I can't imagine why she won't do it."

"Who knows what motivates these bureaucrats? She might think a phone call from us was presumptuous."

"Isn't there anyone who could reason with her?" I asked as I ate my poached eggs.

"Let me think." Arnie poured second cups of coffee for both of us and sipped his slowly. After a few minutes, his face brightened. "I know someone who might be able to help us. What time is it?"

"Nine-thirty."

"Oh, damn. He's probably out to lunch."

"Who? What have you thought of?"

"Dick Riley, my friend from camp. I introduced him to his wife. He's an attorney in Albany. You remember meeting him, don't you?"

I nodded.

"Let me see if I can get him," Arnie said, heading for the phone.

Dick wasn't in the office, but the secretary said she'd have him call as soon as he returned, probably around two o'clock, their time.

We spent the next hour and a half taking care of Alison, almost fighting with each other over whose turn it was.

"You fed her last time—"

"Yeah, but you got to bathe her *and* change her stretchie."

Everything about her was new, thrilling, fascinating.

Dick called back. He knew the woman at the social-service agency. He'd see what he could do and let us know.

We waited. Arnie went down to shop, and I sat next to Alison on the sofa, reading.

I hadn't been out of the hotel room in twenty-four hours, but I felt no restlessness, no yearnings, nothing but a fierce, protective love. A piece of me carved out and given to her forever. A bond of startling intensity.

Strange how fast and deep it formed. After all, there *had* been other babies: Marissa's daughter's baby; the Syracuse baby; maybe a Colombian baby; and, yes, Rachel—there had always been that memory. But from the moment I responded to Alison's first wail of hunger, felt her little body nuzzled against mine, there were no other babies. *Never could there have been any other babies*. She was my daughter, totally and absolutely.

She had just fallen asleep when Dick called. He had gotten permission to make a copy of the letter and would use the airport's special package service for the next jet headed to Los Angeles. He wasn't sure which flight it would make. There was one that arrived at midnight, California time. He'd try for that. Otherwise, it would be on one getting to Los Angeles at 8:00 A.M.

"I'm sorry, but that was the best I could do."

"Sorry? Dick, that's wonderful! How can we ever thank you?"

"Just send us a picture of your little girl. That will be thanks enough."

"Give our love to Jo and the boys," I said, and hung up.

I called Jack Greenberg and told him. He and Katie wanted to come over to the hotel that evening for a quick goodbye drink.

We dressed Alison in one of her few clean stretchies and wrapped her in a matching pink receiving blanket. We ordered some wine and bread and cheese and waited for our guests.

Katie and Jack swore she had grown since the day before. Had it really been just one day? It was hard to believe. Katie begged to feed her; their daughter had given up her bottle a year ago. We sat and talked of babies, formulas, and schedules.

"This is the last interstate adoption I'm going to do," Jack said. "The interstate compact makes it much more work. There were more forms than in *Blumberg's Directory*."

"You can't mean that," I pleaded. "You've changed our whole life. If you hadn't been willing to get involved, we would never have . . ." My voice trailed off. I couldn't say it, or think it.

Alison started making small complaining sounds. "She's probably just being fussy," counseled Katie.

"No, I don't think so. I know her," I said. "She always goes right to sleep. I'd better check her diaper."

I didn't have to do too much checking. Yellowish diarrhea was visible through her stretchie and on the sheet of her carriage. I was concerned as I changed her; diarrhea could be dangerous in an infant, especially one so small. But there was also a part of me that felt proud. I had said that I knew my daughter, and I did.

After Arnie and Jack left for the airport, I started getting our things together and making reservations on several different flights. I made them in the names of both Berg and Schlanger, thinking that some computer would kick out multiple accommodations. If we could leave the next day, TWA had a 7:45 flight and I desperately wanted to be on it. They had nothing left in tourist. I wavered. Then I made reservations in first class. How many times in your life do you fly home with your baby?

It was after 1:00 A.M. when there was a knock at the door. I froze and instinctively glanced over at Alison.

"Who is it?"

"It's me and *we're leaving tomorrow*."

I threw open the door.

"Jack has the letter and we're all set to go. How's Alison?"

"Fine. She's sleeping. No more diarrhea."

Arnie and I packed for another hour or so, then slept for a few hours. But we didn't feel at all tired. We were going home! It was electrifying, energizing. TWA let us board early, and every member of the crew came to take a peek at Alison. Her pediatrician had told us to have her drink during the ascent and descent to reduce the pressure on her eardrums. She took her bottle willingly, then promptly fell asleep. My arm grew numb and warm under her weight, but I didn't move, for fear of waking her. With my free hand I put on the earphones and stayed that way, listening to music, holding Alison, for the entire flight.

The stewardess came by to tell me they were starting the descent. "I've asked the captain to bring the plane down slowly," she said.

"Alison, Alison," I whispered, shaking her gently. She didn't respond at first. A brief feeling of panic swept through me, but in a few seconds her lids opened and she looked at me cross-eyed, trying to focus. Once again she drank with gusto, finishing almost the entire four ounces before we were completely down.

As soon as the plane came to a halt, we put her into the obligatory blue bunting and headed for the ramp. "Enjoy your baby," the flight attendants called, but we were in too much of a rush to give more than an appreciative nod.

Before they saw us, I could see my parents and sister peering anxiously into the crowds. I waved excitedly. Their faces blossomed into smiles. As we approached them, I unexpectedly started to weep. All the fears, the nervousness, the tension of the last few days, flushed out with those tears. A heavyset woman in her late thirties stood nearby. Turning toward us, she smiled and said, "I know how you feel. Two times I flew home with infants. It's quite a trip!"

As soon as we got into the car, my mother undid Alison's hat and looked at her appraisingly. "She really is beautiful. Like a china doll."

I breathed a silent sigh of relief. Arnie, how can you say I need my mother's approval? Not at all!

"Wait until you see the bedroom," my mother said as we entered the apartment.

I stood at the door mesmerized. My eyes swept around the transformed room, slowly, deliberately: the white lace canopy over the crib, the sheets with the tiny pink and blue bowknots, the satin comforter, the stuffed animals waiting to greet her. I tried to stamp it on my memory, knowing, perhaps, that I would never see it quite this way again.

Then my in-laws called, and Susan and Nina came over to see Alison, and Florence came in with an arrangement of flowers. Clara, the baby nurse, arrived, and we were all talking at once, making drinks, celebrating. I'd never seen the apartment so happy.

By nine o'clock everyone had gone. Clara was sitting in the room with Alison, and Arnie and I started making some calls. First on our list was Ron Corwin. We hadn't told him anything yet. "How do you think he'll respond?" I asked as Arnie dialed.

He put his finger to his lips. The phone was ringing. I saw his face become tense and knew someone had picked up. He rushed through the usual greetings and plunged right into our story. His voice told his nervousness. "Well, we *thought* about it, but three babies might be a bit hard to handle. . . ." His voice smoother now, his face loosened and relaxed. He was laughing a little. "Well, as a matter of fact we do. I'll give you a call about that tomorrow."

"What did he say?" I asked before Arnie even put down the receiver.

"He thought we did the right thing. He would have done the same. And he wanted to know if we knew another couple for the baby. I was thinking about Jeanne and Ted."

"So was I. They weren't interested in adopting, but maybe when they hear about this they'll change their minds."

We got no answer in their New York apartment but finally reached them out on Long Island around midnight. Ted waited until I had gone through the entire story, then said: "It sounds fantastic, but we've got some news of our own. Jeanne's pregnant!"

"What!" I screamed. "Arnie, Jeanne's pregnant. Pick up in the kitchen."

"I don't believe this," I said into the phone. "I'm pregnant, too."

Jeanne got on the phone. "Why didn't you tell me?" I scolded. Next to my own pregnancy, hers was the one I'd hoped for most.

"Well, I knew how much you wanted to become pregnant, so I just thought I'd wait a while before saying anything. Now you'll have two children. That's just great!"

We exchanged congratulations and hung up. I crawled into bed and cuddled up to Arnie, sleeping more peacefully than I had slept in two years.

I hadn't been sleeping long when I was awakened by Alison crying. I crept out of bed and peeked into her room. Clara was sound asleep. I had assumed that she would do the night feedings, but what did I know about baby nurses?

I started heating a bottle. Alison was frantic now, crying loudly, flailing her arms and legs. I tried to calm her by walking back and forth, but she only screamed more.

At last the bottle was ready. I sat down with her in our large soft club chair. I held her as close as possible, listening to her small happy sounds. They flowed into me, filling me with pleasure. What a wonderful exchange of needs. It was the start of interdependency, so simple and yet so very complicated.

It seemed like I had just fallen back to sleep when the alarm went off. Arnie was going in to the office for a few hours, then out to Long Island to pick up Laura. I was meeting them for lunch, and together we would tell her about Alison. We wished we could have told her sooner, but everything had happened too fast. We'd had no time for a trip out to Long Island, and we didn't think we should tell her over the phone.

What should we say? "Laura, mommy and I have some *wonderful news* for you"? Well, wonderful to us, but maybe not to her. How about "Laura, mommy and I have some news for you"? No . . . sounds too grave, might alarm her. "We've got a surprise for you"? Wrong again—she'd think it was a present.

"Let's be spontaneous. We'll find the right way," Arnie said.

I met them at the restaurant. Arnie looked a trifle uneasy, and Laura older than two weeks ago. We ordered, then I nodded at Arnie for him to begin. He shifted uncomfortably in his chair. I nudged him slightly under the table. He remained silent.

I reached over and took Laura's hand. "Sweetheart, daddy and I have adopted a baby girl."

She looked startled, but said nothing.

"She's your sister and, at least for the time being, you two will be roommates. I hope that you'll learn to love her, because I *know* that she'll look up to you and idolize you the way I did Lucy when we were children."

She looked pensive for a minute or so, and then said philosophically: "Well, I *knew* that sooner or later you were going to have a baby. I'm glad I didn't know before. This way I had less time to worry about it."

Laura decided to spend the rest of the afternoon with Arnie at his office rather than go directly home with me. Maybe she really wasn't worried, or maybe she was very worried. But I was secretly pleased. I was starting to feel the lack of sleep. Maybe I would just stretch out on the bed and read, or maybe even close my eyes for a few minutes.

But when I entered the apartment I found Clara napping and Alison fretting. I didn't know when she had been fed last, so I gently woke up Clara. She made no effort to hide her annoyance.

"I just fed her an hour ago. She's a hungry baby. You gotta git her into a schedule. Just let her cry."

I felt intimidated. After all, Clara was the expert. She'd been taking care of newborns for twenty-five years. I left the room with Alison's cries in my ears, closed the door to my bedroom, and furtively called Lucy.

"What should I do?" I asked in a whisper.

"Try holding her. If that doesn't work, try feeding her. It's all trial and error at first, but you'll get the hang of it."

I threw back my shoulders and bravely walked into the other bedroom.

"You're gonna spoil that child sure as I'm talkin'," Clara said disdainfully as I lifted Alison up into my arms.

She was warm and damp. "There, there," I soothed protectively, and took her into the living room. How long should you let a baby cry? How often should you feed her? When should you pick her up? Someone ought to invent a "Dial-an-Answer for New Mothers."

I was sitting on the sofa wondering about how to handle Clara when I heard Arnie's key in the lock. "Hi. We're home," he called.

I stood up to greet them, holding Alison out a little so Laura could see her. But Laura took just one peek and walked past me. Straight into the bedroom.

Chapter 11

For ten days we lived with Clara's constant opprobrium. "You're feeding her too much," "You're holding her too much," she'd reprimand.

Soon we felt like fugitives in our own apartment, feeding and playing with our baby behind closed doors. Clara was fond of schedules, but she was also fond of sleep—hers as well as Alison's—so most of the time we were on our own.

It was just as well, since we seemed to disagree with her about everything concerning childcare, and she was not exactly the most pleasant person to have around. I thought about replacing her, but let things ride for a while. Then one morning after I finally had gotten Alison to take a nap, I heard her screaming again. I hurried into her bedroom to find Clara bathing her.

"What are you doing?" I asked dumbly, for anyone could clearly see what she was doing.

"It's ten o'clock. Time for her bath," Clara said definitively.

"But she just fell asleep twenty minutes ago," I protested.

Clara gave me a disgusted look. "You're never gonna git this child into a routine."

It was senseless to argue about it then, since Alison was already wet. I walked into my bedroom, sat down, and raged.

In the long run it probably didn't harm Alison, but new mothers don't see anything in the long run. Everything is immediate and of great consequence. Did she drink three ounces or four? Are her stools yellowish or greenish? Should she sleep on her stomach or her back? At that moment I felt as though Clara had violated the Eleventh Commandment.

I made up my mind to fire her, but I had never fired anyone. It was exactly the kind of confrontation I avoid. Arnie calls me the original soft touch. I end up collecting for every conceivable charity because I can't bear to say no. And in those few instances where I refuse when they call for Mrs. Berg, I feel so guilty about it that by the time they reach me again as Mrs. Schlanger, I give in.

But now, believing that Alison's welfare was at stake, I turned into a lion. Well, maybe not a *lion*, but a pretty determined lamb. I waited for the bath to be finished, and then went into the bathroom where Clara was rinsing out the tub.

"Here, let me help you with that," I said, reaching up above Clara's short arms to hang the white terry-cloth towel on the shower rod. She scowled at me.

I took a deep breath. "I don't think we'll be needing you beyond the weekend," I said in a voice that sounded as if it belonged to a nine-year-old.

Her face hardened, a little angry, maybe a little hurt.

"Uh—my—I mean, my mother-in-law is going to stay with us for a while and she'll help me," I lied, ashamed of my cowardliness.

"Oh, good," she sort of grunted, without really looking at me. "I'll leave Saturday morning."

For the next few days we lived as in a DMZ, but I endured Clara's stony silence with aplomb. Alison was thriving, and she was gaining weight. Her hands were becoming chubby and dimpled, she had a haze of soft blonde hair about her head, and luminescent blue eyes that had an ever-quizzical look. Each morning I would feed her, rocking gently in my old blue chair, and then take her out in the English pram.

The tangerine sun was not yet warm in April, but bright and pretty. And our days were pretty as we strolled together past the newly laden flower shops sweet with orchids, lilies, and gladiolas, and fruit stands overflowing with melons and grapes. I, too, felt sweet and overflowing with my one babe inside and my one outside. I felt good and full and grateful.

As I pushed my sleeping daughter, one eye always alert to the rise and fall of her chest, it seemed that life was finally perfectly aligned, the center and the margins just where they should be. And at home, what happy busy times. So many people came to see Alison, so many gifts. I think there must have been a stampede on Bloomingdale's.

Sometimes Arnie would surprise us by coming home for lunch. We were both fascinated by Alison, wanting to savor every moment of her young life. Arnie and I were having so much fun that I wondered if I should even bother to find another baby nurse. But I remembered Morgan's caution about too much activity and decided I'd better make arrangements. Besides, I needed someone to stay with her when I was teaching and meeting with my students. I phoned another agency.

Ivy arrived, slim, energetic, and very protective of Alison. She even outdid my mother on cleanliness. She changed Alison's clothes at least once an hour, sterilized everything twice, and each day wound a colorful bandanna around her closely cropped curls and scrubbed Alison's bedroom.

Aside from the fact that she was costing us a fortune in laundries, I would have liked her to stay. But she told us the first day that she never remained longer than two weeks. "I become too attached to the baby," she explained. "Besides, there isn't enough to do here."

Next there was Dorothy, who was not attached to anything, except perhaps to her knitting, and left because there was too much to do. Okay. Enough of this fooling around. I had to find someone good. Morgan planned to do a sonogram the next week and, if the fetus

was large enough, schedule me for suturing. I needed to
have a reliable nurse while I was at Hillcrest.

Helga came that Saturday. A short dumpling of a
woman, she immediately took to Alison. She also cooked
delicious chicken paprikash, and, best of all, told us that
she would stay as long as we wanted. She loved to hold
Alison, nestling her in her ample bosom as she sat on the
sofa and talked about her past cases. Most were ficti-
tious, I think. It's hard to believe that she was nurse to
Happy and Nelson's brood, had been asked by Jackie O
to travel to Europe with her, and had taken care of
Amanda and Carter Burden's children before they split.
But I listened mindlessly, murmuring the appropriate
"Oh, reallys" and "How interestings," relieved to have
found her and happy with the affection she felt for our
daughter.

A few days after Helga came, we received a phone
call from one of Arnie's colleagues in Tennessee with
news of another baby available for adoption. We gave
him our regrets, but actually we weren't regretful at all,
about anything. We were extravagantly happy, puffed up
and proud as we paraded with Alison on Madison
Avenue, getting up together for each of her feedings. We
were learning to take care of our baby—reinventing the
wheel, spoke by spoke—and it was marvelous!

But as the date of my sonogram drew near, troubled
thoughts leaped unbidden to my mind. At first I didn't
analyze or answer them; they were oblique, uneasy
moments that passed. But as I waited for the newly
purchased machine to be free in Morgan's office, I
understood what I had been dreading.

I didn't want to see the fetus, didn't want to hear the
heartbeat. I wanted to keep those realities as an idea,
something distant. I didn't want to relate to the fetus as a
living, moving being, a potential baby, all soft and silken
like Alison.

"Barbara," the nurse called. I followed her all the
way down the hall and into a back room.

I won't look, I said to myself as I stretched out on

the table. I don't have to look. No one is forcing me to
look.

"Hey, take a look at that!" Morgan urged excitedly.

I looked. Pavlov, take a bow. I gazed at the tiny form
swimming across the screen.

"It's growing nicely," Morgan said, giving me a
beatific smile. "We'll try to get a suture in next week."

My surgery was scheduled for exactly one year to
the day after the stillbirth. I felt a little superstitious
about it, but decided I was being unduly influenced by
my resident pessimist, that constant forecaster of doom
and gloom that had come to inhabit my psyche in recent
times.

So there I was at Hillcrest refusing pre-op medication with a polite "no thank you" and instructing the
anesthesiologist about my allergies and my reaction to
morphine.

"She doesn't want to take morphine," he reported to
Morgan moments before the procedure was to begin.
One doctor complaining to another about a recalcitrant
patient. But Morgan would have none of that. "Then
give her something else," he said, sounding slightly
superior to his youthful, bearded colleague.

What I got was Demerol. It made me light-headed,
floaty, high. I stayed in that dreamy state for two days,
then left with Morgan's blessing.

"I got a good, tight suture in," he reported. "Take it
easy over the weekend and resume normal activities on
Monday. I'll see you in the office next Friday."

But Friday was a whole other story. Morgan's mood
changed as soon as he examined me. "We got that suture
in just in time. Your cervix is effacing already. I think you
should start complete bed rest. You can do it, can't you?"

I could do it. But why did I have to?

"I don't understand," I sputtered. "Last year the
suture held until my sixth month. I'm only in my third
now, and I have a newborn baby at home."

Morgan shook his head. "It's hard to know. Every
pregnancy is different."

Six and a half months in bed? I *could* do it. But I sure as hell didn't want to. I didn't feel the same way about staying in bed as I'd thought I would. I *had* a baby already, and I wanted to take care of her. If I hadn't been pregnant when we adopted Alison, I would have stopped trying to conceive for a few years, or maybe decided to adopt again.

But I *was* pregnant. I had to try to make it work. The sonogram screen. The picture on it. The large fetal head, the small body, swimming, waving at me. Damn it. I had to stay in bed. What else could I do?

Helga actually seemed a little pleased at the news. She immediately began rearranging my kitchen cabinets —glassware and canned goods. She was the mistress of the house now. I didn't really mind if she wanted to organize my kitchen, but that was where her take-over would end. With the exception of the times Helga took her out, I kept Alison on the bed next to me. My bench from the year before was now stocked with Pampers, stretchies, and bibs. I learned to put on her Pampers while lying down, feed her, and play with her. We even figured out a way for me to help bathe her from my bed.

During the day, she slept next to me or sometimes across my chest. When she was fussy, I sang the standard lullabies and she calmed down and breathed peacefully. Then one day, another song sprang suddenly to my lips.

> *Under my baby's cradle*
> *Sits a golden kid.*
> *The kid goes to Jerusalem*
> *To bring back raisins and almonds.*

I didn't sing this song in English, I sang it in Yiddish, a language I hadn't heard in twenty years. It was the lullaby my grandmother had sung to my mother, and my mother to me. I wept with the recollection of it, and with the sense of being part of that continuum.

While I cared for Alison, Helga found things to do around the house. She loved to cook and offered to make meals for us. The apartment continually smelled from the heavy greasy cooking oil of her own dinners, but the ones she prepared for us were superb.

She wanted to clean too. She was the kind of person who washed the floors once a day and her hair once a month. She looked pasty and a bit untidy, but she so clearly loved Alison, and was relieving Arnie of so much of the burden of caring for me, that we considered ourselves fortunate to have her.

For those first few weeks I was getting up for meals and showers and seeing the doctors every week. I had to go when someone in the family could drive me, so sometimes I saw Morgan and sometimes Davis. This was a Davis day.

"The baby's a good size," he said, pressing on the uterus.

"I've been feeling life now for a few weeks," I said proudly.

Then he moved to the end of the table, put on a rubber glove, and checked my cervix. Still in the same casual voice, he said: "The suture's in trouble."

Well, I knew that already so I wasn't too worried. But he meant real trouble.

"I don't think it's going to take you to term. We might have to resuture you."

"But Dr. Morgan never mentioned the possibility of resuturing me," I said, almost talking to myself.

"Well, it *is* risky." Davis was walking back and forth. He never stood still, not for a second. "Look," he said, drawing a picture on my chart. "Here is where your suture is, here is where we would try to put another one"—he drew a second thick line across the neck of the womb.

"Well, let's see what happens if you restrict your activities even more."

"I know," I said by rote. "No showering, no getting up for meals. . . ." I wouldn't use a bedpan, though; I was too concerned about the risk of infection.

Last year I'd had a good suture and a bad pregnancy. This year I had a bad suture and a good pregnancy. That was progress.

* * *

I was tense the whole week until my appointment with Morgan. I had what Arnie and I call FFAs, otherwise known as free-floating anxiety. I was worried about everything, especially about Alison. In some strange way I felt as though her fate and the baby's were intertwined. Hadn't they both become known to me on the same day, only hours apart? I felt their being was somehow dependent one on the other. Either my life was going to be happy, absolutely, with two children, or unhappy, absolutely, without any children.

So every time Helga said she would be out with Alison for only a half-hour and two hours passed with no key in the lock, I felt frantic: visions of cars jumping the curb, visions of child theft . . . oh, all kinds of crazy, scary thoughts as I lay there watching the clock.

But my nervousness didn't end when I saw Morgan. He thought the suture was all right. "Not enough room on the cervix for a second suture. Probably rupture the membranes trying."

Davis, however, the following week, urged again for resuturing. "I think we might have to take the chance. This isn't going to hold."

Morgan again: "I think it's going to be okay. Besides, resuturing might throw you into labor."

I felt like a yo-yo. Were they examining the same cervix? I knew my anatomy was slightly faulty, but I was pretty sure I only had one cervix.

What was going on? Should I meet them both together? Ask them to confront their differences. No, better yet, I'd go to someone entirely different, someone whose ego was not involved with the condition of my suture or my pregnancy.

I chose J. Wilson Curtis, chief of obstetrics at Northeast Medical Center. I debated whether to tell him I was switching doctors or tell him honestly that I just wanted a consultation. I was honest.

He was Norman Rockwell's image of a doctor. White-haired, tall and lanky, he was professional and pleasant and sympathetic to my predicament.

"I don't think the pregnancy is in imminent danger," he told us. "Strict bed rest might just take you to the point where delivery is possible."

"Could the problem with my cervix have come from the cervical biopsy?" I asked.

He didn't answer at first. The strong, silent type. A doctor playing Gary Cooper. "It's certainly a possibility," he finally said.

"Apparently there was no indication for Dr. Bentley to do it," Arnie said testily.

"Well, no one can say for sure what caused the problem." Curtis played with his letter opener, not looking directly at us.

"Damn that Bentley," Arnie said as soon as we got out to the car. "We should have sued that s.o.b. two years ago."

"But we would have been suing for the wrong thing. The real malpractice was for doing an unnecessary cervical biopsy and not checking me internally during my pregnancy."

"Well, the statute of limitations hasn't run out yet." Arnie was warming to the idea.

"But do you really think you're going to get another doctor to testify against him? Even Curtis started to get nervous when he realized what you were driving at. The old boy network is pretty tight, you know."

I got into bed as soon as I got home, my little pink and blond and blue-eyed baby beside me. She smiled at my presence with her shy, sideways grin. I pulled her to me and nuzzled her neck, breathing the sweet thick fragrance of baby lotion. I watched her curl her fingers around my thumb, feeling as I always felt when I was with her: I can do this. It's not so bad staying in bed.

But Arnie started traveling a lot, back and forth to California. When he wasn't traveling, he was busy at work, making up for the time away.

Helga was sometimes resentful of my insistence upon taking care of Alison; Laura often felt that way too. Her adjustment to her new sister faltered when I had to stay in bed. Before that, with the baby nurse around, Arnie and I could do things with her. But Helga, who had to be with us during the week, took off many weekends, so Arnie had double, or really triple, duty then—Laura, Alison, and me. And Laura, keenly feeling the restraints on his time, took it out by resenting Alison.

"Boy, she sure has a lot of beautiful dresses," she would say, watching Arnie button one of the lacy creations we had gotten as gifts.

"But you have beautiful clothes, too, honey. You *like* to wear jeans all the time."

Sulky silence.

Or she'd ask: "Why does everyone make such a big fuss about her? She doesn't *do* anything."

"Well, it's because she does so little that we get excited about her every accomplishment. You do so much—the flute, dancing, your drawing—we have so many things to be proud of you for."

Did any of this work? Not a bit. Part of the problem was that Alison did attract a lot of attention. The sight of Arnie with his dark, dark hair pushing this golden elf, with her head bobbing and her winsome smile, made people stop. They oohed and ahhed. And Laura resented it. Who says, "My, what an adorable ten-and-a-half-year-old"? But in this city, where babies are scarce, everyone commented on Alison.

Sometimes, though, when Alison was sleeping or my mother took her out for a while, Laura and I would have time that was ours alone, to play Monopoly, read, or draw. One evening late in June, after a long and sweet afternoon together, Laura plopped down beside me and picked up my copy of Dr. Spock. "Is this only about babies or does it have anything about puberty?"

I didn't know. We looked together. It had the standard stuff, but Laura devoured it. What did she want to know?

A few years before, when I was bathing her, she had asked me how babies were made. And I, remembering the golden rule of children's sex questions, had told her as little as would satisfy her.

"A man and a woman make a baby."

"How? With a needle and thread?"

"No, with their bodies."

"Their bodies? You mean with their arms and legs?"

"No, with—with—their . . ." Okay, Barbara, let's see how well you handle this one.

So I had taken her out of the tub, rubbed her dry, put her down on our bed, and sat down next to her. And I told her. I drew pictures, moderating some details, but I did tell her about the birds and bees, the facts of life, the whole lovely thing. And she'd been delighted with it. The next day she sat as close to me as possible, smiling at me knowingly, gratefully. I had told her something really marvelous and she knew it.

But now I sensed some anxiety.

"Do any of your friends get their periods yet?" I ventured.

Laura shook her head. "But I can't *wait* until I get mine. I won't feel like *a woman* until I do."

Ten and a half and she doesn't feel like a woman!

If only I'd get my period, if only I can have a baby, if only someone will like my work, if only someone will say that I'm pretty. If . . . if . . . if . . .

"Laura, honey, you're going to be a wonderful, sweet, delicious woman no matter when you get your period."

She didn't look convinced.

"But you know, sweetie, I worried about it, too, when I was your age."

"You did?" She broke into a huge grin.

So we talked: about what the women's movement was all about, what being a woman meant and didn't mean. A good, warm, open conversation until Arnie interrupted it by bursting into the bedroom.

"How would my girls like some ice cream?"

Laura and I laughed so hard, tears rolled down our cheeks. "Oh, daddy. You're such a male chauvinist!"

Later the three of us lay on the bed, me in the

middle, sandwiched between father and daughter, long lean bodies. "My two noodles," I called them when Laura was young, and maybe when she was a little too old. But not after tonight's conversation. We spooned heaps of ice cream into our mouths and talked and laughed. It was way past Laura's regular bedtime, but we didn't care. This was the last weekend we would see her before she left for camp, and we wanted it to be a good one.

I was flipping through *Vogue* or *Glamour*, one of those magazines, when I came across an article about how hypnosis had been used to increase breast size. Maybe I could hypnotize my cervix to stay closed.

I mentioned it to Dr. Davis sort of jokingly.

"Why not try it? It can't hurt," he said.

It was doubtful that he thought there was any value in it, other than the one that he had recognized early on, my need to feel like an active participant in my condition.

So I lay in bed day after day concentrating on my cervix, willing it to stay closed. And it did.

Then boom, out of nowhere, Arnie was served with papers. Charlotte was suing him for increased child support. We were paying enough, we thought. And with our enormous medical and nursing expenses, we couldn't afford to pay more. But a court battle meant getting lawyers, gathering information, marshaling arguments. We didn't have the time or the money or the interest in it.

It was a bad omen. The next week Morgan told me my cervix seemed a little shorter. Maybe the bad vibes I was sending Charlotte jammed my brain waves to it.

"There's nothing to worry about *yet*," Morgan had said. But that "yet" haunted me.

Then came a phone call from Elmira, New York. Another newborn available for adoption. And the "yet" haunted me even more. Arnie was considering it. "Suppose the pregnancy doesn't work? This way we'll have our two children."

But I couldn't bear to think about the pregnancy not working. I was now in my sixth month, swollen and in love with my unborn child. I felt as tied to its life as to Alison's. It was an active baby, kicking and pushing my belly out in tiny little bulges. We smiled to see my stomach seeming to move on its own, and marveled again and again that human life was so created.

With Helga's rich cooking, I was gaining weight faster this time and felt fleshy and thick with child. But Davis approved. "It's good for the baby," he said as I lay back on the sonogram table that brilliant morning in early August.

The picture flashed on the screen and there was the baby, *my baby*, sucking its thumb. I felt overcome by its vulnerability and by my longing for it. Then Davis examined me and said very calmly, "Your cervix is opening."

"What?" It was more a gasp than a word.

"You're two centimeters dilated and completely effaced."

"In just one week?" I struggled to sit up on the table.

Davis called Arnie back into the room. "We've got to try to get another suture in. I don't know how we'll do it, but we've got to try."

"But what about the risks? Morgan said there was no room—it would rupture her membranes. Do you know where he's vacationing? Maybe we should call him."

"There's no point in that. She's so dilated, I can bounce my finger off the baby. We have nothing to lose. She'll deliver within the week otherwise."

"But would—I mean, *could* the baby survive? I'm in my twenty-sixth week." My voice was trembling.

Davis shook his head and made a doubtful face. "The only hope is another suture. We've got to try even though the odds are stacked against us."

I felt numb. "Go right over to Hillcrest," a part of me heard him saying. "We'll call ahead and reserve a room. And don't let anyone examine you. No one, do you understand?"

I nodded obediently. "Okay. We'll drive home, get my things, and go."

He looked at me strangely, and said carefully, "Barbara, you could deliver this sixth-month, pound-and-a-half baby any minute. You can't go home. You can't do anything. Get right to the hospital, get into bed, and *don't move.*"

Chapter 12

So the whole hideous thing was starting again—the rushing to Hillcrest, the grim looks, the meaningful glances, the aide with the wheelchair. . . . How many times would I go through this? Clenched hands. Quivering lips. How many times would I go to Hillcrest pregnant and come out childless? *Abandon all hope, ye who enter here.*

Arnie stayed downstairs to fill out forms. A nurse helped me into a hospital gown and eased me onto the bed. "I'll be back," she said, resting her hand briefly on my arm. There was something so concerned in her look that I almost burst into tears.

I lay on the bed, my mind racing, trying to absorb what was happening. How could Davis be certain delivery was imminent? Maybe we ought to try waiting just a little longer before resuturing. One month was all we needed. Then the baby might have a chance. If only we could wait one month: one Con Ed bill, one telephone bill, two paychecks, four trips to the super-market. *Just one more month.*

From the hall came the sounds of carts rolling past, of nurses leaving for coffee breaks. Other sounds also came drifting up through the open window—children laughing in a playground, mothers chatting on benches. I heard the hospital sounds through my right ear, the city sounds through my left. And I was in between, feeling a part of neither, part of nothing but my body and the baby it carried.

Suddenly, guiltily, I thought of Alison and remembered I hadn't called home yet. My mother was baby-sitting, and we'd been gone for over two hours.

Her "hello" was quizzical, concerned. Hearing that voice, my mother's voice which had soothed years of scraped knees and hurts, opened the door to my grief. "I'm losing it, I'm losing the baby," I sobbed. For a minute the two of us cried over the phone, sharing a pain beyond words.

I reached for the tissues next to my bed and, as I did, saw a young woman walk in. She was dressed in a low-cut, cream-colored blouse, tan draw-string pants, and sandals, her long blonde hair bleached straw from the sun.

"Hi, Barbara." She pulled up a chair and sat next to the bed.

Still listening to my mother, I turned to look at this newcomer, trying to figure out whether I knew her. A childhood friend? A former student? "I'm Dr. Brody," she explained. And then, ignoring my phone call and my tears: "I'm going to ask you a few questions."

The hell you are, I felt like saying. But restrained myself. Why? Maybe because she was young and inexperienced, or because, in spite of my convictions about patients' rights, I knew the score—knew that I was absolutely confined to my bed and that spelled dependent with a capital *D:* dependent for bedpans, for food and medicine and every kind of monitoring, routine and emergency. And I knew that patients who got "bad reps" for being too outspoken or too demanding also got lousy treatment. *Blessed are the meek, for they shall inherit the sponge bath.*

So I said goodbye to my mother and watched with fascination as Dr. Brody took my medical history. Not that the questions were interesting or new. I'd given my history so many times to so many different residents that I didn't know why they bothered to do it all; surely an asterisk referring the reader to *Berg, May 19, 1978, p. 8* would have been much more efficient. What fascinated me were Brody's nails. Some were bright red, others stripped to white. She continued to peel systematically between writing her notes. Bits of falling polish formed tiny rose petals on the linoleum.

She listened to my heart and lungs; then, taking a needle and syringe from her pocket, she drew blood with such force that an inky blue mark immediately appeared on my arm.

All this she did in a bored, matter-of-fact way, hardly looking at me. But as she put on a surgical glove to do the examination, she became animated. This was her stuff, her specialty. Here she could show me how much she knew. But I wasn't about to let her.

"Excuse me, but I'm not supposed to be examined internally."

"Who said so?"

"Dr. Davis."

She muttered something and left.

I drew my legs tight together. No one, but no one, was going to touch me, even if I had to slither out of Hillcrest on my back.

Moments later Dr. Brody returned with the chief resident, Dr. James Donaldson. He strode into the room with an air of confidence that I would later learn was arrogance.

"So you're the one giving Dr. Brody such a hard time." He made a halfhearted attempt to shake his finger at me, but it came out as a wiggle.

And what did I do—the fiery feminist, the patient advocate, the taker up of all causes except my own? I looked as contrite as possible, apologized for causing so much trouble, and suggested that they speak to Dr. Davis themselves.

But just then Arnie walked in and the opposition melted. Who argues with the husband, the payer of bills, and a lawyer to boot?

Arnie sat next to me on the bed, taking my hands in his. One look at his face told me how much he was hiding, his eyes rimmed with red, his worry lines deep.

Oh, Arnie, what's the use of this? It's over. You know it's over. I know it's over. And Davis knows, too. Then why this extravagant charade? Fetus saved in last-minute attempt. Doctor performs miracle technique. Cover story for *Look* magazine or some obscure medical journal. Why lie to each other? Our marriage is based on truth. All the silly truths, the angry truths, the ugly truths, the wonderful truths that hold us together. Why do we need lies now?

"It's all right, darling," he said. "Whatever happens, it will be all right."

But it can't be all right, Arnie. Not if the baby dies. I can't go through it again. In one deep part of me, it will never be all right.

"I want to see it."

"What?"

"The baby."

"What are you talking about?"

"If it dies, I want to see it. I want to have a funeral."

"Don't be so morbid. Davis said there was a chance."

"A slim chance. I wish Morgan were here, too."

"What could he do?"

"Give us another opinion."

"I'm calling Dr. Curtis."

"You're crazy. We were there three months ago, just for a consultation. He won't talk to you."

But he did talk to Arnie, for forty-five minutes, refusing to send us a bill. He thought there was a clear indication for resuturing. He knew Davis and thought him a fine surgeon, but, of course, if I wanted to switch to the Northeast Medical Center, he'd be glad to take me as his patient.

"What about getting the baby moved?" I whispered. "Northeast has the best neonatal-care unit in the city."

Curtis gave us the name of a neonatologist on the staff of Northeast. He took the call immediately. Twenty-six weeks? He felt our baby would be marginal at best. The biggest risk in premies was respiratory distress.

We'd have to weigh the benefits of having the baby at Northeast against the time it would take to get it there. Of course the ambulances had complete emergency equipment, but an unforeseen traffic jam might mean death. He suggested we talk to the neonatologist at Hillcrest.

And to the police department? And traffic control? What about a helicopter? There we were with lists and phone numbers, trying, trying pathetically, to exert some control, to organize the unorganizable.

By six that evening we had decided that if the baby was born alive we'd keep it at Hillcrest. "I've pulled some through weighing less than two pounds," Dr. Christopher McCarthy told us. Ruddy and red-haired, with a football player's build, he hardly looked like a neonatologist. But he was soft-spoken and reassuring and I trusted him at once. I didn't ask him about birth defects, or abnormalities, so common in premies. I didn't care. I wanted to give birth to a *live baby*. That was all I would ask God for. Later I would bargain for the rest.

Streaks of lightning flashed across the sky. I urged Arnie to go home. He hadn't seen Alison all day, and there was no point in his sleeping at the hospital. Tomorrow would be long enough without our both being exhausted, I argued.

The strange thing was that no one seemed to know exactly what was happening tomorrow. I hadn't seen or heard from Davis since I'd left the office, none of the nurses knew if I was scheduled for surgery, and even the doctor with the wiggling finger was unable to find out.

After Arnie left, I faded into a tense and troubled sleep, and awoke to the glare of light filling my room. My lamp was on, and next to me was a pregnant nurse. How could she be pregnant and work in a hospital? All the germs, all the standing on her feet. And the night shift, no less. Was I crazy for thinking these things, or was she crazy that she hadn't?

"Your 'lytes are low."

"What do you mean? My lights were off until you turned them on."

"No. I mean your electrolytes. Your potassium is way down. You have to drink this." She handed me a cup with thin yellowish liquid and some orange juice.

"But I'm being operated on tomorrow. I'm not supposed to eat or drink *anything*."

"You're not on the OR schedule and it's more important that we get your potassium level up to normal."

Low potassium. Now I was really in style. Potassium was the mineral missing from those zany liquid diets that had caused the death of several women recently.

I drank the bilious brew and worried the rest of the night.

As soon as the day shift came on, I started asking about the OR schedule. No one seemed to know for sure, but, if I was going to be operated on, I wanted to speak to the anesthesiologist while I was still in my room.

I called Arnie at seven, but he was already on his way to Hillcrest. I asked Helga about Alison: What had she eaten? How much? How often had she cried? I really *was* getting crazy.

Arnie arrived about five minutes later. He seemed a little brighter than yesterday. In some strange way, we both were. After three months of different opinions—three months of should we resuture or shouldn't we—we now knew we *had* to, and that was calming.

But as time passed with no word, we became increasingly edgy. Arnie started pacing. Why were they waiting? Every hour was important. My membranes were bulging—a strong sneeze and they could rupture. Maybe Davis had backed down. Too much risk. Too much chance for blame. Those malpractice premiums aren't getting any lower, you know.

Finally Dr. Davis burst into the room. "Where've you been? We've been waiting for you in the operating room for the last forty-five minutes. Why didn't they bring you down?"

I raised my hands in the air. "No one seems to know what's going on here."

"They sure as hell don't. It's so late I don't think I'll have time to do you before my office hours start." He strode from the room.

I reached for my Styrofoam pitcher of ice water and hurled it against the wall.

But ten minutes later, Davis was back with a stretcher cot. "I swiped this from another floor," he told us with a grin. "Help me move her onto this," he said to Arnie. "We'll take her to the OR ourselves."

And so Davis and Arnie pushed me down the corridor and into the elevator with the head nurse running after us yelling, "Hey, you can't take her! The aide's supposed to do that!"

When we got there, I had lost my "spot" in the OR, so they moved me into a labor room to wait. Arnie could stay, but only for a few minutes. He tried desperately to reassure me, while feeling so frightened himself.

I told Davis about the potassium. He grimaced slightly. "The machine's broken. All the electrolytes are coming out too low. But we'll check it again just to be on the safe side." And then expertly, painlessly, he drew another blood sample.

It fascinated me to watch him work—the precision of his directions, his attention to detail. He stopped the nurse, actually taking the needle out of her hand before she could start an intravenous drip. "Look how small her veins are. Why are you using such a large needle?"

So the tone could have been less authoritarian, less chauvinistic. But a doctor who cares if the IV hurts was a rare treat.

"I can put up with a painful IV," I told him.

"Sure, but why do it if you don't have to? I'm really nervous about this," he said, forming a most perfect non sequitur.

"You're nervous? What about me? *Everything* depends on it."

"I know," he replied and walked away.

The anesthesiologist sat and talked to me until the room was ready. Then Davis returned and took my hand. "We'll do our best," he promised.

"What's that?" I asked, pointing to a surrealistic fish tank connected to plastic tubes and monitors.

"Emergency equipment—for the baby, in case you deliver."

"Oh, no," I moaned.

I lay there not knowing. For one unbearably elongated moment, I didn't know.

"Barbara?"

I opened my eyes. Arnie's face close to mine was strained. My heart pounded. It's over. Oh, God, I've lost it.

Then Arnie's voice quietly saying, "He did it. Davis did it."

"What?" I whispered in a choking voice.

"He resutured you. You're still pregnant."

I felt reborn. I reached my free arm toward Arnie and he came to me amid a tangle of tubes and wires. Our faces melted together, wet with kisses and tears.

"Is Davis still here?"

"I'll go find out."

My mind was drifting from the anesthesia. I struggled to stay awake. I had to thank Davis for taking the risk, for being the hero.

"Barb . . . Dr. Davis is here."

I opened my eyes again to a blur of Davis standing by the bed. I touched his arm lightly and fell back to sleep.

Then it started: the dry heaves, the nausea, the sweat, the chills. The potassium was burning its way up my esophagus, bitter in my mouth. I was retching, vomiting. There was no end to it.

Oh, Arnie, I wish you could hold my head the way you do at home. I remember the first time you did it, at that party at Jane's after the Peace March. All of us middle-class kids drinking cheap bourbon, trying to talk like Dylan and act working-class. And I feigned the veteran drinker—me, whose taste in booze was Manischewitz kosher. I remember how sick I got and how you took me back to your apartment and held my head and washed out my blouse and loved me dirty and rancid. And I remember lying shivering under your scratchy old blanket and saying to myself, *Hold on to him, kiddo, this is a man you can trust*.

"Nurse, can I lie on my back? I think it might help."

"No, you have to be on your side. We're giving you heavy doses of Hyperstat to prevent labor. It causes rapid drops in blood pressure."

"Mine's low to start with."

"I know. That's why you have to stay on your side. We don't want to save the baby and lose the mother."

Later, back in my room, Arnie told me how close it had been. That the old suture had opened and was completely nonfunctioning, and that if Davis hadn't acted I would have gone into labor within hours.

"All the nurses are talking about it. They never saw anything like it. He actually reconstructed your cervix on the operating table. If this baby makes it, it'll be a miracle."

"Did he give you any idea what the chances are?"

"I started to ask him, but he had to rush back to finish up office hours. I hope he'll stop by later."

For the remainder of the day we talked about Davis in tones of hushed reverence, as did all the staff members who came into our room. Except for Wiggle Finger. He sauntered in once to check my IV drip and left without so much as a word. But we didn't care. Arnie and I were elated; we broke all our rules of patient/doctor relations: Davis was a god, a super-hero.

Did he believe it of himself? Maybe. Still, he accepted our praise with a fair amount of humility and a greater amount of caution.

"We're not out of the woods yet. You could still go into premature labor. But I think the sutures will give us the time we need."

All the while he was telling us this, he was walking back and forth: frenetic energy, a marathoner who probably did the whole 26 miles, 385 yards on a single morning's rounds.

"Did you pee yet?" he asked suddenly.

I felt the blood rush to my face in what could only be called a blush. I could put up with hearing every part of my anatomy discussed in clinical, medical terms—and God knows it had been—but "Did you pee yet?" still sounded like an indignity to me.

I shook my head. "Why?"

"We have to watch for blood in your urine. I put two sutures in. One to create a posterior lip, the other high up under your bladder. That one could give us some trouble. You have to remember that you have *two* sutures in. One is mersilene, the other is silk. I'll show you." He flipped open my chart. "See, I've attached a piece of each kind of suturing material to this. I want everyone who reads your chart to know that you have *two* sutures in. It's *crucial* that if you go into labor and I'm not around, the doctor on duty remove both immediately. Otherwise we risk hemorrhaging and cervical detachment. Do you understand?"

"Yes."

"Boy, am I tired," he said, at last sinking into a chair. He took a package of Hostess cupcakes from his pocket and offered one to Arnie. "You were so dilated on the table, I could see the baby kicking through the sac."

"Who did it look like?" Arnie asked.

"I only saw the feet."

"If it had calluses, it looked like Barbara."

Night was a snarling beast. The darkened hollow halls, the emptiness, the utter aloneness. My muscles were stretched and torn, everywhere was pain. And even with all the Hyperstat, I was having contractions. Time passed torturously.

Arnie insisted on getting me a private nurse for the next day. She arrived crisp and taut, a tiny cream puff of a hat perched on gray curls so tightly furled that they would have withstood a fifty-mile-per-hour wind. She was schooled in the old way and proud of it. She adjusted my pillows, powdered my back, and made sure no one disturbed my three-hour sleep. When the time came to wake me, she did it quietly and respectfully. "Mrs. Berg . . . I'm sorry to bother you. We have to start your medications now." It embarrassed me that I had called her Elizabeth instead of Miss Everts.

The intravenous drip had been running for about twenty minutes when it seemed to clog. Actually, I had two IVs, the Hyperstat and an antibiotic, both feeding through the same needle. Since the antibiotic was flowing freely, it seemed clear that the needle was all right. The problem was with the Hyperstat tube or bottle.

But it was not clear to Dr. Joanne Brody, who happened to be making her morning rounds just then. Discounting what Everts and I were saying, she pulled the needle from my arm and tried to restart the drip. After six attempts I suggested she ask someone else to give it a try. "I know how to start an IV," she snapped.

What a relief! I'd sure hate to be worked on by someone who didn't know how to start one.

The strange thing was, the more she failed, the more determined she was to get that needle into my vein. I didn't realize then how much ego is tied to every medical decision. How each direction, each order, each prescription, is an extension of the doctor, a symbol of his or her authority, omnipotence. So if Brody said it was the needle, then, goddammit, the needle it was.

But of course, it wasn't the needle. That became apparent when she finally got it into my arm.

"There," she said with obvious satisfaction. And there it was, the antibiotic flowing freely and the Hyperstat clogged in the tube.

"Maybe you could try changing the tube," I suggested deferentially.

"That's what you have a nurse for!" she huffed, and left.

* * *

Two nights later Dr. Morgan came into my room, sun-tanned and hearty from his vacation.

"Boy, some people will do anything to get a change of scene," he teased.

I answered cheerily: "I bet you're glad you were out of town."

"Listen, I may have been away from the office, but I wasn't away from *you*. My wife insisted on reading your book during our vacation. She wants to know why a feminist like you goes to male chauvinists like us."

"She has a good point. And speaking of male chauvinists, don't you think it's time the medical profession changed the name 'incompetent cervix' to something else?"

"What's wrong with 'incompetent cervix'?"

Help!

Finally the contractions stopped, and with that the Hyperstat. I was off all medications now and was starting to feel stronger. I could sleep for more than four hours at a stretch and could eat solid foods.

Days were manageable with their routines of blood pressures, temperatures, changes in shifts. Friends visited, and Arnie, too. He always came in cheerful, brimming with news of Alison and the rest of the world, in that order. I was ravenous for it all, especially since the workers for the *New York Times* had chosen the day I entered Hillcrest to begin their strike.

Arnie and I would share my dinner, which was always cold and congealed on the plate, and sometimes a little extra snack if he'd had time to buy it on the way. For dessert we'd have orange creamsicles, bought by Arnie from the machines in the basement. I don't remember how it started, but it became our ritual.

"I think I'll get going as soon as we finish these."

And automatically, instinctively, my tongue would make slower circles around the pop. How long could I make it last? Ten minutes? Fifteen? I didn't want Arnie to know, didn't want anyone to know, how I dreaded the night.

The aides were obviously indifferent to my calls. They took so long to come into my room that it seemed a contest of endurance. At first I thought I was imagining it, but the pattern was clear, and always the same gruff, put-upon "Yeah, what is it?"

I hated to ask for anything—more water, the air conditioner turned lower. I reduced my requests to the one essential—the bedpan. I rang for it at midnight— nothing—and again at 12:30. Forty-five minutes later an aide appeared at my door. "Yeah, what is it?"

"Nothing. Never mind." I was too humiliated to tell her I had wet my bed.

I lay on the soaked sheets until 6:00 A.M. when Alice, the night nurse, came in to check the fetal heartbeat before going off duty. She was a tiny woman with huge brown eyes, a gleaming chocolate skin, and a husky pack-and-a-half-a-day voice. We had become great friends from my first day there.

"You're gonna make it," she told me, confiding that her doctors had been certain she'd never conceive and that she'd been afraid to tell her boy friend, sure he'd never marry her if he knew. Even now, with her two sons in school, she could still remember how she had felt. How alike were our anxieties and fears and self-doubts!

But now she looked at me incredulously. "You mean you really don't know why they resent you? Honey, to them you're just another white lady asking to be waited on."

"But I'm not like that. You know I'm not like that. I *have* to do this," I protested.

"Sure, but it's a luxury to be able to lie in bed for six months, not to have to work. They'd love to switch places with you. Stick around. You'll learn a lot."

But I didn't want to stick around. I didn't want to hear what Alice was saying. I believed so strongly in a sisterhood of all women, regardless of race or class, it was devastating to be viewed as the oppressor.

"When am I leaving?" I finally asked Dr. Davis.
"Tuesday. I won't be here, though—I'm taking my

kids on a two-week bicycle trip to Vermont. Ronald will discharge you. I want another sonogram done before you leave. I'll order it for Tuesday morning." He started to get up.

I reached for the white paper beside my bed and waved it in the air. "Just a few questions."

He sat down smiling. "Good idea to write them down. Makes our job easier."

"What about checking the baby's development?"

"Well, the sonogram will give us one dimension of growth. Do you mean estriols? Placental function?"

"Yes."

"Too soon. The readings are not meaningful until the eighth or ninth month."

"How restricted should I be at home?"

"Very."

"What about the office visits?"

"Every week."

"No, I mean, won't it be dangerous to be out of bed for so long?"

This caught him off guard. He walked back and forth a few times. "We'll come to your house. Where do you live again? . . . Okay. No problem. We'll take turns every week. If you get a fourth, we can play some bridge."

"Are you going to examine me before you leave?"

"No. I—uh—I have poison ivy."

"Did you have it when you sutured me?"

"I don't know."

Terrific!

I looked forward to Tuesday like a child to a birthday party. In a way I was glad Dr. Morgan was discharging me instead of Dr. Davis. Morgan was always on time or early, while Davis made a point of being late. And now that I knew I was leaving, every extra minute at Hillcrest was unbearable. I kept calling home. "Does Alison know I'm coming? Tell her mommy's coming home."

By the time Morgan came in, I was spruced up and made up and feeling up. Only an hour, maybe less, to go.

But as soon as the examination was over, I knew something was wrong. I'd been through this too many times to miss those body signs: the taut mouth, the avoidance of eye contact, the pale behind the tan.

"The bottom suture's slipping. I don't think the top one will hold either. I don't think you should leave."

I started trembling—visibly, I guess. "But—but how long—how long should I stay?" My voice was shaking so badly I could hardly get the words out.

He sat down looking almost as miserable as I. "It's too tenuous, it's hanging on by a thread. I'm canceling the discharge. Even getting dressed to get into the car could put you in labor. I don't even want you going for the sonogram."

"But *how long* will I have to stay?"

"What?"

He looked straight at me but didn't speak at first. Finally, he said: "I think you should stay for the rest of your pregnancy. I hope it'll be for three months, but let's keep our fingers crossed that we get even three more weeks."

Chapter 13

Furious. I am furious at everyone and everything at Hillcrest: at Davis for promising me the suture would hold and then leaving me here to go on his vacation; at Morgan for giving me the bad news; at the nurses who wake me up at 4:00 A.M. to take my temperature; at Wiggle Finger who enters without knocking; at Dr. Brody who looks through my things and smells my talcum powder while talking to me; at the colorless, tasteless lumps they call food; at the plasticized mattress that makes me drip with perspiration; at the boredom and loneliness and restlessness and muscle aches and sweat and smells; at my helplessness, my dependence, my cervix, my body.

I'll never make it *one* month, forget about three. What's next, God? Boils? Plagues?

Okay. So it's not the worst thing, lying in a hospital bed to have a baby. It's not advanced cancer, after all, or spinal meningitis, not even a broken hip. Guilt. Gratitude. Thank you, God, for making it only this. Only this? *This* is intolerable.

It was my tenth, maybe eleventh, day at Hillcrest, and Alice was doing the morning routine. As usual, she was cursing the fetone machine, which drowned out my baby's heartbeat with its own screeching and screaming sounds.

"Hey, I have the perfect pickup for you," she said as she touched two fingers to my pulse. "There's a woman who's been in and out over the past few weeks with premature contractions. They finally got her stabilized, but she's probably going to have to stay until she delivers."

"When is that?"

"I'm not sure. I think the beginning of November."

"Do you think I should call her?"

"Sure. Her name's Maria Radulovic, spelled just like it sounds."

"How does it sound?"

I kept the slip of paper next to my phone all morning, wondering if I should call. Maybe she would regard it as an intrusion. There was little enough privacy around here anyway without another patient prying into your problems.

I stuck the scrap of paper into one of the nameless, authorless mysteries I was reading.

But then in that deadly, endless, stagnant time between lunch and dinner, I picked up the book and dialed her number.

"Mrs. Radulovic?"

"Yes."

"I hope I'm not disturbing you, but Alice, the night nurse, gave me your number. My name is Barbara Berg."

"Oh, Barbara, hi. Alice told me about you. How in the world are you managing to survive here?"

And so we talked, openly, intimately, like long-lost friends recently united who had to catch up on every detail of each other's life.

She and her husband, Evo, were Argentine citizens, relocated in New York because of his job as an electrical engineer. They'd been here four years and were having a love affair with the city. She was exactly my age, had been married exactly as long, and had been very close to adopting a baby when severe phlebitis threatened to make a pregnancy impossible. We were alike in every way except, perhaps, politically, but bedfellows make for strange politics.

She, like me, was lonely and frightened and venting the rage of her dependency on a hospital that we both knew was no better or worse than most.

We talked for over an hour that afternoon, and she called me back later that day, just as the food trays were being brought in.

"What did you order?"

"Veal. How about you?"

"Beef."

"What does yours look like?"

"Gray and stringy. What about yours?"

"Gray and stringy."

We broke into gales of laughter. Someone had told her she could order "off the menu." Someone had told me I could have a refrigerator in my room. Together we could be quite a team!

The next morning at nine she called again. "Watch out. Old Wiggle Finger is making rounds."

I hung up and quickly slid off the bedpan. I had told her how no one ever knocked and how awful it made me feel to think of being caught on the pot by surprise.

Arnie couldn't understand. "They're doctors, for God's sake. They're accustomed to these things."

"They may be, but *I'm* not."

Minutes later Wiggle Finger came into my room, in starched white and immaculately groomed, as always. He stood a few feet from the bed, his usual spot; he never sat in a chair, never leaned against the wall, but stood there looking down at me, reinforcing the space between us—the doctor and the patient, the woman and the man—rattling off his questions.

"Any contractions?"

"No."

"Any pain?"

"No."

"Any discharge?"

"No."

"Any bleeding?"

"No. There *is* one thing, though. I'm very short of breath. It feels as though there's a lot of pressure on my diaphragm. Do you think it could be from eating practically lying down?"

"No. It's anxiety."

"Mmm . . . I don't think so."

"C'mon, you *have* to be anxious. Aren't you?"

"Well, yes, a little, but—"

"See? I told you." And he turned and left triumphantly.

So I resolved—swore on my charter of NOW—that as long as I remained at Hillcrest, I would never give one of the doctors reason to think of me as anxious. It didn't matter that I cried every morning at four o'clock, or that I panicked, became absoltely terrified, when a few hours passed and I did not feel the baby moving. *They* were never going to know about it. *They* were going to think I was strong and brave and tough. I was going to be a rock about this, a tearless, bloodless rock.

Later that day, when Dr. Roth told me the shortness of breath was caused by the baby pressing on the diaphragm, I felt better. But still later, when a young woman stood at my door introducing herself as Judy Goodman, a staff social worker, my spirits dipped.

A social worker now? Why not after the miscarriage? The stillbirth? Why now?

Ooh, yes, of course. Dr. Donaldson. I could just hear him: "That patient, the one in six-thirty-seven, is a bit anxious. See what you can do to calm her down. It's bad for the baby, you know." Oh, yes, dear old Wiggle Finger.

"Dr. Donaldson, right?"

"Right," she answered, giving me a tentative smile.

I didn't know what to do. I thought it was an intrusion of the worst kind, but she looked so young and earnest that I invited her in.

As soon as Judy left, I called Laura for our afternoon chat, and then Maria. She and I had become an item. Like teenagers, we would whisper and gossip over the phone, exchanging tales and using the nicknames we'd invented for the staff. The assistant supervisor of nursing, with her long tapered nails and cold gray eyes, was the Dragon Lady; Mrs. Watersworth, the buxom, cheerful morning nurse who threw open the blinds and sang as she worked, was the Marching Band; the chief dietician became Miss Piggy.

Were we aware that we were regressing, acting childishly? I'm not sure. But we both knew, *felt* instinctively, that this was the key to our survival: to laugh at the absurd, the outrageous. At least some of the time.

It was strange that we had formed such a bond, that two women who had never even *seen* each other, who could pass in the hall without the slightest recognition, could become so close, could talk for hours each day telling each other their most private thoughts and feelings. But in another way it was not strange at all—for more than Arnie, more than my mother, more than my friends or my doctors, she understood: understood the difference it made if you were given your washbasin at 2:00 P.M. instead of at 9:00 A.M.; understood what it meant if your food tray was plopped down four feet from your bed; understood about back pains and indigestion and heat rash. Who else could you tell these things and have it register in the same way?

I tried to tell Arnie what it was like being confined to bed day after day, confined to my fears, and missing Alison so much that I felt I'd go crazy if I thought about it. But Arnie only heard me with half an ear. With the other half, he was hearing Alison crying and Helga complaining and the phone in his office ringing. His part of the pregnancy!

Was it worse for him? Was it worse for me? Who knows? But we each nurtured secret feelings of being unappreciated and misunderstood.

On Laura's first weekend at the house since summer camp, Helga was off and Alison chose that particular day to scream for five hours straight. Arnie kep phoning me. "Do you hear her? I can't calm her down."

"Did you try holding her?"

"I've tried *everything*."

"Try taking her out for a walk."

"Laura doesn't want to go out now. Oh, never mind—you can't understand how awful this is!"

"What's awful? You don't know the first thing about awful," I retorted.

Why was I even bothering with this whole thing? We'd probably get divorced before I delivered.

"Honey?"

"Arn?"

"Why are we doing this to each other? It's ridiculous."

"And what's more, it's getting boring. It's getting *goddamn boring.*"

This had always been a thing with me—not being bored. I can forgive a person anything except being boring. I almost had written into our marriage vows: "Do you promise to love and to honor and *to interest?*" We weren't going to become one of those couples who sit wordlessly in a restaurant staring straight ahead, one of those couples always escaping to movies, cocktail parties, other people. I didn't ask that it be smooth or perfect or peaceful, I only asked that it not be *boring*.

So it became a buzz word for us. When Arnie took the wrong road going up to visit his parents and we drove for miles in a snowstorm before we could turn around and Laura was crying in the back seat and we were all hungry and tired, he gave me a jaunty smile and said, "At least it's not boring." And when I left my pocketbook in a cab the day before we moved into our new apartment and all the locks that we had just put in had to be changed and all the checks I had written had to be stopped, I turned to Arnie and said, "Well, I may be trouble, but I'm not—"

"I know. You're not boring. Listen, Barbara, when we're sixty-five and living in a retirement community in Florida, do you think by *then* we will have earned the right to have a little boredom?"

"Never, Arnie-dwarmie," I said throwing my arms around his neck and lifting my feet off the ground. "Never."

From then on, whenever one of us started the competitive complaining, started the "It's harder for me . . ." or the "You can't imagine how bad it is . . ." routine, the other put up a hand and said, "Boring. Boring." And we would both begin to laugh. Usually.

It was the week of Labor Day when Maria called me with some wonderful news: Her doctor had given her permission to visit in my room that Sunday. Because her condition was less precarious than mine, she could come in a wheelchair and stay for about a half-hour if we could find a cot for her to lie on.

Arnie would have gone out and bought one if necessary, but it wasn't. The nurses, knowing about our friendship, were so happy and excited that we were at last going to meet that they scanned the floors until they found a chaise longue kind of thing, and kept it hidden for us until Sunday.

I looked forward to Maria's visit the whole week, and Arnie and I spent most of the day preparing. Of course, everything took us a long time: shaving my legs, cutting my toenails, washing my hair—things that are normally routine and easy were for us lengthy projects.

Washing my hair, for example, was a real production. All the furniture had to be pushed away so that Arnie could move the cranked-up bed next to the sink. I was covered with a plastic sheet, and there was so much soap and suds and water around that it was impossible to tell who was doing what to whom. In the midst of all this, Dragon Lady came in. "What in the *world* is going on here?"

"A water orgy," Arnie said. "It's the latest thing."

"Humph." She stormed out the door.

"Oh, Arnie, you shouldn't have. What will she think?" I laughed and got a mouthful of water.

Earlier that week Arnie had stocked the refrigerator with soft drinks and cheese and brought fresh flowers into the room. As eight o'clock approached, I got into a clean nightgown and, for the first time since learning I had to stay at Hillcrest, put on makeup, but I felt somehow apprehensive. Would seeing each other in person somehow change our friendship? After such intimacy, would we be embarrassed on meeting?

There was a knock on the door. "Good evening." In came Evo, tall and broad with a wonderful smile, and Maria in a wheelchair, dark and diminutive, a box of candy in her hands. When she spoke, her eyes flashed, her hands gestured. Each smile broke her face into a million pieces. She was animated, serious and witty, profound and light. I loved her immediately.

"You were the first patient I asked about when I got back." Dr. Davis was sitting in my room, emptying my refrigerator of milk. I'd never seen anyone eat like that. Four containers of milk in a row, cookies by the score. Morgan was the same way, and Maria's doctor also. Arnie swears, absolutely swears, that he came down the hall behind Morgan and Roth and heard one say to the other, "You take the candy rounds, I'll do the cookies."

"So Ronald said you had to stay? What does your insurance company say about it?"

"They'll pay."

"Are you positive?"

"Almost."

He took half a banana off my lunch tray and asked, "Is *that* all you're eating? Cottage cheese and yogurt? I don't want you dieting. How much weight did you gain last year?"

"Eighteen pounds."

"Eighteen pounds to the eighth month!" He was practically screaming. "That's too little, much too little. Low maternal weight gain has been linked to stillbirths. I want you to gain thirty pounds."

I puffed out my cheeks like a balloon. "But I'll be so fat!"

"Thirty pounds, even a little more would be okay. Gain it on complex sugars, grains, fruit, not on ice cream and stuff like that." He started to leave.

"Wait!" I waved my paper in the air like a flag.

He smiled. "I know, your questions." He took the rest of my banana in his hand. "Okay, shoot."

"When can they start checking the estriols?"

"What week are you? Thirty-one? Still too soon. It wouldn't tell us anything until the thirty-fourth at the earliest."

"What else are you going to check?"

"Estriols are really most important. Why?"

"Dr. Morgan thought the stillbirth was caused by an infection. Would doing a white blood count have any value?"

"I still think it was placental malfunction."

"But no one knows for sure."

He thought for a moment. "Okay, we'll do a white blood count, too. Why not? It can't hurt. Next?"

"Should I be lying on my side? I read someplace that lying on your back can put too much pressure on the vena cava."

"I don't think it matters. Jesus! Barbara, what are you doing? Spending all your time here reading about pregnancy?"

"No. Just some of it. Is there anything we can do about the fetone machine? It has so much static, it's impossible to hear the baby's heartbeat."

He nodded. "Try calling the administrative assistant of Ob/Gyn. If you can get a new one, it'll be more than any of us have been able to accomplish."

"And one more thing—what about a sonogram? They never did do it."

"I think you ought to have one." He got up, walked to the door, and then turned back with a grin. "By the way, I hope you're saving these questions."

"No. Why?"

"I think you ought to write a book: *The 100 Most Unusual Questions Asked During Any Pregnancy.*"

The sonogram was scheduled for the next day. I could hardly wait. It would be the first time in over three weeks that I had ventured outside of my room. As the aide pushed my stretcher down the corridor, I felt like a visitor to a foreign land, straining to see the sights—the newborn nursery, the linen closet, the nurses' station, the elevator bank.

Actually we had plenty of time for these last two, as the elevator took fifteen minutes to come. One of the problems was that visitors, staff, and patients all used the same elevators. So in the morning, or during visiting hours, it was like trying to get into the Lexington Avenue subway.

Thirty minutes later I was back in my room. I flipped on the television, caught the end of the "Donahue Show," and then called Helga. This was something I did three or four times a day in order to know everything about Alison. I wanted to know what she ate, what she was wearing, wanted to hear her coos and goos into the phone, but I wanted . . . I wanted more than that. I wanted to hold her and feel her flesh against mine; I wanted to feed her, change her, see her.

I was seized with a new idea. I pressed my button and asked if Miss Wesley, the head nurse, could come in.

"Would it be possible for my daughter to visit?"

"Absolutely not. No children under twelve are allowed in the hospital."

I was glad that Laura looked older than she was and visited regularly. But how could I get Alison in? I called Judy Goodman and left a message for her to call me.

The phone rang. "Barbara?"

"Yes?"

"Matt Davis."

"Oh, hi, Matt."

"I spoke to Karen and the sonogram looks good, baby measures thirty-two weeks. That's great, means so far we're doing fine."

Silence.

"Hey, are you okay?"

"Yes."

"Sure?"

"Well, I'm trying to find a way to get my daughter up here and I'm hitting the wall."

"That's a tough one—hospital rules are pretty strict about it."

That night after dinner, Arnie and I conspired while we watched the city fade into dark.

"What about sneaking her in? I could bring her up through Atlee [the adjoining building] and walk her through to G-Six. We don't have to pass the nurses' station, and if we did it on a Saturday, Wesley wouldn't be here."

"I don't know. . . ." I was hesitant. "If I hadn't asked, it would be one thing, but now that I've gotten a definitive no . . ."

"Well, maybe we can figure out a way to do it within the system. What are they afraid of? Her germs?"

"Yes. They're afraid of bringing her past the new-born nursery."

"That's the stupidest thing I ever heard. She's only five months old. It's not as though she goes to school or is in contact with other children."

"I know," I sighed. I told all that to Wesley, but she wouldn't budge.

"Maybe if we get Dr. Schaffer to write a note saying that he's just examined Alison and she's in excellent health . . ."

"Okay, let's do that and see what happens."

But even the note didn't convince Wesley. "I can't do it. I just can't do it," she said.

"We'll think of something," Arnie promised. But all I could think of was going home. It became . . . how can I describe it? Like a physical craving. I *had* to see Alison.

But it was dangerous, thinking about going home. For the whole month that I'd been here, I never allowed myself to imagine it, to contemplate it. I knew if I did, if I dared to think about it, the whole fragile support system I'd created for myself would crumble—Maria, the nurses, my doctors . . . all the things that were making life tolerable would fade before the vision of being home.

I spoke to Judy and we planned our strategy. It was clear that it was Wesley's decision. She was in charge of the floor and she ran it like the captain of a ship. Davis would never countermand her. But we also knew that in the subtle ways of hospital hierarchy, she would be influenced by his opinion. So it was crucial that we win Davis over, while giving Wesley a graceful way to change her mind.

We asked for a meeting with all four of us present. I began quietly, deferentially, acknowledging that I understood the rules and the importance of them, but that mine was a special case. I felt it was absolutely essential that I see my daughter regularly, vital to her welfare and my own.

Miss Wesley studied her hands for a while. "Well, it certainly is a sticky wicket, but I don't really see what we can do."

Judy spoke next, cautiously at first, then warming to the topic, spurting theories on the effects of long-term hospitalization, the effects of prolonged deprivation—hinting, ever so delicately, at all the different forms of gratification I'd had to relinquish. "Surely it's too much to expect Mrs. Berg to give up her daughter, too." Oh, Judy, I love you.

She went on to hospital responsibility for patient welfare, and the need to treat the whole patient, not just the physical symptoms. She was flushed and breathless when she finished, but I knew she had done it. If I could have, I would have jumped out of bed and thrown my arms around her. Instead I made a circle with my thumb and index finger, and she grinned in return.

Davis looked impressed. He walked over to the refrigerator, picked up a bag of sugar cookies, and said, "Miss Wesley, of course, is right about not bringing the baby past the nursery. But if we can find a way for them to visit that doesn't involve going past the newborns?"

"Perhaps we can arrange for Mrs. Berg to be moved in front of the elevator and she can visit with her daughter out in the corridor for a while," Wesley suggested.

Out in the hall? With everyone around and no place to hold her and cuddle her and play with her, after not seeing her for a month? I looked at Judy pleadingly.

"What about moving Mrs. Berg into an empty room on the other side of the floor for a few hours," Judy suggested. "That way, she and her baby could have a little privacy and Alison wouldn't be anywhere near the newborns."

Davis waited for Miss Wesley to speak.

"Well, we'd probably have to remake the bed in the room after the visit, but I think that could be arranged."

Victory!

The rest of the week the nurses kept tabs on the rooms for me. "Patient in six-thirteen is planning to leave. No, cancel that. Baby has mild case of jaundice." "Patient in six-seventeen running a slight fever—she'll probably stay over the weekend." I felt as though I were managing a hotel.

But then, Friday afternoon, came the word. The patient in 616 was checking out a day early and, barring an on-the-spot baby boom, the room would be empty Saturday.

I was so excited I couldn't sleep, but I was also nervous. Until now all my energies had gone into making the visit happen, but now that it was here, I was scared. Suppose Alison didn't know me? Oh, I would understand, and blame it on the hospital and strange surroundings, but deep down I wouldn't believe that and I would be miserable.

It seemed that everyone wanted to help make the visit a success, wanted to share the excitement: Maria; the supervisor of the labor-and-delivery floor who was covering for Miss Wesley; the nurses; the aide who got me the stretcher cot; and the dietician, who asked if we wanted extra milk. The whole floor was rooting for us.

As Arnie and I reached the room, I could see Alison sitting on my mother's lap, her back to the door.

"Look who's here, Ali," Arnie said. "Look who's here."

I held my breath and waited. She turned and saw me. There was nothing for a second, and then a smile, a smile of recognition—one of her big, grand, marvelous, sideways smiles.

Chapter 14

It was our anniversary, and Arnie came to the hospital early with flowers in one hand and our breakfast in the other. Some glorious days he did this—surprised me in the morning with poached eggs and coffee that didn't taste like Styrofoam.

"I really rushed," he'd say, coming in breathless. "I wanted you to have the eggs while they're still hot." And then he'd stand over me like a watchful mother as I took my first mouthful.

"They're delicious."

"But are they *still warm?*"

"Oh, yes, plenty warm."

Only then would he relax and start eating his french toast, and we'd talk and joke with the nurses and I'd go back to my eggs—which were always *ice cold*.

I made Arnie promise not to buy me a present that year, only a card, and I had one for him, made over a period of days, lying on my side, cutting and drawing and pasting. We were going to exchange them that night. Arnie's first time sleeping over at Hillcrest. He was going to sleep on the cot Maria used at our weekly visits. If we pushed my night table aside and lowered my bed as far as possible, we would be so close I could reach out and touch him during the night.

I hate to sleep alone, the bed stretching out beside me like a vast cold ocean. The first few nights at

Hillcrest, my fingers and toes would creep across the mattress searching for Arnie. I'm this way at home: an inveterate foot cuddler. Arnie is not: He needs room, space. I need security, warmth, physical contact. I begin on my own side of the bed, hugging the pillow, but always end up on his, hugging him.

In layers, I'd become accustomed to it, to the not making love, to the not sleeping together.

"Do you realize how long it's been since we've seen our husbands undressed?" Maria asked.

"Five weeks," I answered gloomily.

We tried not to do this, not to keep track of things: how long since we'd had a real bath, how long since we'd had fresh air. It was like thinking of going home. We were doing time, and, as all inmates know, there's doing easy time and doing hard time. Counting days and weeks meant hard time.

But it had been five weeks without seeing that familiar body, the torso perpetually darker than the lean, tight hips. Five weeks without the silly shared intimacies of married life, like our nightly *quid pro quo:* a backscratch for a hair comb. It had been so long without sharing the bathroom, standing back to back, using our separate mirrors, and every so often reaching behind and touching. So long since we'd really been together.

Where did Arnie come from each morning? He looked like our bed, he smelled like our bed. But was it our bed? I never asked.

Around three o'clock a bouquet of pompoms arrived from Evo and Maria. "What's the occasion?" asked the nurse who was checking the fetal heartbeat.

"Our anniversary."

I waited for one of the usual replies, but she said nothing. I looked at her over the mound of my belly. Her brow was furrowed, her lips pursed.

"Is—is anything wrong?" I forced myself to ask.

"I don't know yet. I'm having trouble getting the heartbeat. I'd better go get a resident." She ran from the room.

A white cold terror gripped me. Moments later, I

pressed my call button. No one was answering. I put my hands over my stomach, poking gently, hoping to feel life, but the baby was still. I pushed the button another time. Where the hell *was* everyone? I picked up the telephone and got information for the nurses' station at Hillcrest G-6. Finally someone answered. They knew about it. They were paging a resident.

I was crying and wringing my hands when Dr. Donaldson walked in carrying one of the large fetal monitors from the labor-and-delivery floor. As always, he was completely calm and in control. Dr. Kildare incarnate.

He felt my stomach, applied a small amount of Surgilube, and put the transducer over it. Immediately the familiar thump, thump sounded, and it was music to my ears. We had re-established radio contact.

All my anger at Wiggles dissipated. Is it always this way? We love the doctor who brings us good news. "The tests came back negative. I won't have to operate." "Oh, thank you, doctor, thank you." Gratitude, loyalty, adoration. "My doctor, he's a *big* specialist, a *big* man in his field." How many times had I heard that expression? In Flatbush where I grew up, they worshiped doctors like the Torah.

He was packing up, still without saying a word to me. I felt a need to talk to him, to have some human interchange. "Excuse me, but I wanted to ask you . . ."

"Yes?" He cleared his throat several times as if in preparation for his answer.

"If the baby had—I mean, what would make a baby just die like that?"

"It's just like anything else," he said, still standing in the doorway. "Millions of women have lumps on their breasts. Why do some turn malignant?" The shoulders shrugged under the starched white coat; the hands went up in the air.

Just like anything else? Good grief!

The second time the nurse couldn't hear the heartbeat, a resident came and found it almost immediately. But the third time, forty minutes passed and no one entered my room. In desperation I called my doctors' office. Maybe *they* could reach a resident.

About fifteen minutes after I hung up, Dr. Roth came bursting in, out of breath and sweating heavily. He had left an office full of patients and had run all the way to the hospital. He came over to the bed and put his fetoscope to his ears. One spot, then another. I kept my eyes closed and my fingers crossed.

"It's okay, I have it. It's okay," he said. He handed me the fetoscope. "Here, you keep this. Now you can check the heartbeat whenever you like and you won't have to depend on a machine that doesn't work and incompetents who don't know how to use it."

I tried using the fetoscope, but it was too difficult; I had to sit up too much and I couldn't hear over the air conditioner. Still, it was an intriguing idea. If I could listen to the heartbeat myself, it would allay a lot of my anxiety. "How about trying to rent a fetone machine?" my mother suggested.

So I had a project. With the Yellow Pages next to me, I started calling all the medical suppliers in the greater New York area. A fetal-monitoring device, however, is not exactly your most popular item. It hardly competes with the hospital bed, wheelchair, or commode in availability. A few places had never heard of it; most did not stock the item; and those that did only had the large units available, which they rented to hospitals or other medical facilities.

But if nothing else, the search was fun, so I kept at it a little longer. "A mini-doppler, that's what you want," the manager of a small hospital supplier told me. "I'm not sure if we can get you one. Call back Monday. The store owner, Dr. Winslow, will be in then."

"I'll go over there and talk to him myself," my mother volunteered. "It's much better in person."

And it was. Dr. Kathy Winslow had had one late miscarriage, then a daughter, who was now five, and difficulty becoming pregnant again. So she knew about the sorority of sufferers. Of course she'd get me a mini-doppler; she'd sell it to me at cost and then try to resell it afterward.

It looked like a large gray flashlight, and had its own traveling case and earplugs. My mini-doppler became the pet of the hall. Everyone wanted to try it: Maria, the nurses, the residents. It kept us entertained at least for a while.

But there was still so long to go. The days seemed to turn back on one another. Still, stagnant, sour. I started to keep a journal.

> I have been here six weeks and it seems as though I am losing my sense of everything but the hospital. Yesterday, Arnie brought me some books for the paper I am supposed to give in December. I looked through them and started to cry. I can't even remember what they're about.
>
> I feel so distant, so detached from everything of importance in my life. My friends visit and I feel as though their lives are beyond my comprehension. My only reality is the changing shifts, which doctor is on, my blood pressure, my urine specimens. . . . How could the act of bringing forth life be so dehumanizing?

Davis had just finished examining me.

"What about the cervix?" I asked. I'd gotten into the habit of saying "the cervix" instead of "my cervix." I was being clinical, objective. It was probably also a way of distancing myself from my condition.

"The bottom suture's almost gone, but the top one's holding. I'm not going to check it anymore. We're not going to resuture you at this point, so why risk an infection?"

He plopped down in the chair, happened to glance in the garbage can, and bolted forward, pointing to three empty paper cups. "Who's been drinking so much coffee?"

"Oh, not me. My sister and parents were just here."

"Okay, good. Gotta watch the caffeine." He was up on his feet, pacing, giving a discourse on the effects of caffeine on unborn children. He was truly peripatetic.

"How's the weight coming?"

"Can't you tell?"

He smiled.

I had really, in the euphemism of pregnancy, *blossomed*. The baby was big, and I had accumulated a layer of soft, milky flesh around my body.

"Next week we start checking the estriols."

"And the white blood cells?"

"And the white blood cells."

"I was wondering . . . after the stillbirth, Dr. Morgan ordered a Kliehauer test to make sure the baby's blood wasn't flowing back across the placenta into my bloodstream. Do you think we ought to do it also?"

"It was next on my list."

So they started. Three times a week—every Monday, Wednesday, and Friday—the blood tests. Three tubes, each with a different-color top: red for the Kliehauer, green for the estriols, and yellow for the white blood count. Sometimes drawn by experts, sometimes drawn by amateurs. And often mislaid, misread, redone. Too often.

"Excuse me, the estriols are supposed to go into the vial with the green cork, not an orange one." Squirt, into the orange. Later that day: "I'm sorry, Mrs. Berg, we have to redo the estriols. Some confusion in the lab." My arms looked like I was a junky.

Arnie had to take Alison to the doctor. She's been running a fever for three days. Dr. Schaffer called to tell me he didn't think it was anything serious. He knows how worried I am. I don't think though that anyone can really know how much I worry about her. It's so awful not to be able to take care of her myself, to have to depend on others. Dependent. That's

really the word. Maria and I were just talking
about it. That's probably the worst part of being
here, having to be so dependent on strangers
and even on our husbands. It's woman writ
large and I guess that's what galls so.

Talk about dependent, for two days my phone was
out of order.
I was absolutely cut off from the outside world.
Maria and I communicated by notes, our nurses gra-
ciously serving as message carriers.

> NOTE FROM MARIA: Don't worry, when Arnie
> learns of this, he'll tackle the whole phone
> company if need be. Did you order eggs
> this A.M.? How do they manage to get the
> yellow like a rock and the whites so
> watery?
> NOTE TO MARIA: Mrs. Watersworth just told me
> that Arnie called the desk, the phone
> company can't promise they'll get to it for
> a few days. She told me to call the patient
> hot line. I can't call them. If I could, there
> wouldn't be any need for me to call them.
> Could you give them a try? I didn't have
> eggs today, Davis wants me to eat bran.
> Ugh!
> NOTE FROM MARIA: I just called, they're assign-
> ing someone to look into it. Are the
> patient reps what you call Lady Bounti-
> fuls? Check out Brody's shirt today. Tauber
> [Maria's doctor] scheduled me for a sono
> on Tuesday. See if you can get one then
> too, we can go down together.

Within an hour—I'm not exaggerating, one hour
later—my phone was fixed. I called the patients' repre-
sentatives to thank them, Maria to tell her about our new
source, Arnie to tell him I was back in business, and
Davis to find out about my next sonogram.
"I scheduled it for Wednesday. . . . You want to go

Tuesday? No problem. You'll be going every week for biparietals."

"What's that?"

"It's a measurement of the baby's skull—gives us another handle on intrauterine growth."

"How are the estriols?"

"Fine, good. I didn't get Wednesday's yet, but Monday's was seven."

"Seven? That's much too low. When my sister was in her eighth month, hers were eighteen."

"Probably done at a different hospital—it depends on whether the measurement is of conjugated or unconjugated estriols. Yours are fine."

"Are you sure?"

"Yep."

"Positive?"

"B-a-r-b-a-r-a."

It wasn't that I didn't trust him, I just wanted to make sure. So when Morgan made his rounds Friday morning, I asked him about my numbers. Three different doctors, a chance to get three independent opinions. Why not?

He must have told Davis that I was still worried, because Saturday afternoon at around three, in what I'd come to view as the desert of the day, when Arnie was with Laura and Alison, and Evo was with Maria, and I was feeling lonely and bored, Davis came strolling into my room. He was dressed in a turtleneck and corduroy jeans.

"You don't look as though you're here on business."

"Only semibusiness. I want to show you something." He took out some folded papers from his back pocket. "These are Xeroxed from a medical textbook. Look at the graph." He pointed to an upward curve. "See? For thirty-four weeks, the estriols should be between six and eight. Your numbers are perfect. You have enough to think about without worrying unnecessarily."

So I looked at the numbers and I looked back at him and I told him what I had been thinking for a long time:

that it was impossible for me to have one hundred percent faith in any doctor, but that I had as much confidence in him as I could possibly have, and the greatest amount of respect for the way he practiced medicine.

He complimented me back, and there we were, complimenting each other, the perfect patient/doctor duo. I liked to *know* and he liked to *tell*. But we worked well together. And that's really the point. Isn't it?

There were other moments, too, of such human compassion that I can't recall them even now without being deeply moved: the large black cleaning woman, who was missing her front teeth, bringing me flowers every day from the empty rooms; the man who ran the TV concession refusing, after the first three weeks, to take any money; Morgan discussing history with me because he thought it important that I keep in touch with that part of my life; and from my family, friends, Laura and Arnie, always much.

There were also moments that set Maria and me convulsing with laughter: Arnie backing into my room one Tuesday morning dressed in a lab coat and carrying a tray of test tubes while I protested that this wasn't my day to have blood drawn; my in-laws buying me a nightgown—a Givenchy, no less—with a pattern so identical to the hospital gown that it was collected with the dirty linen; Laura calling from our house very excited that she had just done a poster on the metric system, using *all* the labels from my canned goods.

And still, so often, moments of despair.

I lie in bed listening to the heartbeat of a baby I may never see. From minute to minute I do not know if it will survive. I feel so hopeless today. Maybe because it's finally happened. I have bedsores. Maria, too. Maybe some new detergent they're using in the laundry. I'm trying not to think of them, but how do you eat resting on your elbows when they are open and raw?

I am so large that I can hardly maneuver on and off the bedpan. Will I always believe that this is worth it? One of my students sent me the book *Anya*, about a Jewish family during World War II. I read it, and I dream that I am in a concentration camp. Her father told her that people can get accustomed to anything. . . . I wonder.

Chapter 15

We were, by all accounts, in the homestretch. My baby was deeply engaged in the pelvis, and Maria's had dropped. She was allowed to take short walks each day; I was allowed to use the toilet and sit up in a chair for a half-hour. I was thirty-five weeks pregnant, five weeks from my due date, and Maria was in her thirty-seventh week. Now we were counting not only weeks but days. Laura's and Alison's visits every Saturday; my blood tests every Monday, Wednesday, and Friday; my biparietals every Tuesday—or supposedly.

Weekly biparietals had been ordered so the doctors could gauge fetal growth, but somehow the sonogram people never managed to get me into a schedule. A day earlier or later didn't seem to matter, but when I'd had my last on a Monday and ten days passed and the sonogram room still hadn't called for me, I called them to ask about it. After all, I was hospital-smart.

Shortly after I phoned, however, Wiggle Finger came bursting into my room, scowling and red in the face. He walked to the chair I was sitting on and stood over it menacingly.

"Did you call the sonogram room?"

"Yes. Matt Davis wants me to have one every week and they forgot to schedule it."

"Patients are not supposed to call the sonogram room," he yelled.

"I didn't know that. When I was an outpatient, Davis's office gave me the number so I *could* call," I answered meekly.

"Well, you're not an outpatient now. Don't you *dare* do it again. We can't have every goddamn patient supervising her own treatment." He was screaming so loudly, a nurse from the room next door came in to see what was wrong.

I felt myself grow pale. I was humiliated, degraded. As soon as he left, I began to cry. And I was still crying fifteen minutes later when Nina came to visit. I was so upset I couldn't even tell her what had happened. I don't know why I reacted so strongly. It's hard for me to be yelled at, it always has been. But I think it was more than that. For nine weeks I had tried in every way I knew how to cling to some shred of dignity, and in five minutes he had wiped it out.

But then the most incredible thing happened. Dr. Donaldson came back into my room to *apologize*, to tell me he'd scheduled the sonogram for that afternoon. By now I was calm and I wasn't going to let him off so easily. It was time he heard what it was like on the other side.

"Do you really believe that patients should relinquish themselves totally to an institution? Are you so tied to the system that you are blind to what goes on around here? Do you know how many times tests are lost, mistakes are made, machines break down? You ought to spend one week flat on your back in this place and you'd realize why patients have to have a voice in what happens to them."

Just then Miss Wesley came in. "I'm sorry to disturb you, Mrs. Berg, but the lab ran the wrong tests. We'll have to redo all your bloods."

I didn't have to say another thing.

Arnie was now coming every morning. We had established our routine: First thing after the kiss hello was listening to the heartbeat, each timing it separately.

"What'd you get?"

"One-forty-six."

"You?"

"One-forty-eight. It's a girl!"

We had no doubt about it. How could it be otherwise? Five grandchildren on Arnie's side and not a single male among them; had my earlier pregnancies worked, there would have been seven girls born in his family.

That finished, we would eat our breakfasts, often with one of our doctors joining us for coffee. Seeing Arnie in the morning sustained me the whole day. He knew how much I looked forward to it—that's why he came. But the strain of his schedule was staring to show. He was thinner, his face hollowed out under the eyes and cheekbones, and recently he had been complaining of stomach pains. Others get migraines or stiff necks or backaches. But when the pressure is on at work or from Charlotte, bingo, the stomach goes into knots. What was causing it now? The accumulated tensions of the last four years, or something specific?

Finally I coaxed it out of him.

"I'm a little worried," he said, smiling self-consciously and I thought a bit sadly, "that I won't be able to stay with you through the labor. That I won't be able to stand seeing you in such pain."

I should have realised this. Arnie's a semi–type "A" American male—driving, demanding of himself, a perfectionist, but possessed of a strong strain of nurture. He sat on the bed and I took him in my arms. God, how I loved him right then.

There was something black on my bed. A piece of dirt or dust. It was too early for me to focus on it. But it was moving. I flipped on the light; it stopped for a moment, then furtively dashed for cover. A cockroach. I looked around; on the wall above my bed, tiny baby cockroaches.

What is this, God? The urban version of locusts?

"Maria, I have cockroaches in my room."

"I've seen a few, too."

"I wonder if there are any in the newborn nursery."

"I'm afraid to ask."

"So am I."

"What time are you visiting today?"

"Maybe at two. Will you be in?"

"I'll try to arrange it."

Maria was pacing. Back and forth, up and down the halls. She was two weeks from her due date and her cervix was sealed shut. She no longer cared if she was early, she just didn't want to be *late*.

So she took a daily constitutional, always stopping for a while to visit. I can still picture her in my room, skinny except for her belly hidden under the folds of a pink and aqua robe. Her hands motioning, her eyes dancing, her legs up on a chair, balancing a tin of cashew nuts on her stomach. Talking about what? The quality of life in Argentina? The quality of our cervical discharge? It didn't matter. We were doing easy time now and we knew it.

Early in October, when I had read every possible book I had ever wanted to read and many that I never wanted to read, and had watched all the reruns of "The Mary Tyler Moore Show," I picked up a pencil and started sketching one of the flower arrangements in my room. I did this casually, on the back of a dinner menu. But Arnie took it seriously. He evaluated the sketch and told me how I could improve it. The next night he came laden with a sketch pad, a tray of watercolors, and a book of impressionist paintings. Arnie loves to give presents and he loves to paint.

So, every night from then on, the two of us would rush through dinner, take out our pads, and draw and sketch and paint. I remember once his getting up from the chair and leaning over to kiss my forehead.

"What's that for?" His eyes were soft and glistening.

"Did you know you were singing? For the first time in three months, you were singing."

The painting did make me happier, the sense of accomplishment, creation. And each painting we hung in the room. What the room looked like had suddenly become a matter of great importance to me. For almost ten weeks I had stared at these same barren gray walls and accepted it as part of the package, but now I felt the need to make it warm, homey. Maria was doing the same, but in crewelwork—hanging butterflies, sunflowers all over her quarters. We were feathering our nests.

We were also preparing for childbirth. Matt gave me the name of one of the nurses who taught the Lamaze classes at Hillcrest. We arranged for her to give both couples private lessons in our room. For three Sundays in a row, Maria and I lay side by side, breathing in and out, huffing and puffing, while Arnie and Evo counted, stopwatches in hand.

The instructor was a sweet, mild woman who had never been pregnant and kept referring to labor as "uncomfortable." She told us about all the possible complications of analgesics and epidurals, implying, ever so slightly, that Hillcrest had a vested interest in giving obstetrical patients anesthesia because it provided income to their staff.

I knew that the word "pain" was the bugaboo of the medical profession. I had even become so jaded as to accept the idea of a conspiracy between obstetricians and anesthesiologists. But I had been through labor twice and I knew that it hurt. It was not uncomfortable, mildly or strongly. It hurt like hell. Still, I was obsessive about this. If I did not have to have a cesarean, I wanted natural childbirth from beginning to end. I wanted nothing. Do you understand? *Nothing*.

"Hi Barbara. How are you feeling today? Yes, I know, no epidural."

And to Arnie, more of the same. "Don't let them give me anything. No matter how bad it is, don't let them. Just keep talking to me about the pioneer women, the Indian women, just keep talking."

I didn't want to be doped, numbed, dazed. I wanted to feel the rhythm of my baby, sense it, savor it, every part of its grinding, grueling journey branded into my gut, my loins. I wanted the last minutes of the pregnancy to be mine.

* * *

Last night for the first time I allowed myself to
fantasize about the baby. I allowed myself to
believe that I would see it, know it, that it
would be born. . . . I am overwhelmed by
my longing and love for it.

I was going to be "induced"—that is, the suture
would be cut, the membranes would be ruptured, and I
would be given a drug to bring on labor. But no one
seemed to be rushing to do this procedure. My doctors
wanted to keep me pregnant as long as possible. Was it
the chocolate chip cookies? Maybe. They, of course,
denied it. "The closer to term, the better. Let's wait
another two or three weeks."

It should have gone slowly, horribly, hideously
slowly. But it didn't. First of all, in spite of myself, I
became involved in watching the World Series. I hadn't
been interested in baseball since I was a child in
Brooklyn. Then we watched, even went to Ebbets Field.
I mean, how could you be from Brooklyn and not have
been a Dodger fan? I remember going to games with my
grandpa, holding his rough, callused hands and eating
popcorn and hot dogs and fibbing about it all to my
mother. Grandpa loved the "Bums" with a passion.

Even after so many years, I felt a little guilty rooting
for the Yankees now. But they put on such a show,
occupied so many nights, coming through for us in the
end, that I have watched them ever since.

"I only wish the Series had gone on another two
weeks," I was telling Davis shortly afterward.

"You want to do something for me?"

"Sure."

"The day before the Marathon, I have to give a
short talk to the American Medical Joggers' Association
on the benefits of running. I don't see how I'll have time
to prepare it. Want to work up a draft?"

Terrific: a research project. Pretty funny, too. I, who
hadn't *walked* in six months, whose legs were now about
the consistency of noodles, writing about the importance
of exercise for mental and physical health.

In the midst of my writing, Jeanne gave birth to a daughter at Hillcrest. It seemed like something out of a grade "B" movie: Two women, childless for so long, become mothers only seven days apart.

"Any preference for days?" Matt asked me shortly after the Marathon.

"Well, the twenty-eighth is Laura's birthday—there'll be enough competition without taking that from her. How about the thirty-first? Halloween."

"Next Tuesday . . . hmmm. We'll have to check the L/S ratio first."

"The what?"

"Lecithin-sphingomyelin Ratios," he said walking over to look out my window. "You see, there's an acute rise in lecithin at thirty-five weeks, and if the lecithin exceeds the sphingomyelin values in the amniotic fluid by a ratio of two to one, the lungs are considered mature. Before that, the newborn is unable to maintain a residual volume of alveolar air and may have respiratory distress that is part of the anoxic syndrome."

All this he said while pacing between the window and the door. I was starting to feel as though I were watching a tennis match.

"Ronald'll do a tap on Monday, and, if we get a go-ahead, Tuesday will be baby day."

From then on, Arnie and I were at the top of our senses. Everything was concentrated: joy, fear, anxiety, hope. It was impossible to believe that it would finally happen, but just as impossible to believe it wouldn't.

We told Davis of Arnie's concerns about the labor, and he reassured us. "You'll be so involved in the birth that you'll forget about the pain. You'll forget about everything except seeing your baby born."

Arnie brought a big pumpkin to the room and we carved it together. We did a mini-review of the different breathing exercises and checked our Lamaze bag again and again.

"Washcloth?"

"Yep."

"Powder?"

"Yep."

"Warm socks?"

"Yep."

"Camera?"

"Yep."

"Comb?"

"Forget the comb. I'm not going to be combing my hair."

"Not even for my pictures?"

"Not even for your pictures."

"Lollipops?"

"Uh-oh. Maria and I finished them yesterday."

"I'll run down and get some. Any favorite flavor?"

"Grape."

Ten minutes later, he was back. "You won't believe this."

"I'll believe anything."

"The police won't let me out of the building. There's a man with a sawed-off shotgun loose and they have all the exits blocked."

"Oh, great! Of all the things I *knew* I'd have to worry about in my pregnancy, I never thought I'd have to worry about being murdered in my sleep two days before the baby was born." It came to mind again, as it had so many times during my stay, that there was no lock on the door. Where else do you sleep so vulnerable? So unprotected?

"Want me to sleep over?"

"No. Just stay for a while. If I see him, I'll hit him over the head with my doppler."

Arnie came with me for the amniocentesis test. It was just for the L/S ratio, not to find out the sex. I told him it wasn't necessary for him to come, but later I was glad he did. It turned out to be more of an ordeal than I had imagined.

My placenta, it seems, was attached anteriorly, covering the baby like a blanket. There was no safe place to put the needle.

Karen kept flashing the picture on the screen. "Here's a spot, doctor."

"No, too close to the artery. Too dangerous."

"How about here?"

"No, too dangerous."

"Doctor,"—exasperation in her voice—"it's fine up here."

"I'm not taking any chances. I don't care if we we wait until she goes into labor."

"Ronald, I'm *telling* you, you can do it up here!"

So I lay there while the two of them disagreed. Was this an honest difference of opinion? A power play? A personality dispute? I lay there listening to them argue and feeling more nervous every minute.

Finally, Morgan found a spot, right near the groin.

"Are you *sure* it's okay?" I asked, stopping his hand with mine.

"B-a-r-b-a-r-a!"

I waited to hear from Davis the whole day—telling my friends not to call, not talking to those who did. I wanted the line free. At 5:15 the phone rang.

"Barbara?"

"Yes?"

"We're on for tomorrow."

I pressed down the button and started to dial Arnie's office. Then I stopped, put down the receiver, clasped my hands over my belly, and smiled.

Tuesday morning I was up early. Or maybe I never went to sleep. I had to keep the vigil, check the heartbeat. Was it strong enough? Steady enough? In the right place? The old magical thinking again, but this was hardly the time to give up superstitions.

All night I bargained with God. I didn't want any screw-ups at the last minute. For some nutty reason I viewed the delivery as the home-free all. Maybe my brain had atrophied along with my leg muscles, or I had become co-opted by the system, but I really did believe in the value of those fetal-monitoring machines with their itchy elastic corsets, their confining, tangling wires, their beeps and readouts.

I suppose it's all, as people are so fond of saying,

relative. Women who have healthy, normal pregnancies look forward to their labor with anxiety. I looked forward to mine with excitement, joy, exultation.

Arnie didn't wholly share my enthusiasm. He came to my room around 7:00 A.M., looking haggard. I didn't notice at first because, from 6:00 A.M., on, the telephone hummed with well-wishers calling in.

"Hey, you're not eating," I said, watching Arnie stare at his breakfast.

"I guess I'm a little nervous. Suppose I can't stay with you the whole time. Will you be disappointed in me?"

Will you be disappointed in me if I don't earn enough? If I'm not as athletic as other men? . . .

"Dwarmie, I could *never* be disappointed in you." I got off the bed and held him as close as my stomach would allow.

"Hey, you're not supposed to do that."

"Why not? Will it put me in labor?" We hugged a little tighter and smiled.

For the next hour or so, we talked about names, deciding on either Caroline or Emily. We didn't even bother thinking of one for a boy. I brushed out my hair, which was now down to my shoulders, pulled it back with an elastic band, donned a clean hospital gown, and waited.

Alice came in with a wheelchair to take me down to Labor and Delivery.

"What are *you* doing here?" I asked. "I thought you'd left already."

"I'm doing a double shift today. Honey," she said in her deep, throaty voice, "I wouldn't miss this for the world."

The labor room was crowded with equipment—machines, IV poles—and another woman, who had been there for hours. The air hung heavy, rank and thick. Each time she screamed, a wave of panic swept through me. Suppose I couldn't take it? Suppose it was too much? I fastened my eyes on Arnie's. "Talk to me about the pioneer women, about the Indian women. Remind me what it was like for them. Just keep talking to me and I'll be all right."

Arnie hung up the picture I was supposed to focus on during labor. A poster of two elephants. How long did they gestate? One year? Two? I felt I'd been at this my whole life.

The nurse started my intravenous drip of glucose and water. "I'm not supposed to have any anesthesia," I told her. She smiled at me benignly.

They let my mother come in for a while. Like me, she talks a lot when she's nervous. She chatted with the nurses, complimenting them on their hairstyles, their uniforms. She was trying to win them over, to say, *Be nice to my daughter. Take good care of her.*

Arnie took some pictures. I smiled for the camera, feeling buoyant. So far, it was fun. So far, nothing had happened.

When Davis arrived, they wheeled me into one of the operating rooms. I breathed deeply of the clean, cold air. With my legs in the stirrups and Mrs. Paterson, the nurse assigned to me, holding my hand, he started to remove the sutures. With each snip I twitched as though an electrical current were going through me.

"Are you hurting?" he asked.

"Don't ask."

When it was over, I asked to see the suture, the top one, the one that had held. Davis washed it off and handed me a heavy opaque cord.

"Can I keep it? I want to show it to Arnie."

"Sure. Hang it in your kids' room. That way you can show them everything you went through."

"When I get out of here, I want to forget about this place. I'm not going to think about it or talk about it."

"Of course you will. And you'll write about it, too."

My membranes ruptured with a great gush of warm wetness.

"Guess how dilated you are."

"Four centimeters?"

"Five."

Wonderful, I thought. I'm halfway there. Having an incompetent cervix has some advantages, after all.

"Start the Pitocin," he told Mrs. Paterson, whom he called Mrs. P, "and page me when she gets going."

For the first hour or so, I was, in the common parlance of Hillcrest, only "mildly uncomfortable." I was doing the deep breathing, able to smile for Arnie's photographs and chat sporadically with the nurses from G-6 who were sneaking downstairs to visit me. Dr. Brody, who, much to my disappointment, was assisting Davis that day, came down to examine me. "Six centimeters," she reported. "How do you feel?"

"Great." I was in control. This was a snap—my belly expanding and tightening in a nice even rhythm. I was riding each contraction like a wave.

Then suddenly, out of nowhere, things went wild. The contractions built and peaked and built and built again. No order. No pattern. A crazy course of its own.

"Is this one almost over? Has it plateaued?" I kept asking Arnie, who was glued to the monitor, timing me, pacing me, soothing me. He didn't have the heart to tell me that a new contraction was starting before the old one had even declined.

I breathed in short, shallow pants. Mrs. P kept me at it even when Arnie forgot. My hands became numb and I had to breathe into a paper bag. I began to shiver and needed blankets; I began to sweat and needed powder.

My stomach was moving by itself, pulling into a rock with a fierce, furious power of its own. There was nothing but the pain. Brazen pain. Knowing no limits, no appeasement.

"Remember the women, the pioneers. . . ." Arnie's voice coached.

I was all women and I was no women. I was a cow and a mare and a beast in the field squatting and groaning and sweating out my young. I was everywhere and nowhere. Drowning in the sea, stranded in space. Swimming and blazing and soaring in pain.

They wheeled me into the delivery room.

"Push," Davis said.

I grasped the poles and pulled myself up and pushed until I thought I would burst.

"Keep going. You're doing fine."

I reached up again and tried to raise my body, but my fingers slipped off the poles and I fell back on the table. Arnie and Mrs. P helped me up, but my legs were trembling. Every bit of strength was seeping from my body.

"You can do it," Brody said.

I shook my head no. Then my eye caught a glimpse of the observation booth. I stared at it. Davis turned to follow my gaze. Judy and Miss Wesley and Alice were standing inside waving at me. Judy jabbed her two thumbs in the air, Alice made a V with her two fingers. They're rooting for me. *Oh, God, they're rooting for me*.

My stomach formed a tight fist. My sides slammed together. "Now," someone said. "Push now."

I drew in my breath and closed my eyes tight and pushed until I felt myself explode into bits of energy and life. I was hanging from the sun and floating with the stars.

"Again."

And I pushed again, screaming in agony and exhilaration.

"Hey, look! Open your eyes."

I looked at the mirror.

"No, not up. Look down, between your legs."

And there was my baby—with damp dark hair, sliding out as though it were the easiest thing in the world.

The next few seconds are lost to me: the first wail of life; the taste of Arnie's face against mine, salty, wet, and sweet, both of us saturated with warm, ragged joy.

"It's a boy," Davis announced.

"What?" But there was our son, upside down and red and shiny and screaming lustily.

"Well, what do you know," said Arnie, looking at him with amazement. "It *is* a boy."

I held him then, his body smooth and bright from birth, his black hair matted down, his temples bruised and swollen. I closed my eyes and opened my eyes and he was still there, breathing on his own. Marvelous, wonderful breaths. "He's breathing," I cried out. *"He's breathing!"* And I was laughing and crying and trembling all over.

I unsnapped the top of my hospital gown and turned to him, lifting him up so he could take my breast. He sucked gently, cleansing me of everything that had gone before. And I felt a part of all that was good and pure and possible.

At 5:00 A.M. the following morning, Arnie crept quietly through the doorway, a bouquet in one hand and coffee in the other. The room was already fragrant and bright with flowers and balloons and cards and gifts. Together we looked at the baby's tiny footprint and waited for the nurse to bring him to us. When she did, he was whimpering slightly, but stopped as soon as I held him. Arnie stretched out on the bed and encircled us both in his arms.

"I've been thinking about names," he whispered.

"So have I. What about either Daniel or Andrew?"

"Andrew," Arnie replied immediately. "He *looks* like an Andrew."

"What do you think, baby?" I asked, gazing down at his sweet face. "Do you want to be called Andrew?"

He made a soft, gurgling sound in return.

We kept Andrew in the room with us all day, loving every bit of his seven pounds, five ounces, and twenty-one inches. We stroked his thick black hair, marveled at his deep blue eyes and long legs, and noticed, for the first time, his one dimple.

My doctors came by to offer their congratulations. "Barbara was just saying she's ready to go through the whole thing again," Arnie told Dr. Morgan.

"She may be, but *we're* not," he said, smiling widely.

Two nights later we gave a party in my room for the doctors and staff. All of us laughed and drank, recalling his or her favorite story of my hospitalization. Evo came by briefly, but not Maria. She was still in the recovery room, having delivered a baby girl a few hours earlier. I sent her some champagne with a note: "I told you I wouldn't leave the hospital with you still pregnant. I'll wait up until you get back to your room so we can celebrate together."

Writing her this note, I felt the sadness of an ending. For I knew that whatever our lives would be on the outside, however much we might "keep in touch," we would never again share that absolute, unadorned intimacy. And as I looked at the faces around me—Alice, Judy, Wiggle Finger, Miss Wesley, the man who ran the TV concession, my doctors, many of the aides—I felt the same strange sadness. My family for three months. They had supported me and opposed me and helped me and sometimes hurt me beyond imagination, but they would be missed.

The next day we got ready to leave Hillcrest. Arnie began to dress Andrew while I got into the clothes he had brought for me. I felt like Rip Van Winkle awakening. I had entered Hillcrest the first week of August wearing a sundress and sandals, and now, in a bleak and wintery early November, with the branches of the trees looking like spiny skeleton arms, I was returning home in a heavy sweater and coat. A loss of ninety days which would take a full year of adjusting to.

Waiting in the lobby while Arnie got the car, I thought of the other times I had sat waiting for him, aching and barren, going home to a house that echoed with emptiness. But now there would be two babies: Alison, with her contagious grin and sparkling eyes; and little Andrew, with his one dimple, who slept peacefully in that special blue bunting in my arms.

Life was sweet and full and perfect.

ABOUT THE AUTHOR

BARBARA J. BERG is the author of *The Remembered Gate: Origins of American Feminism* and several articles on adoption and on women's health care and education. She now teaches part-time at Marymount Manhattan College. She and her husband live in New York City with their two youngest children, Alison and Andrew, and are joined by thirteen-year-old Laura on weekends.

We Deliver!
And So Do These Bestsellers.